Psychological Perspectives on Ethical Behavior and Decision Making

Psychological Perspectives on Ethical Behavior and Decision Making

edited by

David De Cremer
Erasmus University

INFORMATION AGE PUBLISHING, INC.
Charlotte, NC • www.infoagepub.com

Library of Congress Cataloging-in-Publication Data

Psychological perspectives on ethical behavior and decision making / edited
by David De Cremer.
    p. cm.
  Includes bibliographical references.
  ISBN 978-1-60752-105-1 (pbk.) – ISBN 978-1-60752-106-8 (hardcover)
1. Organizational behavior. 2. Psychology, Industrial. I. De Cremer,
David.
  HD58.7.P79 2009
  174'.4–dc22

                                                           2009011494

Printed in the United States of America

*This book is dedicated to those who stood close to me
when fairness was hard to find.*

CONTENTS

PART IV

THE SOCIAL CONTEXT AND ETHICAL BEHAVIOR

PART I

INTRODUCTION

CHAPTER 1

PSYCHOLOGY AND ETHICS

What It Takes to Feel Ethical
When Being Unethical

David De Cremer
Erasmus University

The last 15 years the media has almost constantly reported on issues of fraud, corporate scandals, and other types of unethical behavior. Indeed, the numerous scandals in business such as witnesses with Enron and Worldcom made all of us concerned about the emergence of ethical and moral behavior in organizations. More recently, this concern has even become stronger due to the world-wide financial crisis in which it became explicitly clear that the irresponsible (and unethical) behavior of managers and organizations inflicts pain on society and its members. These high-profile scandals and crises ironically have promoted interest in the scientific field of business ethics. Business ethics is the field that "deals with questions about whether specific business practices are acceptable" (Ferrell, Fraedrich, & Ferrell, 2008, p. 5). The examples referred to above clearly violate prescriptive norms, which dictate that we should act and do business in responsible ways that does not hurt the interests of others and

Psychological Perspectives on Ethical Behavior and Decision Making, pages 3–13
Copyright © 2009 by Information Age Publishing
All rights of reproduction in any form reserved.

shows respect to society at large. This idea, for example, aligns well with Kant and his categorical imperative (Hill, 2000, p. 39), which holds that moral behavior should be an end in itself because of "a rational moral requirement for everyone that is not based or conditional on its serving one's contingent personal ends."

In light of this business ethics approach it is interesting to observe that the key players in many of these business scandals claim that they are not unethical people and that they did not intend to inflict harm upon others. These actions indicate that many of these business men are aware of the prescriptive approach (often communicated by their companies' code of conduct), but nevertheless they have clearly failed to act as responsible and ethical individuals. How can we explain this? Early explanations focusing on the underlying causes of these ethical failures promoted the idea that most business scandals were the responsibility of a few bad apples. This assumption is intuitively compelling and attractive to use as it is a simple and straightforward solution and at the practical level it facilitates identification and punishment of those deemed to be responsible. However, more recent ideas note that many of the ethical failures witnessed in society and organizations are not characteristic of this specific group of so-called bad apples but may apply to all individuals. Rather, the idea is launched that all of us may commit unethical behaviors, given the right circumstances. This latter idea is one of the major assumptions used in the emerging field of *behavioral ethics*.

Treviño, Weaver, & Reynolds (2006, p. 952) recently defined behavioral ethics as a notion that "refers to individual behavior that is subject to or judged according to generally accepted moral norms of behavior." Tenbrunsel and Smith-Crowe (2008, p.) interpret this definition as saying that "behavioral ethics is primarily concerned with explaining individual behavior that occurs in the context of larger social prescriptions." Because of its focus on the actual behavior of the individual (i.e., advocating thus a descriptive approach rather than a prescriptive one!), it becomes clear that research in behavioral ethics largely draws from work in psychology. The field of psychology is indeed referred to as the scientific study of human behavior and thought processes (p. 2, Quinn, 1995). As such, it follows that the application of psychological insights will be necessary to promote our understanding of why it is the case that good people sometimes can do bad things as well. Along the same lines of reason, Bazerman and Banaji (2004, p. 1150) recently also noted "that efforts to improve ethical decision making are better aimed at understanding our psychological tendencies." (see also Messick & Bazerman, 1996).

PSYCHOLOGY AND THE ETHICAL BEHAVIOR
OF INDIVIDUALS

In this chapter, I advocate the view that research building on work in psychology may help us significantly to deepen our understanding why individuals sometimes do not recognize moral dilemmas and subsequently display behavior violating accepted moral standards. When this negative event happens, the question is often asked whether those unethical individuals have no moral awareness. According to Rest (1986) moral awareness can be seen as an interpretative process wherein the individual recognizes that a moral problem exists in the situation one is involved in. If such recognition is present then the individual should realize "that his or her potential decision or action could affect the interests, welfare, or expectations of the self or others in a fashion that may conflict with one or more ethical standards" (Butterfield, Treviño, & Weaver, 2000, p. 82). Recent research by Reynolds (2006a, 2008) further demonstrates that individual differences exist in the manner in which people recognize and interpret moral issues. An important assumption of these perspectives is that they all underline the idea that moral awareness is a rational process. Thus, according to this literature, people do interpret moral dilemmas in a conscious manner in which cognitive corrections can be applied. This view is, however, recently challenged by research on the notion of "bounded ethicality."

The concept of bounded ethicality is derived from earlier research on the notion of bounded rationality in which it is argued that people are not perfectly rational self-interested players in society. Instead they have bounded rationality in a way that they are also influenced by, for example, concerns of fairness. In a similar vein, bounded ethicality refers to the idea that our moral and ethical concerns are colored by self-favoring interpretations (e.g., I am fairer than others), making that people may easily display behavior that contradicts ethical standards (Banaji, Bazerman, & Chugh, 2003). In fact, because such self-favoring motivations are often automatic, it follows that people do not interpret their unethical behavior as unethical. In other words, bounded ethicality leads people to be able to see themselves as ethical persons while making unethical decisions (Chugh, Bazerman, & Banaji, 2005). Examples of such automatic self-favoring perceptions include the tendency of seeing oneself as more moral than others (Epley & Dunning, 2000) and interpreting fairness of allocations in an egocentric manner (Messick & Sentis, 1983). These egocentric tendencies thus significantly influence ethical behavior and decision making without people being aware that they are behaving unethically.

The fact that these processes often do not happen at the conscious level, which is in contrast to the dominant perspective that moral reasoning is a primarily reflective and rational process (Kohlberg, 1984), is further supported by recent research on morality, intuition and affect. Indeed, in this recent perspective, moral judgments and interpretations are argued to be the consequence of relatively automatic and intuitive affective reactions (Haidt, 2001). Haidt (2001, p. 818) defined moral intuition as "the sudden appearance in consciousness of a moral judgment, including an affective valence (good-bad, like-dislike), without any conscious awareness of having gone through steps of searching, weighing evidence, or inferring a conclusion." Applying these insights to our egocentric tendency to evaluate larger shares for ourselves to be fair indicates that a larger share is intuitively valued positive and as such subsequently biases our fairness evaluations. As Chugh, Bazerman and Banaji (2005, p. 83) put it, "this sequence suggests that "automatic egocentrism" precedes an evaluative moral judgment." The importance of intuitive and automatic processes has further provided support by research in the field of social neurocognition, showing that affect often plays a much bigger role in our judgments than initially thought (Gaudine & Thorne, 2001) and that its influence on ethical decisions may depend on the different subsystems within the brain (Reynolds, 2006b).

Another important psychological process that biases people's moral awareness concerns the concept of moral disengagement (Bandura, 1999). Moral disengagement can be defined as "an individual's propensity to evoke cognitions which restructure one's actions to appear less harmful, minimize one's understanding of responsibility for one's actions, or attenuate the perception of the distress one causes others" (Moore, 2008, p. 129). In a way moral disengagement can thus be seen as a buffer that allows people to free themselves from feeling guilty and uneasy with the idea that they may have violated accepted ethical standards. Moreover, moral disengagement is particularly successful to reduce feelings of dissonance that would normally occur if an individual has strong moral awareness when harming the interests of others (i.e., then a moral conflict would be very salient). Overall, the psychological influence of processes such as bounded ethicality and moral disengagement impact on individual's tendency to experience less conflict in the case of a moral dilemma (i.e., moral awareness is reduced). Or, in other words, these psychological processes clearly activate the phenomenon referred to as "ethical fading." As Tenbrunsel (2005, p. 96) notes, ethical fading is "a process that removes the difficult moral issues from a given problem or situation, hence increasing unethical behavior (Tenbrunsel & Messick, 2004)." The moral implications of one's decisions thus fade away because of the underlying dynamics of people's self-serving and self-deceiving perceptions.

THE IMPACT OF THE SITUATION ON ETHICAL BEHAVIOR
AND DECISION MAKING

The above makes clear that psychological processes significantly influence people's perceptions, interpretations and ultimately their behaviors. This observation therefore strongly suggests that behavioral ethics researchers need to devote attention to the egocentric biases that influences individual's behavior. Of course, this focus is particularly concerned with the cognitive, motivational and affective processes that take place within the individual (i.e., an intra-individual approach). As we know from social psychology (Snyder & Cantor, 1998), human behavior, however, is not only influenced by what one feels, thinks and wants, but also by the situation one is interacting in (see also Treviño, 1986). In line with this view, Tenbrunsel, Smith-Crowne, and Umphress (2003) elaborated on the impact of the situation on people's unethical behavior and decision making by emphasizing the importance of looking at organizational elements that are specific to the setting. According to Tenbrunsel and colleagues, specific organizational features may frame the organizational setting in ways that prevent unethical behavior and decision making. In the present chapter, I discuss three of such elements.

The first organizational feature that has the potential to significantly frame the working setting of employees is the employment of sanctioning systems (i.e., punishment of unethical behavior; Mulder, Van Dijk, De Cremer, & Wilke, 2006). In the literature, generally two reasons are identified why unethical behavior should be punished (Carlsmith, 2006). A first reason concerns the idea of *retribution*, in which punishment is seen as an end in itself. As such, punishment of unethical behavior is morally justifiable regardless of its subsequent consequences. Moreover, the view of retribution uses the important principle of moral proportionality—the punishment evoked should be of the same degree that moral offence was created by the transgressor. The second reason concerns the idea of utility, in which punishment is used to limit future transgressions. The idea is that the costs of the punishment should negatively impact how attractive a rational transgressor evaluates the act of future unethical behavior. The notion of utility indeed seems to be an important heuristic used by lay people. For example, research by Treviño and Ball (1992) showed that observers consider punishment of individuals acting unethical more fair when the punishment is more severe. Other research also shows that depending on one's own position in the punishment process (i.e., being the one who punishes or is being punished) utility may be determined more by process or outcome concerns. For example, research by Butterfield, Treviño and Ball (1996) illustrated that managers consider the procedural fairness of the delivery of the punishment the most important thing whereas those subordinates being punished evaluate distributive justice the most important. Lastly, punishment does not always represent a formal organizational procedure but can also be delivered in informal ways. For example, those acting unethical can also become ostracized by their peers as such denying them belongingness to the group or organization. Important with respect to this type of punishment is, however, that acts of ostracism may influence future ethical behavior in two ways. First, it may act as a motive for the wrongdoer to start behaving in line with the norms of the group and thus to display more ethical and prosocial behavior. Second, it may, however, also backfire in a way that feeling excluded will thwart the belongingness needs of the wrongdoer motivating him or her to act in a more hostile and unethical manner (see also Pillutla & Thau, this volume).

The second organizational feature concerns procedural fairness. Procedural fairness refers to the perceived fairness of the procedures enacted to allocate outcomes (Thibaut & Walker, 1975; Tyler, 1988) and has been shown to positively promote cooperative, trustworthy and prosocial behavior in groups and organizations (De Cremer & Tyler, 2005). Authorities using fair procedures promote perceptions of organizational members in ways that the organization is evaluated as a neutral and ethical decision maker. In fact, according to Tyler, Dienhart, and Thomas (2008), the enactment of fair procedures signals to employees that the organization considers the value of morality as an important one. Furthermore, Tenbrunsel et al. (2003) note that organizations are able to create procedural justice climates, which should have the potential to affect employees' perceptions and expectations that others in the organization act in moral and ethical ways. In a related manner to the procedural justice climate, another organizational feature of importance is the presence of an organizational ethical climate. Such a climate provides a broad sense of what type of behavior the organization strives for and how unethical behavior will be corrected. From this perspective, organizational climates can be seen as the basic dimension used to support the ethical infrastructure within organizations at different levels (Tenbrunsel et al., 2003).

OUTLINE OF THE BOOK

The book is divided into three relatively coherent sections that focus on understanding the emergence of (un)ethical decisions and behaviors in our work and social lives by adopting a psychological framework.

Section 1

The first section focuses on reviewing our knowledge with respect to the specific notions of ethical behavior and corruption. These chapters aim to provide definitions, boundary conditions and suggestions for future research on these notions.

Reynolds and Ceranic review the ethical decision-making literature and conclude that, despite other beliefs in the literature, we do not know quite a bit about the causes and conditions of ethical behavior. As a response, these authors consider theoretical, methodological, and institutional factors that limit our ability to make revolutionary gains in our understanding of the causes and conditions of ethical behavior. The chapter is concluded by offering recommendations that could increase our knowledge in this specific field of research.

Moore advances the argument that the literature on the psychological aspects of organizational corruption is not well developed because the primary focus has been to treat corruption as an organization level phenomenon while denying the individual-level—and in particular, psychological—influences that create the conditions under which corruption thrives within organizations deserves a closer look. Her chapter takes a psychological view on how corruption is successfully initiated, diffused, and institutionalized in organizational contexts, and makes recommendations about how future research at the individual level can contribute to our understanding of this inherently organization level phenomenon.

Section 2

The second section focuses on the intra-individual processes (affect, cognition and motivation) that determine why and how people display unethical behavior and are able to justify this kind of behavior to a certain extent. In these chapters the common theme is that given specific circumstances psychological processes are activated that bias perceptions of ethical behavior and decision making.

Zhong, Cain, and Liljenquist explore why good people do bad things and how they survive such indiscretions with an intact moral self-image. It is suggested that morality is a salient aspect of the self-image that undergoes constant revision. One's moral self-image is affected not only by past behaviors, but also expected behaviors and aspects of the self that are not directly related to ethics and morality (e.g., cleanliness). To account for this observation, the authors propose a general model of moral licensing, exploring behaviors or situational factors that promote unethical behavior by affirming a positive moral identity.

Cameron and Miller propose that the idea that losses loom larger than gains (prospect theory) has implications for ethical behavior. In this chapter the authors explore the reasons why loss aversion may in fact lead people to cheat more, or to take a greater number of what they call ethical shortcuts. A review of the relevant literature is presented, as well as evidence from their own research in which it is demonstrated that idiosyncratic definitions of losses and gains lead individuals to cheat more to prevent losses, involving falling behind an established financial or performance standard, than to achieve gains relative to a similar standard.

De Cremer, van Dijk, and Reinders-Folmer attempt to tackle the question whether leadership elicits concerns of social responsibility or entitlement when allocating valuable resources. These authors present compelling evidence that being labeled the leader automatically seems to activate beliefs of entitlement, consequently motivating those being in charge to take unfair and larger shares for themselves (referred to as the instant entitlement bias). Furthermore, a series of studies is discussed illustrating the boundary conditions of this entitlement bias.

Pillutla and Thau draw from evolutionary perspectives to develop a framework for individuals' propensity to engage in unethical behaviors in groups. They distinguish between actual exclusion, i.e., when people are actually excluded by their group members and potential exclusion, i.e., when people are at risk of being excluded by their group members and suggest that they differ in terms of their impact on the nature of unethical behaviors. More specifically, they advance the argument that people who are actually excluded are more likely to respond by taking actions that harm the group, while those at risk take actions that they believe will help the group.

Gollwitzer and Rothmund present a model that explains under what conditions a need to trust may result in unethical behavior. Their model departs from assumptions derived from research on trust and on fear of being exploited and their effects on uncooperative or egoistic behavior. These authors suggest that people differ with regard to their sensitivity towards environmental cues that suggest that other people harbor mean intentions—a personality construct that they call Sensitivity to Mean Intentions (SeMI).

Boksem and De Cremer focus on the importance that neurocognition research may have for the study of behavioral ethics. They review recent research exploring the neural components of fair and moral behavior in games and moral dilemmas. They illustrate that our strong prosocial sentiments have evolved from basic attachment to important others in our social group, which allows for morality to be a driving force in our social setting. As a result, our behavior is guided away from pure self-interest and towards interests that we share with significant others.

Section 3

The third section explores how organizational features frame the organizational setting and climate. These chapters focus on how employment of sanctions, procedurally fair leadership and a general code of conduct shapes perceptions of the organizational climate in ways that it becomes clear to organizational members how just, moral and retributive the organization will be in case of unethical behavior.

Mulder addresses the question of how the use of sanctions affects moral norms by presenting a model aimed at understanding when sanctions increase and when they decrease moral norms. The model specifically argues that the influence of a sanction depends on whether the sanction is interpreted as a retributive message or a compensatory one, which, in turn, is determined by various aspects of the sanction and the situation in question.

Mayer, Kuenzi and Greenbaum explore the topic of *ethical climates:* (a) by reviewing the empirical research that has emerged since Victor and Cullen's original conceptualization of ethical climate; (b) to critique the extant ethical climate literature on definitional, operational, theoretical, and methodological grounds; and (c) to prescribe a number of useful directions for future research to help ensure that ethical climate research continues to thrive—and ultimately gets integrated into mainstream organizational behavior.

Tyler and De Cremer examine evidence for the argument that ethical values shape rule adherence in groups. These authors argue that from a group perspective ethics are important, in part, if they motivate people to follow group rules and standards for appropriate conduce. This issue is considered within the framework of several important organizational settings and it is argued that, in both, ethical values have an important influence upon rule following behavior.

REFERENCES

Banaji, M. R., Bazerman, M., & Chugh, D. (2003). How (Un)ethical are you? *Harvard Business Review, 81,* 56–64.

Bandura, A. (1999). Moral disengagement in the perpetuation of inhumanities. *Personality and Social Psychology Review, 3,* 193–209.

Bazerman, M. H., & Banaji, M. R. (2004). The social psychology of ordinary ethical failures. *Social Justice Research, 17,* 111–115.

Butterfield, K. D., Treviño, L. K., & Ball, G. A. (1996). Punishment from the manager's perspective: A grounded investigation and inductive model. *Academy of Management Journal, 39,* 1479–1512.

Butterfield, K. D., Traviño, L. K., & Weaver, G. R. (2000). Moral awareness in business organizations: Influences of issue-related and social context factors. *Human Relations, 53,* 981–1018.

Carlsmith, K. M. (2006). The roles of retribution and utility in determining punishment. *Journal of Experimental Social Psychology, 42,* 437–451.

Chugh, D., Bazerman, M. H., & Banaji, M. R. (2005). Bounded ethicality as a psychological barrier to recognizing conflicts of interest. In D. A. Moore, D. M. Cain, G. Loewenstein, & M. H. Bazerman (Eds.), *Conflicts of interest: Challenges and solutions in business, law, medicine and public policy* (pp. 74–95). Cambridge: Cambridge University Press.

De Cremer, D., & Tyler, T. R. (2005). Managing group behavior: The interplay between procedural fairness, self, and cooperation. In M. Zanna (Ed.), *Advances in Experimental Social Psychology* (Vol. 37, pp. 151–218). New York: Academic Press.

Epley, N., & Dunning, D. (2000). Feeling "holier than thou": Are self-serving assessments produced by errors in self- or social prediction? *Journal of Personality and Social Psychology, 79,* 861–875.

Ferrell, O. C., Fraedrich, J., & Ferrell, L. (2008). *Business ethics.* Boston: Houghton Mifflin.

Gaudine, A., & Thorne, L. (2001). Emotion and ethical decision-making in organizations. *Journal of Business Ethics, 31,* 175–187.

Haidt, J. (2001). The emotional dog and its rational tail: A social intuitionist approach to moral judgment. *Psychological review, 108,* 814–834.

Hill, T. E. (2000). *Respect, pluralism, and justice.* Oxford: Oxford University Press.

Kohlberg, L. (1984). Moral stages and moralization: The cognitive developmental approach. In L. Kohlberg (Ed.), *Essays on moral development: Vol. 2. The psychology of moral development: The Nature and validity of moral stages* (pp. 170–205). San Francisco: Harper & Row.

Messick, D. M., & Bazerman, M. H. (1996). Ethics for the 21st century: A decision making approach. *Sloan Management Review, 37,* 9–22.

Messick, D. M., & Sentis, K. (1983). Fairness, preference and fairness biases. In D. M. Messick & K. S. Cook (Eds.), *Equity theory: Psychological and sociological perspectives* (pp. 61–64). New York: Praeger.

Moore, C. (2008). Moral disengagement in processes of organizational corruption. *Journal of Business Ethics, 80,* 129–139.

Mulder, L., Van Dijk, E., De Cremer, D., & Wilke, H. A. M. (2006). Sanctioning systems in social trilemmas. *Personality and Social Psychology Bulletin, 32,* 1312–1324.

Pillutla, M. M., & Thau, S. (this volume). Actual and potential exclusion as determinants of individuals' unethical behavior in groups. In D. DeCremer (Ed.), *Psychological perspectives on ethical behavior and decision making.* Charlotte, NC: Information Age.

Rest, J. R. (1986). *Moral development: Advances in research and theory.* New York: Praeger.

Reynolds, S. J. (2006a). Moral awareness and ethical predispositions: Investigating the role of individual differences in the recognition of moral issues. *Journal of Applied Psychology, 91,* 233–243.

Reynolds, S. J. (2006b). A neurocognitive model of the ethical decision-making process: Implications for study and practice. *Journal of Applied Psychology, 91,* 737–748.

Reynolds, S. J. (2008). Moral attentiveness: Who pays attention to the moral aspects of life? *Journal of Applied Psychology, 93,* 1027–1041.

Snyder, M., & Cantor, N. (1998). Understanding personality and social behavior: A functionalist strategy. In D. Gilbert, S. Fiske, & G. Lindzey (Eds.), *Handbook of social psychology* (Vol. 1, pp. 635–679). New York: McGraw-Hill.

Tenbrunsel, A. E. (2005). Commentary: Bounded ethicality and conflicts of interest. In D. A. Moore, D. M. Cain, G. Loewenstein, & M. H. Bazerman (Eds.), *Conflicts of interest: Challenges and solutions in business, law, medicine and public policy* (pp. 96–103). Cambridge: Cambridge University Press.

Tenbrunsel, A. E., & Messick, D. M. (2004). Ethical fading: The role of self-deception in unethical behavior. *Social Justice Research, 17,* 223–236.

Tenbrunsel, A. E., & Smith-Crowe, K. (2008). Ethical decision-making: Where we've been and where we're going. *Academy of Management Annals, 2,* 545–607.

Tenbrunsel, A. E., Smith-Crowe, K., & Umphress, E. E. (2003). Building houses on rocks: The role of the ethical infrastructure in organizations. *Social Justice Research, 16,* 285–307.

Thibaut, J., & Walker, L. (1975). *Procedural justice.* Mahwah, NJ: Erlbaum.

Tyler, T. R. (1988). What is procedural justice?: Criteria used by citizens to assess the fairness of legal procedures. *Law and Society Review, 22,* 103–135.

Tyler, T. R., Dienhart, J., & Thomas, T. (2008). The ethical commitment to compliance: Building value-based cultures. *California Management Review, 50,* 31–51.

Treviño, L. K. (1986). Ethical decision making in organizations: A person-situation interactionist model. *Academy of Management Review, 11,* 601–617.

Treviño L. K., & Ball, G. A. (1992). The social implications of punishing unethical behavior: Observers' cognitive and affective reactions. *Journal of Management, 18,* 751–768.

Treviño, L. K., Weaver, G. R., & Reynolds, S. J. (2006). Behavioral ethics in organizations: A review. *Journal of Management, 32,* 951–990.

PART II

REFLECTIONS ON (UN)ETHICAL BEHAVIOR

CHAPTER 2

ON THE CAUSES AND CONDITIONS OF MORAL BEHAVIOR

Why is This All We Know?

Scott J. Reynolds
University of Washington

Tara L. Ceranic
University of San Diego

As a result of the many scandals that have recently hit the headlines, organizations are becoming increasingly aware of the role that moral[1] behavior plays in creating a successful business. A recent review of the literature on ethical decision-making by Treviño, Weaver and Reynolds (2006) found that a great deal of research has been conducted on the topic. Moreover, a recent meta-analysis of this body of work (Gephardt, Harrison, & Treviño, 2007) indicates that the field has identified many specific personality traits and organizational conditions that are able to foster more moral behavior. To be specific, Gephardt, Harrison and Treviño's (2007) findings show that

Psychological Perspectives on Ethical Behavior and Decision Making, pages 17–33
Copyright © 2009 by Information Age Publishing

individuals higher in cognitive moral development, lower in Machiavellianism, with a more internal locus of control, a less relativistic moral philosophy, and higher job satisfaction are less likely to plan and enact unethical behaviors in the workplace. Furthermore, in organizations with benevolent climates, strong ethical cultures, and (enforced) codes of conduct, fewer unethical choices occur.

Although many researchers look at results such as these and conclude that the field knows a great deal about the causes and conditions of moral behavior, we draw a very different conclusion. Indeed, we marvel that after many decades with hundreds if not thousands of scholars conducting research on the topic, the body of knowledge regarding moral behavior is fairly sparse and rather unsurprising (e.g., would we expect Machiavellianism to be positively associated with moral behavior? Should a strong ethical culture correlate with immoral behavior?). Granted the literature contains specific findings that are quite surprising on their own (e.g., Reynolds & Ceranic, 2007), but on the whole, the quantity and quality of knowledge that we have acquired about why individuals act ethically and unethically is incredibly low, particularly when considering the critical importance of the topic.

In this chapter, we examine why that is the case. We consider theoretical, methodological, and institutional factors that limit our ability to make revolutionary gains in our understanding of moral behavior. We then offer suggestions for dealing with these obstacles. Ultimately, we conclude that researchers must realize that many of the most significant factors limiting our knowledge of moral behavior are inter-related, and that dramatically improving our knowledge of moral behavior could require significant changes in our overall approach to our research and to our profession.

THEORETICAL OBSTACLES

Cognition

Several significant challenges to developing a rich and complete body of knowledge regarding moral behavior are rooted in the theoretical bases for the field. The study of moral behavior is deeply entrenched in a cognitive approach (Haidt, 2001; Reynolds, 2006b) and has focused primarily on understanding how individuals process and analyze information. This reality can undoubtedly be traced to ethical philosophy, which for centuries has given primacy to rational thought (e.g., Kant, 1785/1994). More directly, though, the attention paid to cognition is largely a product of Kohlberg's (1981) theory of moral development.

Kohlberg (1981) provided what is generally regarded as the first and most thorough psychological treatment of the ethical decision-making process. The depth and breadth with which he covered the phenomenon provided a foundation upon which others could build. Whether they were pursuing or criticizing his theory, other scholars used cognitive moral development as the central stake upon which to pitch their research tent. While Kohlberg's theory created a remarkable surge in ethics research, it also entrenched the field into this cognitive approach, and unfortunately, the approach has two major limitations. First, it emphasizes the role of rational thought to the point of excluding other decision-making processes such as intuition and emotions. Second, it fails to adequately account for the role of contextual factors. We will briefly discuss each of these limitations in some detail.

Whereas scholars recognize that many decisions are the result of, or are at least impacted by, rational assessments of right and wrong, a growing body of research acknowledges other processes that can affect decision-making and behavior. For example, Reynolds (2006b) argued that reflexive, automatic, or non-conscious decision-making processes dramatically influence the choices that individuals make. Colloquially referred to as moral intuition, these automatic processes are pattern-recognizing mechanisms of the brain that allow individuals to quickly and efficiently process otherwise overwhelming amounts of information. Hence, just as an individual can instantly recognize a dog and "know" that it pants and barks, the individual can instantly recognize a bribe and "know" that it is morally wrong. Even though such processes account for a significant proportion and perhaps the vast majority of ethical decision-making events, these processes have yet to be explored empirically in any great detail.

Similarly, the cognitive approach does not adequately account for the role of emotions in the ethical decision-making process. Generally speaking, scholars have acknowledged that emotions are critical to the survival of the species because of their adaptive value and their ability to enable humans to react to their environment (e.g., Darwin, 1896). Emotions have been considered in disciplines from which ethics draws quite heavily. Numerous philosophers, including Plato, Aristotle, Descartes, and Hume (Solomon, 2003), have contemplated the place that emotions have in daily life. Additionally, psychologists (James, 1884; Lange, 1885) and organizational behavior theorists (Ashforth, 1993; Ashkanasy & Daus, 2002; Grandey, 2003; Pugh, 2001; Rafaeli & Sutton, 1987; Simon, 1987; Tan, Foo & Kwek, 2004; Wharton & Erickson, 1993) have each dedicated a great deal of research to understanding emotions. Believed to arise from the appraisal of significant objects (Lazarus, 1991; Roseman & Smith, 2001; Scherer, 1993; Smith & Ellsworth, 1985), emotions provide the individual with a form of judgment (Solomon, 1976, 1988) indicating how to respond to any given situation.

Despite wide-spread acknowledgement that emotions affect judgment, there is a dearth of emotions research within the business ethics domain.

Gaudine and Thorne (2001) provided the most comprehensive account of emotions and moral behavior to date by offering testable propositions regarding positive and negative affect and ethical dilemma recognition. Yet, empirically speaking, the ethics literature is just beginning to investigate the effect of emotions on ethical decision-making behavior. Rozin, Lowery, Imada and Haidt (1999) utilized four experiments in a test of the "CAD Triad Hypothesis" and demonstrated that three emotions (contempt, anger, disgust) map onto three moral codes (community, autonomy, divinity). Ceranic (2008) empirically examined the effects of (moral) emotions on ethical decision-making behavior and found that eliciting moral emotions (guilt, contempt, compassion, inspiration) in a context that encourages emotion significantly impacts the occurrence of moral behavior. Beyond these studies, though, little is known about the role of emotions in shaping ethical decisions. Given that the closely-related field of justice has benefited a great deal from the increasing attention its scholars have paid to emotion (de Cremer, 2007; de Cremer & van den Bos, 2007), the lack of knowledge and research on the relationship between emotions and moral behavior seems particularly glaring.

The second major limitation of a cognitive approach is the lack of attention it pays to context. Despite very relevant theories in other closely-related fields (Bandura, 1977, 1991; Fiske & Taylor, 1991) and explicit attempts to steer research in this direction (Treviño, 1986), business ethics research has generally failed to adequately address the interaction between the individual and the environment. Milgram's (1974) studies of authority have fascinated students of psychology because they demonstrated the extent to which individuals will commit heinous acts (i.e., shocking others to death). What is often lost in the discussion of these findings, however, is the extent to which a broad array of contextual conditions affected the participants' behavior. Milgram conducted multiple iterations of his experiment and found that symbols of authority (e.g., lab coats), the physical proximity of the victim, and even the location of the experiment influenced individual reactions. Granted, more and more research is taking into account the role of context in shaping moral behavior. For example, Butterfield, Treviño, & Weaver (2000) demonstrated that the language used to describe an issue impacts the extent to which an individual recognizes the issue as a moral issue, and Greenberg (2002) found that the perceived cause of a personal injustice impacts decisions to steal. Such findings notwithstanding, ethical decisions do not occur in vacuums, and to the extent that the cognitive approach tacitly elevates the individual and his or her cognitions without fully acknowledging the role that the environment plays in shaping behavior, our research is unable to capture the complete picture of moral behavior.

Normative Issues

Another significant obstacle in the study of moral behavior involves the normative aspects of the topic. Moral behavior is a unique social scientific construct in that it can strongly imply or even demand what behavior ought to occur (Moore, 1903). Social scientific theory, however, often struggles to incorporate or even address these kinds of normative concerns (Weaver, & Treviño, 1994). Two notable exceptions are Kohlberg's theory of moral development (Kohlberg, 1981) and stakeholder theory (Freeman, 1984). Kohlberg argued that individuals can progress from one stage of cognitive moral development to another, supplanting existing decision-making frameworks with more complex and sophisticated decision-making rubrics with each stage. He also made a normative assertion claiming that greater complexity and sophistication made higher stages morally superior to lower stages (Kohlberg, 1984). In a similar fashion, stakeholder theory argues that organizations are dependent upon both owner and non-owner entities for survival, and that addressing the interests of "stakeholders" relates directly to the bottom-line success of the organization. Furthermore, the theory adds, addressing stakeholders' interests is not only financially prudent, but also morally required (Freeman, 1984; Donaldson & Preston, 1995). Thus, these theories not only describe what is, but also proffer positions on what ought to be.

In contrast, the vast majority of theories applied in ethics research make little or no attempts to establish what ought to be, and as a result they are consistently agnostic in their tone. Although, proceeding as though ethics were like any other social scientific topic might have advantages from an empirical point of view, we argue that any knowledge gained from the resulting empirical work will be inherently limited. Ultimately, the research must return to the topic's normative domain to assert the relationship between is and ought (Moore, 1903). As evidence of this argument, consider the research on justice. Several decades ago, researchers seemingly set aside the philosophical origins of the topic, and, following social scientific norms, generated theory and gathered data about perceptions of distributive, procedural, and other forms of justice as if the normative aspects of these concepts did not exist (or at least were irrelevant). Now, with volumes and volumes of justice data at their disposal, some in the field have begun acknowledging that these findings explain only part of the story. Currently, there is a slow but growing movement to address the normative issues that are the foundation of justice in organizations (e.g., Cropanzano, Goldman & Folger, 2003), a return that to us was inevitable. On a study by study basis, it might be reasonable for an ethics researcher to set aside normative concerns so that he/she might better understand a facet of moral behavior, but a theory of moral behavior cannot thoroughly explain and predict behavior without ultimately and effectively accounting for the normative elements of the phenomenon.

Free Will

A final issue for researchers to consider is the free will. With few exceptions, social science is exceedingly deterministic, treating every phenomenon as though it were the effect of a cause and the cause of yet another effect. Indeed, the field is essentially built upon a deterministic assumption that if a phenomenon exists, something must have caused it to be, and even if no cause is apparent, it can become apparent with the proper methodology. Determinism, however, is an ontological assumption about the nature of reality, and though determinism is a shared belief that defines the discipline, its veracity has long been debated outside the field. For philosophers, the anti-thesis of determinism is the free will—the individual's capacity to choose, to decide, and to initiate motion. Kant's (1785/1994) ethical philosophy, for example, a central pillar of many ethical decision-making theories (e.g., Kohlberg, 1981), was dependent upon the concept of a free will in that he argued that acts are only moral to the extent that they were the result of a free choice to do what is right (Hudson, 1994). Social science assumes that moral behavior is the result of some factor, whether it be a cognition, an emotion, a peer, a policy, or some other force, but outside of our deterministic paradigm lies the possibility that moral behavior can be the result of a spontaneous display of the free will, a choice of origination—the creation of an entirely new beginning and an escape from the past. Though a social scientist might be able to model free will as a contingency or a possibility in a chain of events, by definition a free will is free of cause and therefore contrary to the fundamental assumptions upon which the social science of moral behavior is built. Given these conditions, ethics scholars should recognize that though they speak of trends and statistical significance, it is possible that our knowledge of the causes and conditions of moral behavior will never be absolute, not as long as individuals have the potential to choose independent of causal forces.

METHODOLOGICAL OBSTACLES

In addition to theoretical obstacles, our ability to generate knowledge about ethical decision-making is also hampered by several substantial methodological concerns, three of which we consider here. First, the construct of moral behavior is incredibly broad. As Treviño, Weaver, and Reynolds (2006) addressed in their review of the literature, moral behavior encompasses all behaviors that involve larger social norms, expectations or prescriptions. Thus, the construct represents behaviors that violate moral or social standards (e.g., cheating, stealing), meet those standards (e.g., honesty, driving at the speed limit) and exceed those standards (e.g., volunteering, donating). Given the variety of behaviors that exist within and across those three domains, it can be difficult to justify generalizing the findings of any study of moral behavior. For example, it would be nice to assume that if levels of factors X and Y contribute to stealing money then comparably low levels of X and Y will foster the donation of money, but this is probably not true. Researchers in other areas of study purposefully define their constructs with sufficient precision in order to make these kinds of leaps in logic. Unfortunately, the breadth of the moral behavior construct effectively limits this kind of generalization from the start.

Second, the measurement of moral behavior can be particularly challenging. This is true for a variety of reasons, but we suggest that the principal reason why moral behavior is so difficult to measure is because of the nature of its defining characteristic: social norms. Social norms can be somewhat paradoxical in that they tend to be widely acknowledged but not necessarily uniformly defined. For example, nearly everyone recognizes the principle of honesty, and yet there is disagreement about how honesty is displayed at work (e.g., what constitutes an honest response to an ineffective boss who requests feedback?). Furthermore, for many, a primary characteristic of moral behavior is the intention of the focal actor as he/she responds to that social norm. As illustrated in the famous Heinz dilemma utilized in measures of moral judgment (Kohlberg, 1981), most consider stealing for oneself to be immoral, but many can consider stealing for the sake of another to be morally justifiable, if not morally required. From a methodological point of view, there is no measure of stealing that can account for the intention of the actor. Thus, an observer, unaware of the true intention of the individual committing the act, cannot determine whether the act truly constitutes immoral behavior or not. Strategy researchers can state unequivocally that the firm has made a profit or not, but ethics researchers must acknowledge that because of inconsistent definitions and unknown intentions, they can never truly verify that their subject has acted unethically.

A final methodological obstacle worth considering is the challenge of demonstrating the construct validity of moral behavior measures. In particular, we are referring to the challenge of measuring those behaviors that are most prototypical of the phenomena we claim to be studying. Leadership scholars study managers as they lead groups and teams, and turnover scholars study employees as they quit. Thus, their constructs have strong face validity. The headlines that grab our attention and initially spark moral decision-making research detail behaviors such as embezzlement, blackmail, securities violations and so forth. But for a variety of reasons (many of which are discussed in the following section), social scientific research often focuses on more trivial behaviors, such as stealing pennies (Greenberg, 2002), donating cans of food (Aquino & Reed, 2002), and addressing panhandlers (Taylor, 1998). Unfortunately, any disconnect that exists between the phenomena that drives moral decision-making research and the actual behaviors that researchers study immediately discounts the power of any conclusions that might be drawn from the research results. Stealing a penny is hardly equivalent to embezzling a million dollars, and until such gaps are addressed, researchers will struggle with the challenges that follow from discussing one behavior while measuring another.

INSTITUTIONAL OBSTACLES

Beyond theoretical and methodological obstacles, many of the challenges facing the field are institutional in origin and have unique characteristics and dynamics. For example, perhaps the most critical factor affecting the amount of knowledge we have of moral behavior is the academic market's willingness to "pay" for that knowledge. In order to acquire any knowledge the academic market must acquire that knowledge by setting aside resources necessary to generate it. The most critical of these resources are tenure-track and doctoral student positions—from these positions most every other resource will flow. As a general rule, the best research comes from the best institutions, and a quick glance at the best schools reveals that very, very few have tenure-track positions dedicated to ethics researchers. Granted, many organizations have faculty with "ethics" in their titles, but oftentimes such titles are more representative of the institution's interest in appearances rather than the qualifications of the faculty member or the primary purpose of that position. Some might argue that an academic market with few ethics tenure-track positions merely reflects the principles of supply and demand, and that so few positions exist because demand from the business community is so low. The frequency of ethical issues in headlines, however, would suggest otherwise. Others flip the supply and demand argument to claim that there are so few positions because there are so few qualified researchers to fill them. This is a compelling argument (especially when considering the theoretical and methodological obstacles listed above) until we recognize that the academic market is a fairly unusual creature in that the consumer is basically responsible for the supply—universities admit and train doctoral students who then become the market from which they select faculty. To the extent that top institutions dedicate resources to admit and train the next generation of ethics scholars, they create their own pool of highly-skilled ethics researchers. Ultimately, what seems to be the most clear explanation is that academia (and its stakeholders) simply does not value this knowledge as much as those within it might like to believe.

A second challenge facing ethics research is the tenure process. In most institutions, tenure decisions are based on a host of criteria, but it is no stretch of the imagination to say that in many schools this process can be simply characterized as a publication-counting exercise. The emphasis on sheer numbers often places researchers in situations where they feel pressure to get their research to press, which means that they must make difficult choices regarding the objectives and the processes of their research. Sometimes these choices result in substantial sacrifices. For example, sacrifices might surface in decisions regarding samples; the difference between small, convenient, homogenous student samples and large, theoretically-driven, diverse managerial samples could mean the difference between two quick publications and one more time-consuming publication, which could have significant implications for a tenure decision. Unfortunately, this choice also holds profound implications for the usefulness and the meaningfulness of the knowledge generated. Other sacrifices might involve the kinds of measures and manipulations employed, the extent of the analyses conducted, and the number of studies included in one research article. Revolutionary research is expensive. From a researcher's point of view it requires time, energy, and other tangible resources, and if institutions do not recognize nor reward the expenditure of these resources, then the field will continue to reap what it sows.

Given the characteristics of the market and the tenure process, another major limitation of ethics research is, to be frank, the researchers themselves. To fully explore moral decision-making and moral behavior, a scholar should ideally have formal training in psychology, philosophy, economics, sociology, physiology, anthropology, statistics/methods, and (of course) since most business ethics scholars operate in business schools, management. Needless to say, it is the rare individual who has training in all of these areas, and thus it is typical that ethics scholars will prioritize. One common trend that we see is that some who consider themselves to be theoreticians tend to ignore statistics/methods—our distress over this approach is explained in the next section. Another common trend that we find even more alarming is when researchers and institutions act as though philosophy is the least important of these areas. More and more ethics researchers have little to no formal training in philosophy, an ironic twist given that the field has been dominated by philosophers for more than 2,500 years. Many seem to believe that a self-education is sufficient to glean from philosophy what is necessary to conduct ethics research. But of course this is the same logic the managers use to reject ethics training. The fact that ethics researchers are resisting (if only passively) philosophy is entirely consistent with the field's avoidance of the normative aspects of moral behavior, but we believe that to the extent that the field continues to devalue philosophical perspectives and philosophical training in its researchers, our ability to understand moral behavior will likewise become increasingly limited.

A final and somewhat unique hurdle for ethics researchers are existing Institutional Review Board (IRB) policies and procedures. IRB policies and procedures are a study in and of themselves on ethics. They are designed to ensure that both the participants in ethics research are safe and that the institutions supporting such research are not exposed to any unnecessary or avoidable risks. It is true, though, that protecting the interests of participants and institutions comes at the expense of knowledge. Given free reign, a great deal of knowledge could be gained by subjecting participants to intense moral experiences. Indeed, it is no coincidence that two of the most famous and thought-provoking studies in the history of ethics research, Milgram's (1974) obedience studies and Zimbardo's (Haney, Banks, & Zimbardo, 1973) prison simulation, both occurred before the institutionalization of IRB principles. This is not to advocate the dismissal of such review bodies or policies, but rather to make explicit the principle of trade-offs at work in these situations: Our ability to gain knowledge of moral behavior is limited by the need to safeguard the rights of those involved in the research. Given this dynamic, we admit that there is likely no "solution" to this tension. Nevertheless, we do not advocate surrender. Rather, we simply point out that uncovering revolutionary knowledge while still following these principles will obviously require more effort, more sophisticated research methods, and more creativity than ever before.

INTER-RELATEDNESS

As all of these obstacles come into view, it becomes apparent that many are inter-related. Clearly, theory has implications for methods, and institutions impact the research process from start to finish. Nevertheless, it is worthwhile to illustrate the extent to which these forces interact to shape our current understandings. An excellent example of the inter-relatedness of these factors can be found in the world of the Defining Issues Test (DIT). The DIT is a paper-and-pencil instrument that presents five hypothetical situations to individual participants and asks them to indicate the extent to which 12 statements about the moral issues in the situation match their own thoughts and beliefs. Typically completed in 15 to 30 minutes, the DIT provides scores related to the individual's stage of moral development.

Clearly, using the DIT represents a choice of the individual researcher, and to its credit the DIT has many attributes that make it attractive to researchers. For example, the DIT is a product of Rest's work on moral development (1986), but its origins can be traced back to Kohlberg's theory. Thus, its theoretical basis is the cognitive approach which places it in the predominant research paradigm, thereby increasing the chances that others (colleagues, reviewers, and editors) will be familiar with its premises and thus more receptive to it. It is also very easy to administer, which allows the researcher to gather large amounts of data in a short period of time. Additionally, it can provide a single score for each participant, which the researcher can easily use to conduct correlational analyses. Finally, the instrument deals with hypothetical situations and can be taken anonymously, which means it can easily pass even the most taxing of IRB hurdles. For a researcher who is facing a tight promotion timetable (the institutional context), these theoretical and methodological attributes make the DIT very attractive. Subsequently, it is not surprising to learn that, according to the test's developers and owners at the University of Minnesota, approximately 400,000 people have taken the DIT and its variants.

Such a choice, though, does have consequences. Theoretically, the DIT does not account for intuition, emotion, or other non-cognitive aspects of ethical decision-making. Also, the cognitive perspective downplays the role of context, so DIT scores are generally (if only implicitly) emphasized over the role of contextual matters or interactions with contextual factors. Furthermore, the DIT involves hypothetical situations, which are far-removed from behaviors that make headlines. This is not to suggest that the use of the DIT represents a poor choice. Indeed, as an instrument the DIT is undoubtedly the single greatest contributor to knowledge in the field. Rather, we are simply calling attention to the fact that institutional forces such as promotion pressures and IRB constraints make an easily-administered, easily-replicated, easily-scored instrument such as the DIT an attractive choice, and with that choice comes theoretical and methodological issues that have profound implications for the larger body of knowledge. Clearly, the obstacles to revolutionary knowledge are inter-related, and so achieving such gains will require that scholars: (a) sufficiently recognize the forces that drive them to conduct a particular type of research; and, (b) more thoroughly consider the theoretical, methodological and institutional implications of the choices they make.

RECOMMENDATIONS

In some cases, the paths to coping with these obstacles seem apparent, but others are less so. In this next section we offer both obvious and less obvious recommendations with regards to all three types of obstacles, proceeding in reverse order.

Institutional

With regards to institutional obstacles, our recommendations are fairly straightforward. First, we would like institutions to demonstrate that they value ethics research by investing in tenure-track positions dedicated to the topic and in admitting and training doctoral students with interests in the area. We recognize that faculty lines are rare and valuable vehicles, but we also adhere to the old adage, "you get what you pay for." If institutions are interested in more complete, more thorough, and more rich understanding of moral behavior, such knowledge does not come cheaply. Clearly, such changes will require leadership within and by institutions.

Second, there is much that individuals can do to affect institutional forces. Individuals can defend existing ethics-directed resources and push for more. Additionally, individuals would do well to be more cognizant of the forces that make sacrifices in their research so alluring. Of course, we are not suggesting one particular course over another; we are simply advocating greater awareness of the long-term and systemic consequences of individual decisions.

Finally, researchers would do well to better prepare themselves to complete first-rate research. It is becoming increasingly difficult for any researcher to publish "A" level work, and in the field of ethics, the standards of what constitutes "A" level work are rising quickly. For example, "A" level work these days typically requires that researchers provide a strong theoretical basis for the researcher's central arguments, a thorough defense of every measure's construct validity (via discussion and empirical analyses within-sample and/or with other samples), a large sample representative of the target population (i.e., managers), and evidence of generalizability (e.g., multiple ethical behavior measures, multiple studies). Perhaps the strongest trend is a greater emphasis on the measurement of behavior (i.e., donating, stealing, etc.) rather than just intentions. Meeting these rising standards requires a great deal of time and energy. Most importantly, it requires a willingness to develop the skills necessary to conduct this kind of high level research. To the extent that researchers are willing to prepare themselves and their research to meet these standards, they will have greater influence within the academic community and within their institutions to make other changes beneficial to the field.

Theoretical

From a theoretical perspective, the field is awakening to its reliance on the cognitive approach and is branching out. We fully support this movement. Nevertheless, we also note that, "While we may have perhaps over-relied on cognition in the past, we did so for good reason. As the field moves towards other areas…it is wise to integrate into those new areas what research based on the cognitive perspective has already established" (Reynolds & Ceranic, 2007, p. 1622).

Similarly, scholars would do well to focus more on the interaction between individuals and the context. Both individual and contextual characteristics influence behavior (Chatman, 1989; Treviño, 1986) and so examining one without the other seems futile. For example, since the study of moral awareness is deeply rooted in the cognitive perspective, research has generally assumed a one-way relationship wherein the issue exists and the individual is either aware of its ethical qualities or is not (Sparks & Hunt, 1998). Jones (1991) challenged this view to suggest that the nature of the issue matters, and Reynolds (2006a) demonstrated an interaction effect between individuals and issue characteristics—not only do both individuals and context matter, but they work together to shape moral awareness. In this spirit, Reynolds (2008) went even further, demonstrating that individuals vary in their everyday attentiveness to moral issues, and thus they vary in their capacity to construct moral issues and to behave morally. Often a difficult undertaking in ethics research, an interactionistic perspective is nevertheless very likely to yield the most revolutionary of results (Chatman, 1989).

Methodological

Scholars should also focus on developing more rounded or more generalizable studies. There are multiple ways in which to do so. Generally speaking, we advocate a multiple-study approach to ethics research. Multiple studies can demonstrate different nuances of the central principles or hypotheses of the research. For example, additional studies could employ different samples, different measures of the key variables, or different analyses. One example of this approach is Reynolds and Ceranic's (2007) recent work on moral identity. They argued that moral identity and moral judgment interact to shape moral behavior. They then provided empirical evidence of this argument using two different samples and three different measures of moral behavior, which did much towards establishing the generalizability of their findings. To the extent that researchers provide more evidence of their central hypotheses the greater the contribution that their work can make to the field.

Finally, we suggest that the field would benefit by a greater sense of the inter-relatedness of theoretical and empirical work. As a field, business ethics scholars tend to be tangibly divided between those who focus on theory and those who focus on empirics. This seems less than ideal. In our view, knowledge is best generated in an iterative process, wherein theory is developed, tested, modified based on those tests, and subjected to more empirical tests. Several groups of scholars have modeled this process. For example, Mitchell, Agle and Wood (1997) developed a theory of stakeholder salience arguing that stakeholders garner attention based on their power, legitimacy and the urgency of their claim. Then, Agle, Mitchell and Sonnenfeld (1999) provided an empirical test of these arguments. This started an iterative process wherein others have been able to develop and test other related ideas (e.g., Reynolds, Schulz & Hekman, 2006; Ryan & Schneider, 2003). Similarly, Jones (1995) theorized about the instrumental value of adopting an ethical perspective on business, and later conducted tests with colleagues related to those arguments (Berman, Wicks, Kotha, & Jones, 1999). Granted, not every scholar has the skill set necessary to fully develop and then rigorously test theory (this is why we have co-authors), but on the whole the field would be better off if every theorist proactively considered the empirical steps that followed the theory and if every empiricist would thoroughly consider the significance of research results for the principal theory.

CONCLUSION

Moral behavior is a critically important topic to life in general and to businesses in particular. As such, business ethics scholars should focus their energies on conducting the most pertinent research possible. This chapter has outlined some of the obstacles that we in this endeavor face and has presented possible resolutions to these impediments. In summary, we are recommending two basic steps. First, revolutionary research requires a greater understanding of the inter-relatedness of our obstacles and a greater awareness of the ramifications of our individual choices. Second, individually we need to make choices that most effectively further our knowledge. The field has the capacity to make the world a better place, and we hope that as others consider, enact, and expand upon these suggestions, that collectively we make a dramatic move towards that end.

NOTE

1. We consider the terms ethical and moral to be synonyms.

REFERENCES

Agle, B. R., Mitchell, R. K., & Sonnenfeld, J. A. (1999). Who matters to CEOs? An investigation of stakeholder attributes and salience, corporate performance, and CEO values. *Academy of Management Journal: 42*, 507–525.

Aquino, K., & Reed, A., II. (2002). The self-importance of moral identity. *Journal of Personality and Social Psychology, 83,* 1423–1440.

Ashforth, B. E. (1993). Emotional labor in service roles: The influence of identity. *Academy of Management Review, 18,* 88–126.

Ashkanasy, N. M. & Daus, C. S. (2002). Emotion in the workplace: The new challenge for managers. *Academy of Management Executive, 16,* 76–86.

Bandura, A. (1977). *Social learning theory.* Englewood Cliffs, NJ: Prentice Hall.

Bandura, A. (1991). Social cognitive theory of moral thought and action. In W. M. Kurtines & J. L. Gewirtz (Eds.), *Handbook of moral behavior and development* Vol. 1, (pp. 45–103). Hillsdale, NJ: Lawrence Erlbaum.

Berman, S. L., Wicks, A. C., Kotha, S., & Jones, T. M. (1999). Does stakeholder orientation matter? The relationship between stakeholder management models and firm financial performance. *Academy of Management Journal. 42,* 488–506.

Butterfield, K. D., Treviño, L. K., & Weaver, G. R. (2000). Moral awareness in business: Influences of issue-related and social context factors. *Human Relations 53,* 981–1018.

Ceranic, T. L. (2008). *Bridling emotions: Exploring emotions and ethical behavior.* Unpublished dissertation manuscript: University of Washington.

Chatman, J. A. (1989). Improving interactional organizational research: A model of person-organization fit. *Academy of Management Review, 14,* 333–349.

Cropanzano, R., Goldman, B., & Folger, R. (2003). Deontic justice: The role of moral principles in workplace fairness. *Journal of Organizational Behavior, 24,* 1019.

Darwin, C. R. (1896). *The expression of emotion in man and animals.* New York: D. Appleton.

De Cremer, D. (Ed.) (2007). *Advances in the psychology of justice and affect.* Charlotte, NC: Information Age.

De Cremer, D., & van den Bos, K. (2007). Justice and feelings: Toward a new era in justice research. *Social Justice Research, 20,* 1–9.

Donaldson, T. & Preston, L. (1995). The stakeholder theory of the corporation: Concepts, evidence, and implications. *Academy of Management Review, 20,* 65–91.

Fiske, S. T. & Taylor, S. E. (1991). *Social cognition* (2nd ed.). New York: McGraw Hill.

Freeman, R. E. (1984). *Strategic management: A stakeholder approach.* Boston: Pitman.

Gaudine, A. & Thorne, L. (2001). Emotion and ethical decision making in organizations. *Journal of Business Ethics, 31,* 175–187.

Gephardt, J., Harrison, D. A., & Treviño, L. K. (2007). The who, when, and where of (un)ethical choices: A meta-analysis. *Academy of Management Best Paper Proceedings 2007.*

Grandey, A. A. (2003). When the "show must go on": Surface acting and deep acting as determinants of emotional exhaustion and peer-rated service delivery. *Academy of Management Journal, 46,* 86–96.

Greenberg, J. (2002). Who stole the money, and when? Individual and situational determinants of employee theft. *Organizational Behavior and Human Decision Processes,* 89, 985.

Haidt, J. (2001). The emotional dog and its rational tail: A social intuitionist approach to moral judgment. *Psychological Review, 4,* 814–834.

Haney, C., Banks, W. C., & Zimbardo, P. G. (1973). Study of prisoners and guards in a simulated prison. *Naval Research Reviews, 9,* 1–17. Office of Naval Research: Washington, DC.

Hudson, H. (1994). *Kant's compatabilism.* Ithaca, NY: Cornell University Press:

James, W. (1884). What is an emotion? *Mind, 9,* 188–205.

Jones, T. M. (1991). Ethical decision making by individuals in organizations: An issue-contingent model. *Academy of Management Review, 16,* 366–395.

Jones, T. M. (1995). Instrumental stakeholder theory: A synthesis of ethics and economics. *Academy of Management Review, 20,* 404–437.

Kant, I. (1785/1994). Grounding for the metaphysics of morals. In *Ethical Philosophy,* (2nd ed.). (translated by J.W. Ellington). Indianapolis: Hackett.

Kohlberg, L. (1981). *The philosophy of moral development.* San Francisco, CA: Harper & Row.

Kohlberg, L. (1984). *The psychology of moral development: The nature and validity of moral stages.* New York: Harper and Row.

Lange, C. G. (1885). *The mechanism of the emotions.* Boston: Houghton Mifflin.

Lazarus, R. (1991). Cognition and motivation in emotion. *American Psychologist, 46:* 352–367.

Milgram, S. (1974). *Obedience to authority; An experimental view.* NY: Harper & Row.

Mitchell, R.K., Agle, B. R., & Wood, D. J. (1997). Toward a theory of stakeholder identification and salience: Defining the principle of who or what really counts. *Academy of Management Review, 22,* 853–886.

Moore, G. E. (1903). *Principia ethica.* New York: Cambridge University Press.

Pugh, S. D. (2001). Service with a smile: Emotional contagion in the service encounter. *Academy of Management Journal, 44,* 1018–1027.

Rafaeli, A., & Sutton, R. (1987). Expression of emotion as part of the work role. *Academy of Management Review, 12,* 23–37.

Rest, J. R. (1986). *Moral development: Advances in research and theory.* New York: Praeger.

Reynolds, S. J. (2006a) Moral awareness and ethical predispositions: Investigating the role of individual differences in the recognition of moral issues. *Journal of Applied Psychology, 91,* 233–243.

Reynolds, S. J. (2006b). A neurocognitive model of the ethical decision-making process: implications for study and practice. *Journal of Applied Psychology, 91,* 737–748.

Reynolds, S. J. (2008). Moral attentiveness: Who pays attention to the moral aspects of life? *Journal of Applied Psychology, 93,* 1027–1041.

Reynolds, S. J., & Ceranic, T. L. (2007). The effects of moral judgment and moral identity on moral behavior: An empirical examination of the moral individual, *Journal of Applied Psychology, 92,* 1610–1624.

Reynolds, S. J., Schultz, F. C., & Hekman, D. R. (2006). Balancing stakeholder interests: The constraining effects of resource divisibility and stakeholder saliency. *Journal of Business Ethics, 64,* 285–301.

Roseman, I. J., & Smith, C. A. (2001). Appraisal theory: Overview, assumptions varieties, controversies. In *Appraisal processes in emotion: Theory, methods, research.* (Ed.) K. R. Scherer & T. Johnstone (pp. 3–19). New York: Oxford University Press.

Rozin, P., Lowrey, L. Imada, S., & Haidt, J. (1999). The CAD triad hypothesis: A mapping between three moral emotions (contempt, anger, disgust) and three moral codes (community, autonomy, divinity). *Journal of Personality and Social Psychology, 76,* 574–586.

Ryan, L. W., & Schneider, M. (2003). Institutional investor power and heterogeneity. *Business and Society, 42,* 398–429.

Scherer, K. R. (1993). Studying the emotion-antecedent appraisal process: An expert system approach. *Cognition and Emotion, 3,* 325–355.

Simon, H. A. (1987). Making management decisions: The role of intuition and emotion. *Academy of Management Executive, February,* 57–64.

Smith, C. A. & Ellsworth, P. C. (1985). Patterns of cognitive appraisal in emotion. *Journal of Personality and Social Psychology, 48,* 813–838.

Solomon, R. (1976). *The passions: Emotions and the meaning of life.* Indianapolis, IN: Hackett.

Solomon, R. (1988). On emotions as judgments. In *Not passion's slave: Emotions and choice* (pp. 92–114). New York: Oxford University Press.

Solomon, R. (2003). *What is an emotion? Classic and contemporary readings.* New York: Oxford University Press.

Smith, C. A., & Ellsworth, P. C. (1985). Patterns of cognitive appraisal in emotion. *Journal of Personality and Social Psychology, 48,* 813–838.

Sparks, J. R., & Hunt, S. D. (1998). Marketing researcher ethical sensitivity: Conceptualization, measurement, and exploratory investigation. *Journal of Marketing, 62,* 92–109.

Tan, H. H., Foo, M. D., & Kwek, M. H. (2004). The effects of customer personality traits on the display of positive emotions. *Academy of Management Journal, 47,* 287–296.

Taylor, C. J. (1998). Factors affecting behavior toward people with disabilities. *The Journal of Social Psychology, 138,* 766–771.

Treviño, L. K. (1986). Ethical decision making in organizations: A person-situation interactionist model. *Academy of Management Review, 11,* 601–617.

Treviño, L. K., Weaver, G. R.., & Reynolds, S. J. (2006). Behavioral ethics in organizations: A review. *Journal of Management, 32,* 951–990.

Weaver, G. R.., & Treviño, L. K. (1994). Normative and empirical business ethics: Separation, marriage of convenience, or marriage of necessity? *Business Ethics Quarterly, 4,* 129–143.

Wharton, A. S., & Erickson, R. J. (1993). Managing emotions on the job and at home: Understanding the consequences of multiple emotional roles. *Academy of Management Review, 3,* 457–486.

CHAPTER 3

PSYCHOLOGICAL PROCESSES IN ORGANIZATIONAL CORRUPTION

Celia Moore
London Business School

INTRODUCTION

The number, scale and persistence of corporate scandals in the last decade have provided cynics about business ethics quite a lot of fodder. Enron and Worldcom, the classic cautionary tales from the early 2000s of corporate practice gone wrong, are presently being supplanted by more recent stories, from rogue traders losing billions at Société Générale and Credit Suisse to the multinationals currently implicated in the collapse of the sub-prime mortgage market. All of these juicy accounts have given rise to serious and legitimate interest among academics in corporate corruption; however, the literature on corruption has remained of inconsistent quality, lacking cohesion, and at the fringes of organizational scholarship (see the commentary in Ashforth, Gioia, Robinson, & Treviño, 2008a).

There are a number of reasons why research on corruption has remained on the outskirts of organizational research. First (and perhaps most important), the construct itself is muddy and overly broad. Corruption hasn't

Psychological Perspectives on Ethical Behavior and Decision Making, pages 35–71
Copyright © 2009 by Information Age Publishing
All rights of reproduction in any form reserved.

only been ill-defined in the organizational literature; it has hardly been defined at all, with preference shown for terms such as "organizational illegality" (Baucus, 1989; Szwajkowski, 1985) when speaking of illegal acts of corporations, and, broadly, "deviance" (Bennett & Robinson, 2003; Robinson & Greenberg, 1998) when speaking to the morally questionable acts of individuals. Looking outside the organizational literature to sociology, criminology, law and political theory adds depth to our understanding, but the overall consensus even within those fields is that "we still lack firmly grounded theories of corruption" and that corruption itself remains a "highly contested concept" (Williams, 2000: xi) with "few shared understandings" (Kleinig & Heffernan, 2004: 3). Corruption can refer to a wide variety of actions and/or behaviours, which makes establishing a clear definition difficult (see Bloch & Geis, 1962; Geis, 1962; Quinney, 1964).

A second complicating factor is that corruption is an inherently *multilevel* phenomenon. Individuals can be corrupt: embezzlers, for example, are typically individuals working in isolation (see Cressey, 1953). Groups can be corrupt: for example, successfully carrying out large scale fraud within organizations often requires the complicity and active involvement of groups of informed individuals (see McLean & Elkind, 2003). Organizations can be corrupt: for example, an organization's business model, processes or policies can require or depend on illegal behaviour on the part of their employees (see Eichenwald, 1995). Finally, industries can be corrupt: representatives from multiple firms within an industry might collude to fix prices, for example (see Baker & Faulkner, 1993).

The third complicating factor is that corruption refers both to a *dynamic* process, as well as the *outcome* of that dynamic process (Ashforth et al., 2008a). Though organizational researchers are typically more comfortable studying outcomes (as static and measurable) than processes (as dynamic and difficult to capture empirically), it remains an underappreciated fact that corruption refers to both. Given all of these complications, the necessity of clearly specifying what is meant in any particular discussion of corruption—how corruption is being defined, at what level of analysis it is being studied, and whether it is being focused on as a product or as a process—is heightened. This chapter, therefore, starts with fundamentals, and returns to the original definition of corruption in the *Oxford English Dictionary* for clues on how to proceed.

The origin of the word corruption is a Latin verb *corrumpere*, which means to "break in pieces, destroy, ruin, spoil, mar, adulterate, falsify, draw to evil, seduce, [or] bribe." The fact that corruption has its roots as a verb means that it perhaps more accurately understood as a process rather than as an outcome. Interestingly, corruption has less often been studied as a process, even though the true puzzles we need to unravel in order to understand (and undo) corruption are about the *processes* that deliver corruption, rather than the end result of those processes (Ashforth et al., 2008a; Darley, 2005). Therefore, this chapter will focus on understanding corruption dynamics rather than more simply on outcomes.

In terms of the second complication, the definition of corruption does not imply any particular level of analysis. The majority of the work on corruption to date has focused on the more macro perspectives—corruption at the state, industry, or organization level (Douglas, 1977; Heffernan & Kleinig, 2004; Jong-sung & Khagram, 2005; Miller, Roberts, & Spence, 2004; Simon, 1999),[1] with organizations conceptualized as the "deviant" actors (Coleman, 1996; Ermann & Lundman, 1996; Pfarrer, DeCelles, Smith, & Taylor, 2008; Pinto, Leana, & Pil, 2008). Corruption at the group or individual level is less well understood (two excellent exceptions: Ashforth & Anand, 2003; Brief, Buttram, & Dukerich, 2001). However, corrupt firm behaviour is necessarily underpinned by the actions of individuals and groups of individuals, and these actions are motivated by a wide range of psychological processes. This chapter, therefore, focuses on the psychological processes that underpin corruption, and how they lead to corruption at higher levels of analysis.

Finally, returning to the original problem, given the broadness of the corruption construct, how is it best to define corruption here? Remembering that this chapter is going to focus on psychological processes that speak to corruption as a dynamic process, this chapter defines corruption as: *a process which perverts the original nature of an individual or group from a more pure state to a less pure state.*[2] Appropriately, this definition is inherently tied to notions of morality (Kleinig & Heffernan, 2004), which is challenging because of ongoing debates about what constitutes ethical behavior (Tenbrunsel & Smith-Crowe, in press), but allows us to connect this conversation to behavioural research on ethical decision making (Tenbrunsel & Smith-Crowe, in press; Treviño, Weaver, & Reynolds, 2006), even though the ethics and corruption literatures are not well-integrated (see Baucus, 1994).

The question that then drove the rest of this chapter was this: how can we understand the ways in which individuals and groups become perverted from their original natures, to move from more pure to less pure states? To look more closely at the *Oxford English Dictionary*, one finds that corruption has nine different definitions, including: "spoiling" and "moral deterioration" (OED definitions 1a and 4, respectively), the "perversion or destruction of integrity" (OED definition 6), "infection, contagion, taint" (OED definition 2), and "the oxidation or corrosion of a body" (OED definition 1b). These definitions suggested a framework for organizing current literature relevant to corruption processes: two types of processes at the individual level, and two at the group level, two that work internally, and two that work externally (see Table 3.1).

TABLE 3.1 Psychological Processes in Organizational Corruption

	Internal (inside→out) Processes	External (outside→in) Processes
Individual level	**Compulsion** "Moral deterioration"	**Compliance** "Perversion or destruction of integrity"
	Small unconscious steps towards corrupt outcomes (i.e., driven by bounded ethicality), become a slippery slope towards larger transgressions	Conformity with corrupt group norms or demands from authority figures become unconscious and routinized within individuals
Group level	**Contagion** "Infection, contagion, taint"	**Corrosion** "Oxidation or corrosion of a body"
	Incremental changes occur within a social network which then slowly spread throughout the social systems	Structural or systemic (i.e., organizational or environmental) forces motivate corruption at the group levels and facilitate neglect of the ethical dimensions of decisions

The first two types of psychological processes discussed operate at the individual level. Corruption as "moral deterioration" is reflected in the notion of *compulsion*. Compulsion works from the inside-out, due to the various ways in which our rationality (and ethicality) is bounded, and facilitates small, unconscious steps that start us on a slippery slope towards more corrupt behaviours. Corruption as the "perversion or destruction of integrity" is reflected in the notion of *compliance*. Compliance operates from the outside-in, and encompasses the ways in which individuals respond to pressures to obey authority or conform to group norms.

The second two types of psychological processes operate at the group level. Corruption as "infection" is represented by the notion of *contagion*. Contagion operates from the inside-out, and refers to ways in which incremental changes can occur within social networks and gradually spread through social systems. Corruption as "oxidation" is represented by the notion of *corrosion*. Corrosion refers to the ways in which structural or systemic forces can create external pressure on groups, providing incentives for groups to engage in behaviours towards corrupt ends. I now discuss each of these types of corruption dynamics in turn.

COMPULSION IN ORGANIZATIONAL CORRUPTION

The first definition of corruption in the *OED* is "the spoiling of anything"; the fourth is "moral deterioration." Both definitions imply a process that occurs without intention. Fruit and vegetables spoil simply by being left out in the air. The apple can't help it—spoiling is an inevitable outcome of the natural features of the fruit interacting with its natural environment. Though deterioration may be halted (to continue with the fruit analogy, through refrigeration, for example), left to their own devices, some things, through no intentional or conscious participation, simply deteriorate. One way to understand how "moral deterioration" might function at the individual level is to look at how people, in their natural environment and simply succumbing to natural human weaknesses, are *compelled* towards corruption. This represents, at the individual level, a process that works from the inside out: without vigilance or intervention, it is simply in the nature of some things to become corrupted.

There is quite a substantial body of literature that both directly and indirectly addresses how individuals deteriorate towards corruption in these unintentional and unconscious ways. This human compulsion towards corruption has been addressed directly in the work on bounded ethicality (Chugh, Bazerman, & Banaji, 2005), ethical fading (Tenbrunsel & Messick, 2004), and moral seduction (Moore, Tetlock, Tanlu, & Bazerman, 2006)—all of which draw heavily on more basic social psychological research on general decision making biases and framing effects (originally stated and best overviewed in Kahneman, 2003b; Kahneman & Tversky, 2000; Tversky & Kahneman, 1981). Three important ways in which individuals are susceptible to corruption—our tendency towards self-serving or self-enhancing biases and attributions, our inability to appropriately judge outcomes of our behavior, and the way in which our choices are driven by how decisions are framed—are briefly discussed here.

Self-serving biases. Self-interest is natural to the human condition, even if we can often disregard the drive towards it (Miller, 1999). There are many obvious reasons, both evolutionary and psychological, why our evaluations of events and perceptions of decisions should favour the self. These biases are natural to the human condition in part because they are self-protective: in evolutionary terms, self-serving helps ensure one accumulates the resources necessary for survival; in psychological terms, self-serving assists in the development, maintenance and security of self-esteem and identity, and helps reduce the threats to self-esteem and identity presented by others (Sedikides & Strube, 1997). However, this biased perspective can be dangerous to the extent that it can hinder consideration of interests we might be obligated to serve outside our own. Operating from a self-interested perspective is particularly insidious because, as Moore and Loewenstein note:

> [S]elf-interest is automatic, viscerally compelling, and often unconscious. Understanding one's ethical and professional obligations to others, in contrast, often involves a more thoughtful process. The automatic nature of self-inter-

est gives it a primal power to influence judgment and makes it difficult for people to understand its influence on their judgment, let alone eradicate its influence. (2004, p. 189)

The direct relationship between the human tendency towards self-serving biases and unethical behavior has been discussed at length theoretically (Johns, 1999; Moore & Loewenstein, 2004), and is confirmed by empirical work. Leaders in particular use self-serving biases to make unfair resource allocations to themselves because positional power creates feelings of entitlement (De Cremer & van Dijk, 2005, see also De Cremer, van Dijk, & Folmers, this volume) A series of experimental studies have shown that people are good at justifying outcomes which unfairly advantage the self (Diekmann, Samuels, Ross, & Bazerman, 1997), and work in the medical literature has indicated that doctors are swayed against offering their best medical advice by gifts and influence attempts from the pharmaceutical industry (Dana & Loewenstein, 2003; Wazana, 2000). People are also particularly likely to act unfairly towards others if they have had a recent opportunity to bolster their self-image as a fair and honest person, leading to an argument that humans might be cognitively predisposed towards moral hypocrisy as a way of succumbing to biases while maintaining one's moral identity (Batson, Kobrynowicz, Dinnerstein, Kampf, & Wilson, 1997; Batson, Thompson, Seuferling, Whitney, & Strongman, 1999). These biases become more worrisome when thinking about how individuals can be unconsciously compelled towards increasingly serious corruption. Once we have approached information in a biased way, it is hard to reinterpret the same information in a less biased way (Babcock, Loewenstein, Issacharoff, & Camerer, 1995), which makes it easier for us to "deteriorate" or "spoil," as it were.

Inability to judge outcomes. The human weakness in evaluating the future outcomes of our decisions represents a second unintentional and unconscious way in which individuals can be compelled towards corruption. Thirty years of research show that people are more likely to make decisions when consequences are known and predictable rather than unknown and unpredictable, even when the risks of the decisions outweigh those of other options (Tversky & Kahneman, 1981, 1992; Tversky & Wakker, 1995). Since many of the benefits of corrupt behaviour are immediate, tangible, and easy to predict (i.e., direct personal gain and securing immediate organizational goals), and many of the risks of corrupt behaviour are less visible, have a longer time horizon, and are difficult to predict (i.e., the threat of detection, exposure and criminal liability), the human tendency to be poor outcome evaluators represents a second compelling force towards corruption.

Framing. Finally, it is important to understand how the cognitive frames we use to approach problems influence the choices we make (Kahneman

& Tversky, 2000: Part IV). Much of the work on framing has focused on our tendency to be to be risk-seeking in situations which are negatively framed in order to avoid possible losses (Kahneman & Tversky, 1979, 2000; Tversky & Kahneman, 1981). This inclination towards risk seeking when events are negatively framed implies dangerous consequences in ethically intense situations, since these types of situations are likely to create negative frames due to their high risk of loss, and thus encourage risk-taking. As a result, decision frames are increasingly being considered as a key factor in ethical decisions (Tenbrunsel & Smith-Crowe, in press).

There are good theoretical arguments to support the notion that using an economic or business frame helps shield ethical concerns or outcomes from our decision sets (Ferraro, Pfeffer, & Sutton, 2005). Empirically, studies of outcomes in prisoner's dilemma games have shown that creating conditions in which business frames (rather than ethical frames) are adopted significantly decreases the likelihood that individuals cooperate (Tenbrunsel & Messick, 1999). From a more grounded perspective, it is easy see how job design and job training (i.e., the way you are communicated to about your job) could be a powerful force influencing how individuals frame decisions at work. Gioia discusses the ways in which his job at Ford in the 1970s trained him not to recognize the ethical risk involved in deciding against a recall of the Pinto car, which was susceptible to gas tank rupture and explosion in low impact collisions (Gioia, 1992). This framing, which helped to "script" Gioia's behavior and which dramatically affected his decision making in an unconscious way, facilitated the seemingly risk-averse choice not to recall the Pinto, when in fact best estimates are that the decision not to recall the car eventually cost Ford well over $100 million (Bromiley & Marcus, 1989).

Anchoring is a phenomenon closely related to framing which also can compel individuals towards corruption. The psychology and behavioural economics literatures both attest that our judgments are strongly influenced by the information that is most available and accessible; this information provides *anchors* which influence the evaluation of available behavioural options (Cain, Loewenstein, & Moore, 2005; Strack & Mussweiler, 1997; Tversky & Kahneman, 1981). In other words, "perception is referent-dependent" (Kahneman, 2003a, p. 1449). Organizations, superiors, peers and co-workers all have the opportunity to present information in ways that can unconsciously influence individuals towards corruption. However, research specifically testing how anchors can influence ethical decision making have yet to appear in the literature (though the way organizational goals operate to anchor behaviour will be discussed in the section on corrosion).

These three tendencies of the human condition—self-serving biases, poor outcome evaluation, and issue framing—all represent obvious ways in which human cognitive and evaluative weaknesses can unconsciously compel individuals toward corruption. However, they represent given (i.e., static) factors that have the potential to influence individuals towards less ethical decision making. Yet if corruption is a *process*, a deterioration or a spoil*ing*, then what are the dynamics that these conditions play in to at the individual level which *compel* people towards corruption? In the next section, I discuss two dynamics which speak more directly to how individuals can be compelled towards corruption: the slippery slope, and escalation of commitment.

The slippery slope. A number of researchers in related areas have written about the process of individuals descending into corruption as a "slippery slope" process (Ashforth & Anand, 2003; Cain et al., 2005; Moore & Loewenstein, 2004; Tenbrunsel & Messick, 2004). The common thread in this work is that it is easier for individuals to take small steps towards corrupt ends, hardly noticing the shifts in their behaviour, and thus paving the way for larger corrupt actions. Moral seduction theory, for example, makes the case that descending into corruption will most likely occur gradually, in a number of successive steps, each of which swings individuals' behavioural anchors farther from their original starting position (Moore et al., 2006). Individuals first cross into a morally ambiguous zone, and as behaviour within that zone becomes acceptable, it then becomes easier to extend the boundaries of moral ambiguity out farther into previously unconsidered territory. Ashforth and Anand's work discusses this slippery slope as "incrementalism," which they define as the process of being "induced to gradually escalate [one's] corruption," and consider it one of the main routes of corruption normalization (2003, p. 28).

The slippery slope represents a process of personal anchor-shifting: as actions of decreasing ethicality are accepted by an individual, their moral standards erode. To put it another way, once an "initial" act is committed, the distance between that act and a second (more corrupt) act shrinks (Darley, 2005; Tenbrunsel & Messick, 2004). Empirical tests of the hypothesis that individuals' moral standards are most likely to erode gradually over time are rare. However, it is easy to find anecdotal evidence of the mobility of personal anchors of morally acceptable behaviour. Sabrina Harman, the Specialist in the U.S. Army who took some of the famously exploitative photographs at the prison at Abu Ghraib, attests to this. A recent article quotes her as saying:

> In the beginning...you see somebody naked and you see underwear on their head and you're like, 'Oh, that's pretty bad—I can't believe I just saw that.' And then you go to bed and you come back the next day and you see something worse. Well, it seems like the day before wasn't so bad. (Gourevitch & Morris, 2008, p. 51)

Dozens of regular army and reservist personnel have now been implicated in this major abuse of human rights (Hersh, 2004; Scherer & Benjamin, 2006), a recent example of corruption to which 'otherwise normal' individuals can become acclimated (though the Holocaust remains the primary example of the extremity of the abuses to which ordinary people can be compelled to participate, see Arendt, 1963/1994; Darley, 1992, 2005; Lifton, 1986).

The shifting anchors phenomenon can be found in less horrific examples of incremental adaptation to corruption as well. For example, in order to more easily reach earnings targets during a period of financial duress surrounding an IPO at Kurzweil Applied Intelligence Company in the early 1990s, sales people were initially permitted to post sales which were to come in a few days after the fiscal quarter closed (Maremont, 1996). As this practice became normalized, salespeople began booking sales earlier and earlier, until finally they would forge clients' signatures when sales were simply likely to come through (Maremont, 1996). In this example, allowing sales which were to come in a few days after the end of the quarter shifted the boundaries of acceptable behaviour in an unethical direction. As these anchors of acceptable practice are repositioned, so are the internal moral standards of the actor. As Darley writes:

> Each step is so small as to be essentially continuous with previous ones; after each step, the individual is positioned to take the next one. The individual's morality follows rather than leads. Morality is retrospectively fitted to previous act by rationalizations..." (1992, p. 208)

Once a less ethical set of practices becomes "normalized" (Ashforth & Anand, 2003), practices that are similar to it, and even less ethical, become normalized as well—by proxy, as it were. In other words, if X is acceptable, then a marginally worse version of X called Y is probably acceptable as well; if Y is acceptable, then a marginally worse version of Y called Z is then probably acceptable as well; and so on. Tenbrunsel and Messick call this the "induction mechanism" (2004, p. 228) which makes new and increasingly corrupt practices acceptable.

One of the reasons this slippery slope is so compelling is because there are enormous psychological pressures—of self-justification, dissonance reduction, and the maintenance of one's self-image as a moral person, among others—to continue down a path one has started down. As Kelman has written, once an initial step has been undertaken, an individual is:

> in a new psychological and social situation in which the pressures to continue are quite powerful...many forces that might have originally kept him out of the situation reverse direction once he has made a commitment...and now help to keep him in the situation. (1973, p. 46)

It has proven very difficult to study in more controlled settings how this process might work, since both the content and the dynamic nature of the process of interest are difficult to capture empirically. However, related research from other areas of psychology confirms that people are a little reminiscent of "boiling frogs." Frogs, the story goes—though the veracity of this story is disputed—will simply jump out of a pot of boiling water, but won't notice temperature changes as long as the water is brought up to the boiling point slowly. Similarly, we tend not to notice changes in our surroundings—even if those changes direct or constrain our behaviour—as long as the changes are sufficiently incremental (e.g., Levin, 2002; Thorson & Biederman-Thorson, 1974).

One recent study has attempted to replicate slippery slope processes in a laboratory setting (Gino & Bazerman, 2007). Participants were asked to approve a series of estimates made by others of the number of pennies in a jar, and provided with an incentive to approve high estimates while also having to "sign" a statement that they believed the estimate they were approving was within 10% of the true number of pennies in the jar. Participants were significantly more likely to approve over-estimations which increased incrementally rather than over-estimations which increased in an obvious leap (Gino & Bazerman, 2007).

Escalation of Commitment. Similar to the slippery slope, escalation of commitment is a *process*, and one in which individuals are *compelled* to engage, as a result of common weaknesses in human psychology. Escalation of commitment is triggered by decisions which have led to "questionable or negative outcomes" (Staw & Ross, 1987: 43), but for which "withdrawal involves substantial costs" or for which "persistence holds at least the prospect for eventual gain" (Staw & Ross, 1987: 40). Though typically studied in the context of poor financial decision making (Ross & Staw, 1993; Staw, Barsade, & Koput, 1997), the research findings and frameworks developed in nearly 30 years of research on the topic (Staw, 1981, 1997; Staw & Ross, 1989) provides a fruitful if underused paradigm within which to study corruption processes.

The implication that escalation of commitment might lead to an increased likelihood of unethical behaviour has been noted in theoretical statements of the escalation phenomenon (Street, Robertson, & Geiger, 1997). Escalation has also been discussed in ethical contexts such as the decision to remain in Vietnam (Staw, 1997; Staw & Ross, 1989). To date, only one study has ever specifically shown that unethical behaviour is a likely outcome of escalation situations (Street & Street, 2006), yet it is easy to see how escalation might apply in ethically charged situations. For example, in the circumstances at Kurzweil Applied Intelligence Company, escalation of commitment was likely a factor in the fraud perpetrated there because taking sales out of a future quarter in order to increase the sales figures of the current quarter meant that the actions needed to make that next quarter acceptable to the balance sheet became even more desperate (Darley, 2005).

The idea of escalation as a continuing source of questionable decisions that becomes more and more difficult to unwind from fits well with the narrative that accompanies stories of "rogue traders" as well. The autobiography of Nick Leeson, the man who brought down Barings Bank in 1995 after accumulating trading losses of more than £800 million, provides a classic narrative of the process of escalation, from a series of small mistakes that required larger cover-ups, which then led to increasingly risky decisions, and which eventually leading to the demise of London's oldest investment bank (Leeson, 1996; Ross, 1997). Leeson describes how the incremental decisions he made, including the ongoing use of dummy trading accounts in order to cover his errors and losses, became "an addiction" (Leeson, 1996: 64). Early reports of the recent £5 billion losses incurred at Société Générale by the newest addition to the "rogue trader" gallery, Jérôme Kerviel, attest that escalation of commitment may have also played a role in taking on the level of risk which he did (Gauthier-Villars & Mollenkamp, 2008). A comprehensive account of the rogue trader phenomenon has yet to appear, though with new "rogue traders" appearing repeatedly in the press—including the post-Société Générale discovery of traders at Credit Suisse covering up £1.4 billion in losses in order to protect their bonuses (Winnett, 2008a)—the time is ripe for one.

What psychological mechanisms involved in escalation of commitment might be particularly salient in situations where the commitment escalates to increasing levels of corruption? It is a human tendency to selectively choose reasons which justify behaviour in which we have already engaged. Psychologically, this has been called defensive bolstering (Tetlock & Lerner, 1999; Tetlock, Skitka, & Boettger, 1989) or self-justification (Brockner, 1992; Staw, 1976). Escalating corruption might be particularly likely for actors who initiate the early corrupt acts; for example, when Jérôme Kerviel first started making bets outside the daily limits imposed on him by his supervisors, he would have been particularly committed to ensuring those bets became profitable, since he would need to convince himself he had made the right move by overextending his positions. Changing one's course of corrupt action might be particularly difficult when a series of ethically tenuous decisions is made by an individual who is particularly ambitious, since achievement striving has been found to be positively linked to escalation of commitment decisions (Moon, 2001).

These slippery slopes are unconscious due to a number of psychological processes which kick in as we slide, and which permit us to continue to think of ourselves in a positive light during the journey. Often, these psychological processes involve bracketing ourselves off from our own agency. For example, in the social identity literature, depersonalization describes how the draw of identifying with prototypical group members effectively brackets off one's original behavioural or attitudinal standards as an individual (Hogg & Turner, 1987; Turner, Hogg, Oakes, Reicher, & Wetherell, 1987). Milgram termed the process passing into an "agentic state" (Milgram, 1974), in which "the conscience has been switched off in the individual" (Darley, 1992: 206). Similarly, Bandura describes moral disengagement, as a process wherein individuals become habituated to cognitive mechanisms which "disengage" the self-sanctions that ought to compel us to behave morally (Bandura, 1990a, 1990b, 1999, 2002). In other words, when we are compelled towards corruption, our psychology operates in ways which shields our consciousness from the worst of its own behaviour.

COMPLIANCE IN ORGANIZATIONAL CORRUPTION

The sixth definition of corruption in the *Oxford English Dictionary* (OED) is the "perversion or destruction of integrity." This definition implies yielding to some outside force. While the factors relevant to *compulsion* processes were internal to the individual, including weaknesses in human cognition, evaluation, or perception, the forces relevant to *compliance* processes are external to the individual. These forces can be explicit, as in direct pressure faced by authority figures or groups, or tacit, as in socialization processes. Both of these types of compliance—explicit pressure from authority or groups, and tacit pressure from socialization processes—will be discussed in turn.

Explicit pressure from authority or groups. There is a long history of research on how individuals are strongly drawn to submit to pressures from authority figures (Kelman & Hamilton, 1989; Milgram, 1974). The ease with which authority figures can coerce individuals into corrupt actions was most dramatically shown in Milgram's obedience experiments in the 1960s (Milgram, 1963, 1974), and findings both empirical and anecdotal about the human propensity to conform to the wishes of authority figures have continued to accumulate since then (i.e., Kelman & Hamilton, 1989). Within organizations, the pressure both implicit and explicit to follow the behavioural norms set by organizational superiors should not be underestimated. When in two separate surveys nearly 20 years apart *Harvard Business Review* readers were asked to rank the importance of multiple factors in influencing their potential unethical behaviour, the behaviour of supervisors came out as the most important factor both times (Baumhart, 1961; Brenner & Molander, 1977).

The psychological literature on how individuals are easily manipulated into conforming to group norms is as substantial as the research on the pressure to conform to authority (Asch, 1951, 1955; Janis, 1983). The ease of getting people to conform to group norms has been explained by our need to socially identify with others in our groups (Hogg & Turner, 1987; Turner et al., 1987), as well as by the strong desire to belong (Baumeister & Leary, 1995) and the related desire to avoid social exclusion (Kurzban & Leary, 2001). How this conformity pressure plays out through the desire to feel identified with one's work group is dramatically described by Michael Lewis, in his description of the three years he spent as a salesman at Salomon Brothers (1989). Early in his career, when he was triggered to question certain normative practices of the firm, he was told that his option was either to become a "jammer," a person who was willing to unload whatever stocks would most benefit Salomon Brothers' (regardless of their worth or benefit to the client), or to be labelled a "geek" or "fool" (Lewis, 1989). It is difficult in such situations to make the decisions that not only result in social exclusion but also risk one's job; it is both easier and less assaulting to one's identity to do what it takes to comply with existing group norms.

Outside the psychological literature, an entire branch of criminological theory—differential association—is devoted to the influence that groups have in facilitating the criminal behaviour of individuals (Sutherland, 1939). Differential association is really a social learning theory of criminal behaviour, which posits that unethical behaviour is encouraged, modelled, and normalized through the process of interacting with one's peer groups (Sutherland, 1939). A study of rule-breaking at an insurance company supports this differential association perspective: whether an employee joined in the rule-breaking, such as misrepresenting the true cost of policies to clients, or selling policies to clients using the cash value or dividends from already-purchased policies ("churning"), depended on, in the words of one study participant, "who you were learning from" (MacLean, 2001: 176).

Differential association theory has not found much traction in the ethical decision making literature, though it forms an integral part of Ferrell and Gresham's influential model of ethical decision making in marketing research (1985) and inspired two empirical studies developed with that model in mind (Zey-Ferrell & Ferrell, 1982; Zey-Ferrell, Weaver, & Ferrell, 1979). In these studies of marketing managers and advertisers, Zey-Ferrell and her colleagues found that individuals' perceptions of their peers' behaviour were a more powerful predictor of self-reported unethical behavior than were the individuals' own beliefs (Zey-Ferrell & Ferrell, 1982; Zey-Ferrell et al., 1979). In other words, the people to whom one looks to model appropriate behaviour—one's referent others—are a key explanatory variable in one's own behaviour. There is a great deal we might learn from better understanding how one chooses moral referents, particularly at work. Though the importance of moral referents has been proposed, both in moral approbation theory (Jones & Ryan, 1997) and in recent theory that explores ethical decision making from an organizational sensemaking perspective (Sonenshein, 2007), how individuals both choose and use moral referents in their own decision making is not well understood.

Socialization. Having been reminded that there is substantial evidence that both authority figures and peers have separate coercive effects on the corruption of individuals, we now turn to the joint effects of pressure from multiple agents in one's environment. Experimental evidence indicates that when authority figures and peers both exert an influence towards corrupt behaviour, their effect is amplified (Jones & Kavanagh, 1996). As the pressures from superiors and peers coalesce, the effects move from direct pressure to comply towards a more subtle form of compliance pressure: socialization.

In a way, socialization is compliance without looking like it. It is a natural human tendency to search out normative behaviours in groups to which we belong, and then work to meet those norms. People tend to act in ways that they have answered the question: "What does a person like me do in a situation like this?" (Messick, 1999; Weber, Kopelman, & Messick, 2004). When norms are not immediately apparent, people tend to transpose norms from past experience in similar situations (Bettenhausen & Murnighan, 1985). All of these efforts to discover and operate in normatively appropriate ways help individuals fit in, figure out one's job, and meet the expectations of relevant others inside organizations—key ways in which individuals reduce the stress and uncertainty of starting new jobs (Saks & Ashforth, 1997; Van Maanen, 1976). As Milgram wrote in his overview of his studies on obedience to authority:

> Obedience does not take the form of dramatic confrontation of opposed wills or philosophies but is embedded in a larger atmosphere where social relationships, career aspirations, and technical routines set the dominant tone. Typically, we do not find a heroic figure struggling with conscience, nor a pathologically aggressive man ruthlessly exploiting a position of power, but a functionary who has been given a job to do and who strives to create an impression of competence in his work. (Milgram, 1974, p. 187)

This quote, from the classic analysis of how pressure from authority figures drives people to act in ways they would not normally, is really a statement about socialization. Often, in an effort to meet the requirements of organizational roles, we unconsciously comply with behavioural expectations we would never have consciously set for ourselves.

The term "compliance" remains appropriate when thinking about socialization because the corruption that results from socialization can not be credited to factors *within* the individual the way that it could when thinking about compulsion processes. The corruption that results from socialization can only be attributed to factors *outside* the individual, factors within one's social environment. Or, as Darley has noted:

many evil actions are not the volitional products of individual evildoers. Instead, they are in some sense societal products, in which a complex series of social forces interact to cause individuals to commit...evil. (Darley, 1992, p. 204)

Socialization processes are key to the institutionalization of corruption, forming one of the three "pillars" which Ashforth and Anand consider central to the normalization of corruption within organizations (2003, pp. 25–34). There are many reasons why socialization is such an effective route to corruption. Corrupt firms reward individuals for conforming to corrupt norms, through promotion or other types of organizational rewards, as they did at Prudential-Bache Securities in the 1980s (Eichenwald, 1995). Corrupt firms also punish non-conformers—either with symbolic punishment like social ostracization or ridicule, as we just noted with Lewis' choice to become a "jammer" or a "fool" at Salomon Brothers (Lewis, 1989), or with forced or encouraged dismissal, as has been shown in a study of accounting firms (Ponemon, 1992). Coercive socialization can be pre-emptive as well: individuals who are unlikely to effectively socialize into corrupt norms simply aren't hired by those who control entry into corrupt organizations. An ethnography of corrupt dock workers indicates that foremen were disinclined to permit the hiring of workers who were unlikely to be effectively socialized into their norms of pilferage (Mars, 1974, 1982).

So how does the process of socialization to corrupt norms work? There are two main avenues, representing two ways in which immersion in an environment eventually alters the individuals within those environments. The first avenue is *seduction*, which operates in a similar way as the previous section described moral seduction theory, in that incremental shifts gradually change the general behaviour and attitudes of the focal actor, except in this case people are seduced by their external environment rather than their own internal tendencies towards self-serving biases and framing. The second is *surrender*, where individuals eventually relent after facing continued social pressure to be or act a certain way.

Seduction. As was just mentioned, seduction can be motivated both internally, through biases and ways of perceiving situations that are difficult to resist, and externally, through immersion in an environment which one doesn't notice is slowly changing one's moral attitudes or ethical standards. Often, these two seduction forces work in tandem, such that individuals do not notice how their environment is seducing them to change, because the attractiveness of changing plays into all the internal reasons why people are also seduced to corruption. Over time, compliance with the expectations of one's immediate referent others (peers, workgroups) erodes one's moral standards, and one's understanding of acceptable behaviour widens to include previously proscribed acts. This process has also been called habituation, in which "exposure to different stimuli of increasing aversiveness weakens reactions to the stimuli" (Ashforth & Anand, 2003, p. 13), and has had the most thorough empirical examination in the marketing literature, in a body of work on foot-in-the-door processes.

Taking a metaphor from the practices of travelling salesmen, the idea is that if you can just get your foot through someone's doorway, their compliance with future requests becomes significantly easier to secure.[3] A body of empirical work beginning in the 1960s finds relatively consistently that individuals are more likely to agree to a larger request after having already agreed to a smaller one (Freedman & Fraser, 1966). For example, individuals are significantly more likely to allow an imposing billboard promoting safe driving in their front yard if they have previously agreed to display a small safe driving sign in their window (Freedman & Fraser, 1966), or make a donation to cancer research if they have previously agreed to wear a daffodil on their lapel (Pliner, Hart, Kohl, & Saari, 1974).

Surrender. Succumbing to the pressures of socialization can also happen consciously, raising the white flag against the relentless pressure to conform to given norms, and meeting the expectations of unethical models. This process has also been called desensitization, in which "repeated exposure to the same stimulus progressively weakens reactions to the stimulus" (Ashforth & Anand, 2003, p. 13). In qualitative work on how individuals become socialized into white collar criminality, individuals speak about a process of surrender to a momentum they feel powerless to change: an "if you can't beat them, join them" mentality. For example, Sutherland describes a young salesman, who quit his first two jobs after graduating from college over what he perceives to be unethical business practices (Sutherland, 1949/1983). Upon entering his third job, he relents to the pressures he has come to view as inescapable, saying "the game was rotten, but it had to be played" (Sutherland, 1949/1983, p. 241). As Leonardo Da Vinci has been quoted as saying, "It is easier to resist in the beginning then at the end" (cited in Cialdini, 1984, p. 57).

Starting in the 1970s, a practice related to foot-in-the-door, termed door-in-the-face, has also been found to be successful in securing desired behaviours from individuals. Door-in-the-face strategies differ from foot-in-the-door strategies in the same way that desensitization differs from habituation. As foot-in-the-door experiments showed that agreeing to a *small* request could lead to higher rates of agreement with *larger* requests (habituating the individual to a target behaviour), door-in-the-face experiments demonstrate that making a *large* request of individuals, which is typically declined, increases the likelihood of securing agreement to a *small* request later on (desensitizing the individual to a target behaviour) (Cialdini et al., 1975). For example, individuals who first turned down a request to make a commitment to volunteer on a weekly basis for two years were more likely to agree to accompany a group of juvenile delinquents on a trip to the zoo, than were individuals who asked only to go on the zoo trip (Cialdini et al., 1975). In other words, it is difficult to persist over time in denying "favours" individuals request of you.

Interestingly, neither the foot-in-the-door paradigm nor the door-in-the-face paradigm has ever been applied to requests to engage in unethical behaviour. The majority of foot-in-the-door studies have been undertaken in the context of attempting to gain compliance with *prosocial* behaviour such as making donations (for money or blood) or volunteering (for various charitable or environmental causes) (Dillard, Hunter, & Burgoon, 1984). Both of these paradigms offer interesting opportunities to better understand how individuals can be coerced into corruption through different types of socialization patterns.

CONTAGION IN ORGANIZATIONAL CORRUPTION

The second definition of corruption in the *OED* is "infection, contagion, taint." That corruption can be viewed as a contagious danger is not new (Darley, 2005). Where compliance involves changing newcomers to behave in the normative ways of a pre-existing context, contagion involves introducing something new to a pre-existing context which changes the norms within it. In other words, in compliance with corruption, the individual is the new element being introduced to an already corrupted environment, and in contagion of corruption, a corrupt practice or behavior is the new element being introduced to an otherwise uncorrupt environment. In the former case, the individual becomes corrupted, and in the latter, the environment becomes corrupted. It is therefore more appropriately conceptualized as a psychological process that occurs at the group level, one that focuses on how a group can become "infected."

Contagion has been widely though disparately studied. From the psychological perspective, contagion has been examined in terms of emotions, attitudes, and behaviours; however, much of the research has tended to stay in the realm of social psychology rather than crossing the fence in to organizational studies (though Barsade, 2002, is an exception). Organizational research has tended to characterize contagion research as diffusion (Rogers, 2003), and has typically focused at more macro levels of analysis. I will discuss both diffusion research and contagion research, and will follow with a discussion of how the way groups are organized can facilitate or hinder the contagion of corruption.

Diffusion research. From an organizational perspective, the context in which contagion has been most comprehensively studied is in terms of the diffusion of innovations (Rogers, 2003). Early diffusion research looked at how new practices such as the use of hybrid seed corn among farmers

(Ryan & Cross, 1943), new drugs among physicians (Coleman, Katz, & Menzel, 1957), or family planning methods among rural women (Berelson & Freedman, 1964) are diffused through populations. The epidemiological literature is unsurprisingly comprehensive in their studies of behavioral contagion, in particular in studies of suicide (i.e., Mercy et al., 2001) or high risk behaviours that could lead to disease (i.e., Christakis & Fowler, 2007; Cleveland & Wiebe, 2003). Though this work abstracts significantly away from the psychology underlying contagion processes, understanding how practices become successfully diffused through environments remains an important building block in understanding corruption dynamics.

Early work on diffusion tended to view "success" simply as the adoption of the new practice, but diffusion processes can also be viewed as yet another incarnation of the slippery slope, with small corrupt actions undertaken by individuals leading to tolerance for larger corrupt actions at the group level. This perspective is captured by the criminological theory of broken windows (Wilson & Kelling, 1982), which makes the argument that street crime can follow patterns of contagion, with small contraventions of rules easily snowballing into larger crimes. A quasi-empirical test of broken windows theory occurred in New York City from the mid-1980s through the end of the 1990s, when one of its major proponents, George Kelling, was hired by the NY Transit Authority to help turn around a system which had fallen into chaos (Gladwell, 1996, pp. 140–145). Kelling, and later William Bratton, who took over the New York City Police Department, applied broken windows theory in their respective domains and strategically targeted "quality-of-life" crimes in order to reduce the epidemic of violent crime in the city (Bratton, 1998). The result (though not uncontested, see Levitt & Dubner, 2005, Chapter 4) was that community policing helped reverse the criminal contagion process, and reorient behavioral norms in the communities under their watch.

Contagion research. From the psychological perspective, the literature on contagion is extensive, though it is considered poorly integrated and conceptually muddy (Levy & Nail, 1993). Many of the psychological processes that were relevant in the prior two sections at the individual level remain relevant here at the group level. For example, the section on compulsion discussed escalation of commitment at the individual level, with individuals making poor decisions as a result of questionable outcomes of prior decisions when there are substantial sunk costs. However, escalation of commitment can occur in groups as well: for example, group contexts are required in order to initiate "auction fever" (Ku, Malhotra, & Murnighan, 2005)—circumstances where individuals (bidders) in a group (at an auction) make irrational and poor decisions as a result of the rivalry, time pressure, and social facilitation offered by the context. One can imagine that in certain results-oriented environments, where employees are pitted against each other and forced to perform in contexts of intense time pressure, a version of auction fever in which the poor decisions were ethical violations rather than overbidding could result.

Similarly, the section on compliance discussed the natural tendency of individuals to conform to group norms. This natural tendency at the individual level is especially worrisome when coupled with what we know about group processes over time: groups can operate in insidiously risk-seeking ways. The group think literature has demonstrated that groups can be strongly drawn towards consensus views without critically examining all the available options (Janis, 1972, 1983). The literature on group polarization has documented that groups can unintentionally end up taking riskier positions and more extreme perspectives than individuals (Isenberg, 1986; Mackie & Cooper, 1984; Moscovici & Zavalloni, 1969). The tendency towards risk and extremes means that even in the absence of a pre-existing corrupt group norm (which would more appropriately speak to a socialization process), groups can develop more corrupt norms than the individuals within those groups might enact independently. Both of these literatures point to ways in which groups have the potential to "infect" themselves towards more corrupt outcomes.

The insidiousness of group processes in encouraging negative outcomes unintended by any one group member can also be seen in one of the only empirical examinations of the diffusion of "corruption" in a group. In his study of delinquent boys, Matza (1964) found that even though on an individual level the boys did not approve of delinquent behaviour or think it was "right," group interaction facilitated an overall shift towards delinquent norms. This "drift" (as he termed it) towards greater delinquency was a result of individually low thresholds against delinquent behaviour counteracting with the positive benefits the boys accrued from delinquency, such as appearing masculine towards one's peers (see also the discussion in Granovetter, 1978, p. 1435).

Contagion has also been examined in the context of social learning theory (Bandura, 1977; Hamblin, Miller, & Saxton, 1979; Pitcher, Hamblin, & Miller, 1978). This is an interesting approach to contagion, since it assumes the mechanism of "infection" is indirect; individuals, operating as behavioural models, "legitimize" behavior for others, who then take up that behaviour and become models for yet others to imitate. As Hamblin and colleagues have written, "Everyone makes[...] decisions, not just on the basis of his own individual experiences, but to a large extent on the basis of the observed or talked about experiences of others" (1979, p. 809). Thinking about contagion in terms of social learning theory helps explain the quick rise of behaviours through populations since every new adherent to a practice becomes both a contributor to that behaviour and a model of it. Social learning explanations of diffusion have been used in the analysis of airplane hijacking, anti-Semitic vandalism, and civil disorder, among other forms of collective violence (Pitcher et al., 1978). The qualitative study cited earlier of how rule-breaking became endemic in an insurance agency provides further support that corrupt business practices can become diffused through social learning processes (MacLean, 2001). This type of contagion has been termed "disinhibitory contagion" (Levy & Nail, 1993), in that witnessing individuals engage in certain behaviours frees individuals to engage in those behaviours themselves.

Avenues of contagion. Diffusion research shows that the successful spread of practices is especially dependent on interpersonal relationships, the influence of nearby peers, and the role of central "opinion leaders" (Coleman, Katz, & Menzel, 1966; Rogers, 2003). This focus on relationships provides a psychological lens through which to consider diffusion research. The importance of network centrality in successful diffusion is a consistent finding in diffusion research—which hints that most diffusion processes are "trickle-down" (i.e., from leaders to employees) rather than "trickle-up," and empirical research confirms that individuals with higher status are more effective at spreading new practices (Coleman et al., 1966; Ryan & Cross, 1943; Wheeler, 1966). The diffusion literature, however, remains largely focused on the adoption of *positive outcomes* such as innovations (Rogers, 2003; Strang & Soule, 1998), and there is some indication that "trickle-up" processes are more likely to manifest when the behavior being diffused is counter-normative (see Abrahamson & Rosenkopf, 1997, p. 294), as would be the case with the contagion of corruption.

Mobility is another key mechanism in the contagion of corruption. Corrupt practices can be disseminated in a contagious fashion though inter- or intra-organizational mobility (Ashforth & Anand, 2003, p. 10). In terms of inter-organizational mobility, Granovetter noted 20 years ago that the mobility across organizations afforded by modern industrialized capitalism creates opportunities both for malfeasance as well as trustworthy behavior (1985). Many types of corruption, such as bid-rigging and price fixing, depend on social relations (Baker & Faulkner, 1993), and provide an example of how economic action is embedded within social networks that extend across organizations (Granovetter, 1985). A recent way in which inter-firm social networks have been used to spread corruption is through a practice known as swaps—illegal reciprocal "back-scratching" trades between companies which artificially inflate revenue—a behavior that led to the bankruptcy of companies like Qwest Communications and Global Crossing, and serious investigation of many others, including AOL Time Warner (Berman, Angwin, & Cummins, 2002). Intra-firm corruption also often requires organized coalitions with strong social ties. An example of this type of corruption can be seen in an ethnographic study reported by Dalton (1959), which described how employee collusion supported the misrepresentation of inventory in an internal audit.

Group composition also has an important influence on the effectiveness of contagion. Granovetter's threshold model of collective behaviour presents a simple example to illustrate this point (Granovetter, 1978). His model shows how nearly identical groups of individuals can result in radically different end outcomes, with minor changes in group composition. Imagine two groups of 100 people. In the first, Person 1 will riot even if no one else is rioting, Person 2 will riot as long as one other person is rioting, Person 3 will riot as long as two other people are rioting, and so on. The composition of this group is such that eventually, all 100 members of the group will eventually riot. Now imagine exactly the same group, except that Person 2 as well as Person 3 require two other people to riot in order to join the uprising. The composition of this group leads to an outcome where Person 1 riots by him- or herself. These two groups are nearly identical, but for the rioting threshold of Person 2, and yet have completely different outcomes.

Granovetter's model demonstrates both the attraction and the limits of one of the main fantasies about the contagion of corruption: the idea that one bad apple can spoil the barrel. One bad apple might spoil the barrel, but only with exactly the right confluence of additional factors, including a facilitating group composition. Other research adds to this list of contextual requirements for the "bad apple" fantasy: suggestibility and ambiguity. In simulations developed by Johnson and Feinberg to model how consensus emerges in crowds (Feinberg & Johnson, 1988; Johnson & Feinberg, 1977), there is evidence that lone "agitators" aren't enough to sway the behavior of crowds: people have to be suggestible enough to succumb to the influence of the agitator, and the context needs to be ambiguous enough for them to be suggestible. The importance of contextual ambiguity in similar processes, such as bandwagon effects (Abrahamson & Rosenkopf, 1997), or increasing competitiveness/decreasing cooperativeness in groups (Weber et al., 2004) also serve as reminders that "bad apple" theories need to always attend to context in order to be true reflections of reality (see Treviño, 1986; Treviño & Youngblood, 1990).

While it is rare to be able to track how actual behavior operates in a contagious way within organizations, computer simulations provide opportunities to test how differences at the individual level might translate into group-level outcomes. Macy has used computer simulations to show that communities attain the benefit of collective cooperative action through serial interaction with other group members, in which people take their behavioral cues from what the group as a whole is doing (1991). Contributions are still likely to come from a core of highly interested members (Oliver & Marwell, 1988), but especially when there is not a high cost of participating, group equilibria tend to shift toward whatever behaviour is gaining normative momentum. Though these simulations were used in the explanation of collective cooperative action (a positive outcome), it is not difficult to transpose similar processes onto an organization like Enron, in which a group of highly committed "activists" created corrupt conditions under which it was not costly for the main body of organizational members to participate.

CORROSION IN ORGANIZATIONAL CORRUPTION

The final type of corruption dynamic had been termed "corrosion," tracking another among the first set of definitions of corruption in the *OED*: "the oxidation or corrosion . . . of a body." This definition is particularly interesting, because it highlights the necessity of an interaction between a "body" and its external environment in the process of becoming corrupt.[4] Therefore, this section begins with a discussion of some basic systemic forces which provide corrupting influences on groups. Interestingly, the corrosive elements that operate to corrupt group norms can simply be external incentives facilitative of the internal compulsion processes discussed earlier. Organizations can be designed in ways which both encourage self-serving behaviour at the group level, and frame issues for groups and individuals in ways which obviate moral concerns. The design of goals and incentives (which often support corrupt self-serving biases at the group level), and the design of jobs and routines (which often support corrupt ways of framing at the group level) are two important ways external forces can corrupt groups, and will be discussed at the end of this section.

In many ways, this quadrant of the typology harkens back to classic sociological theory and its interest in unanticipated consequences of certain types of social organization. Max Weber and Karl Marx both had interestingly consistent views about how bureaucratic organizations in capitalist economic systems would involve negative and unanticipated consequences for individuals and society, though Weber was more concerned with the effects of bureaucratic organizations, and Marx with capitalist systems. In both cases, social structures "take on a life of their own," and since "people lack control over them, structures are free to develop in a variety of totally unanticipated directions" (Ritzer, 2000, p. 252). As Marx wrote, "while we are highly successful in bringing about the immediate results of our conscious intentions, we still too often fail to anticipate and forestall the undesired remoter consequences of those results themselves" (cited in Venable, 1945, p. 76). In other words, there is no intention on the part of the systems to encourage a slow descent into corruption, but the systems create environmental conditions that result in corruption unintentionally.

Much of the work on corruption and like concepts such as organizational crime or deviance has looked exclusively at the organizational level, minimizing detailed analysis of the role (and responsibility) of individuals in corruption processes (Cochran & Nigh, 1987; Ermann & Lundman, 1996; Finney & Lesieur, 1982; Gross, 1978, 1980; Shover & Bryant, 1993). In fact, a body of work in critical sociology has made the claim that profit-seeking enterprises are "inherently criminogenic" (i.e., Gross, 1978: 78; Needleman & Needleman, 1979). This is really an argument about structure, about how organizations can be designed in ways which discourage reflection about anything which doesn't directly contribute to their sustainability, growth, and profitability. In a supportive vein, critical legal theorists have voiced concern that the way corporations are legally structured encourages a restrictive focus on shareholder value to the point where ethical concerns are marginalized (Bakan, 2004; Mitchell, 2001).

Theorists from these traditions stress how organizations restrict the actions of individuals within them (Ermann & Lundman, 1996). Organizations effectively create:

> positions in a structure of relations, the persons who occupy the positions are incidental to the structure. They take on the obligations and expectations, the goals and resources, associated with their positions in the way they put on work clothes for their jobs. (Coleman, 1990, p. 427)

Even though Coleman himself had a much more complex and nuanced view of the relations between individuals, groups and social systems than this quote suggests, the quote itself seems to strip individuals of all agency in their own actions. In an extreme form, this theoretical tradition can neglect the fact that these organizationally designed and imposed "restrictions" do have psychological effects at the group and individual level, which deserve an independent assessment.

An application of this theoretical argument can be seen in the work of Moore and his colleagues, who show that occupational and political pressures have operated in a way which erodes the independence of financial auditors (Moore et al., 2006). They argue that incremental changes at the industry level (now partially but not completely addressed by recent legislative changes including Sarbanes-Oxley) have created conditions which undermine an auditor's ability to deliver truly independent assessments of their clients' financials, leading to difficulties in the auditing profession with conflicts of interest (Moore et al., 2006). Nick Leeson's experience at Barings Bank also points to systemic corrosive elements which supported and directed him in his fraud. First, even when his superiors had strong indications that the operation in Singapore was in trouble, they turned a blind eye to it, because the numbers coming out of the regional office allowed the bank to post great profits; second, Leeson was in charge both of the front office and the back office, structurally creating opportunities which facilitated his escalating losses (Leeson, 1996).

These examples clearly show that there are a number of systemic factors which have the potential to corrode groups of individuals within organizations. In the rest of this section, we focus on two, because of the way in which they represent systemic elements facilitative of the internal compulsion processes discussed earlier at the individual level: organizational goals and incentives, which play into how we succumb to biasing at the individual level, and job design and routines, which facilitate particular ways of framing.

Goals and incentives. The evidence that goals motivate behaviour is overwhelming (Locke & Latham, 2002), and the evidence that they can do so in morally insidious ways is substantial and growing (e.g., Barsky, 2004; Schweitzer, Ordóñez, & Douma, 2004; Tenbrunsel & Messick, 1999). Research has shown that when we exist in contexts where the goals set for us are ethically agnostic, we are likely to do what it takes to meet those goals without worrying about their ethical implications (Schweitzer et al., 2004). Additionally, when individuals have incentives to act unethically, they are also more likely to make negative ethical attributions about others' intentions (Tenbrunsel, 1998), compounding the effect that goals may have as motivators of unethical behaviour.

Performance goals or revenue targets may actually—perversely—cause a neglect of the moral implications of the actions we take to meet them. A series of studies on goal shielding show that individuals are better able to focus on and meet specific goals when alternate, and potentially competing goals, have been "shielded" from immediate relevance, and as such, leave more cognitive room to focus in a targeted way on the goal of interest (Shah, Friedman, & Kruglanski, 2002). One can imagine a strongly organizationally relevant goal such as meeting quarterly sales targets (which typically aligns nicely with a personally relevant goal such as earning a large bonus or commission) might be better met if individuals weren't simultaneously concerned with a secondary goal such as ensuring that the actions involved in meeting those sales targets didn't violate moral codes of behaviour.

Recent trading scandals, including those at Société Générale (Gauthier-Villars & Mollenkamp, 2008) and Credit Suisse (Gow, 2008; Winnett, 2008b), attest that the desire to earn large bonuses was a direct and traceable cause of the corruption that led to the behaviour that lost their respective firms billions of dollars. There can really be no question that the way that individual traders are incented at large banks increases their likelihood of falling into traps of taking on too much risk in the pursuit of personal gain. At the group level, the excitement of the chase of the big score might mimic "auction fever" situations, in which decision making is impaired by the context's defining features, such as rivalry, social facilitation, and time pressure (Ku et al., 2005). In many organizational contexts, individual jobs and rewards are constructed in ways which impair decisions in exactly these ways—team members compete with each other over bonus pools, promotions, and other organizational rewards—and may lead to corrupt activities in order to ensure that the rewards are accrued in a way which benefits the self (Sivanathan, 2009).

Routines and job design. The role of routines and job design in corruption has been discussed mostly at a theoretical level; for example, in understanding how functionaries were able to carry out their duties in Nazi concentration camps (Bergen, 2003: 229), or how executioners are able to carry out the death penalty in the U.S. (Johnson, 1998). Routines also played a corrosive role in the Ford Pinto recall (Gioia, 1992), by scripting Gioia's behaviour in ways which drew his attention away from the moral implications of the actions required by his organizational role. Routines facilitate framing one's actions as being outside one's own agency, leading to "it's not me, it's my job" rationalizations. For example, in a study of penitentiary personnel actively involved in the execution process, the efforts that are made to routinize the process in the greatest detail, however absurd (for example, using an alcohol swab on an inmate's arm before administering a lethal injection) have been shown to help people perform these jobs in a way which mitigates their distress (Osofsky, Bandura, & Zimbardo, 2005). Regardless of one's personal beliefs about the acceptability of executions, the fact that routines can play an active role in normalizing negative outcomes to individuals in these roles remains relevant.

Job design, especially over-specialization, also corrodes group members' ability to appropriately determine how individuals are responsible for the outcome of group tasks. Task specialization diffuses individual responsibility for outcomes, so that it becomes difficult to attribute responsibility to anyone, while triggering individuals to morally disengage from the actual outcomes they are playing a part in causing (Bandura, 1990a, 1990b, 2002). Diffusion of responsibility has been blamed for the Challenger launch decision (Vaughan, 1996), as well as other decisions where many individuals played a small role in the eventual failure of important technologies, such as airline brakes (Vandivier, 1996).

At the organizational level, once this type of responsibility diffusion has become embedded in organizational routines, "it takes more conscious effort to *dis*continue it than to continue it" (Ashforth & Anand, 2003, p. 11). At the individual level, once someone has been successfully socialized into corrupt routines, following these routines has a script-like quality that goes unquestioned, and just becomes "part of the everyday" (Benson, 1985: 591). In other words, if individuals' jobs are designed or incentivized in a way which obligates them to ethically tenuous actions, they are more likely to be compelled to meet the obligations of their jobs than the grander (more distal, vague, and uncertain) obligations to meet those expectations ethically, and they will be able to do so without distress.

CONCLUSIONS AND FUTURE RESEARCH DIRECTIONS

So what does all of this teach us about corruption dynamics? By offering a typology of four processes—compulsion, compliance, contagion, and corrosion—as they relate to corruption, this chapter has aimed to clarify our understanding of how psychological processes play into the dynamic nature of corruption.

The first conclusion that seems fair, though disappointing, is that as a construct, corruption is unlikely to become any more central than it currently is in organizational research. As viscerally gripping as corruption phenomena are, they are simply too varied, span too many levels of analysis, and represent too many things to too many people to facilitate a clear or cohesive literature. Coherent literatures typically spring from well- and narrowly-defined constructs that are measurable and empirically tractable. Corruption is simply too unwieldy to be pinned down in that way. That said, the attraction of corruption as a concept is only growing (Ashforth, Gioia, Robinson, & Treviño, 2008b), and is unlikely to abate soon. So the task then becomes: how might we further our understanding of processes *relevant* to corruption, rather than trying to pin down "corruption," as the more meta-phenomenon, itself.

This leads directly to the second conclusion reached in this chapter: it seems clear that there are many paradigms in psychology, both theoretical and empirical, which are exceptionally relevant to corruption dynamics, but which to date have not (or hardly) been applied in those contexts. In the discussion of compulsion processes, both slippery slope processes and escalation of commitment were discussed as relevant to corruption but rarely studied in that way. The discussion of compliance highlighted the promise of research on foot-in-the-door and door-in-the-face phenomena as representative of seduction or habituation to corruption and surrender or desensitization to corruption, respectively. The discussion of contagion noted how diffusion processes have focused almost exclusively on the diffusion of positive outcomes, when it seems obvious that corrupt outcomes can also be diffused through populations. The discussion of corrosion highlighted the need to take a more expansive view of how choices at macro levels influence group- and individual-level psychological processes. While there may be a lot to learn about corruption, there is certainly no shortage of germane research opportunities for creative researchers.

This brings me to my third conclusion—which has been drawn before, but without much follow-up: the difficulties in studying these phenomena empirically continue to hinder advancement of research on this topic, both because accessing quality data is a perennial challenge, and because studying corruption as a dynamic phenomenon requires gathering this difficult-to-access data over time as well. However, this chapter has surfaced a number of different research paradigms that provide reason for optimism about future research, in two specific ways. One, we have covered a number of applicable research paradigms—such as escalation of commitment, foot-in-the-door, and door-in-the-face—which are relevant to corruption but which have hardly been studied with corrupt outcomes in mind. And two, new methodologies provide additional opportunities to try to model corruption dynamics in new ways. In particular, computer simulations of contagion and diffusion processes have much promise (Oliver & Myers, 2002), but thus far have had few takers, particularly in the ethical decision making literature. A couple of exceptions, in philosophy (Alexander, 2007) and law (Picker, 1997), represent the rare projects with relevance to corruption using computer simulations. Which leaves me to close on both a cautiously positive and optimistic note: much work to do, but a path paving the way there.

NOTES

1. NGOs Transparency International and the World Bank also collect data on corruption at the national level.
2. Underpinning all the definitions of corruption, whether they refer to the process of *becoming* corrupt or the state of *being* corrupt, is an assumption that the corrupted entity has "an original state of purity" (Corruption, *Oxford English Dictionary*, definition III). Therefore, psychological research that assumes an original state of *impurity*—for example, trait-based approaches in explaining corruption outcomes, such as looking at Machiavellianism (Wilson, Near, & Miller, 1996)—won't be addressed here.
3. This type of process is actually rife with metaphors including the "thin edge of the wedge," or "giving an inch and taking a mile."
4. I would like to thank Holly Arrow for working through this metaphor with me.

REFERENCES

Abrahamson, E., & Rosenkopf, L. (1997). Social network effects on the extent of innovation diffusion: A computer simulation. *Organization Science, 8,* 289–309.

Alexander, J. M. (2007). *The structural evolution of morality.* Cambridge, UK: Cambridge University Press.

Arendt, H. (1994). *Eichmann in Jerusalem: A report on the banality of evil.* New York: Penguin. (Originally published in 1963)

Asch, S. E. (1951). Effects of group pressure upon the modification and distortion of judgments. In H. Guetzkow (Ed.), *Groups, leadership and men: Research in human relations* (pp. 177–190). Pittsburgh, PA: Carnegie Press.

Asch, S. E. (1955). Opinions and social pressure. In A. P. Hare, E. F. Borgatta & R. F. Balles (Eds.), *Small groups: Studies in social interaction* (pp. 318–324). New York: Alfred A. Knopf.

Ashforth, B. E., & Anand, V. (2003). The normalization of corruption in organizations. *Research in Organizational Behavior, 25*, 1–52.

Ashforth, B. E., Gioia, D. A., Robinson, S. L., & Treviño, L. K. (2008a). Re-viewing organizational corruption. *Academy of Management Review, 33*, 670–684.

Ashforth, B. E., Gioia, D. A., Robinson, S. L., & Treviño, L. K. (Eds.). (2008b). Special topic forum on organizational corruption [Special issue]. *Academy of Management Review, 33*(3).

Babcock, L., Loewenstein, G., Issacharoff, S., & Camerer, C. (1995). Biased judgments of fairness in bargaining. *American Economic Review, 85*, 1337–1343.

Bakan, J. (2004). *The corporation: The pathological pursuit of profit and power.* Toronto, Canada: Penguin.

Baker, W. E., & Faulkner, R. R. (1993). The social organization of conspiracy: Illegal networks in the heavy electrical equipment industry. *American Sociological Review, 58*, 837–860.

Bandura, A. (1977). *Social learning theory.* Englewood Cliffs, NJ: Prentice-Hall.

Bandura, A. (1990a). Mechanisms of moral disengagement. In W. Reich (Ed.), *Origins of terrorism: Psychologies, ideologies, states of mind* (pp. 161–191). New York: Cambridge University Press.

Bandura, A. (1990b). Selective activation and disengagement of moral control. *Journal of Social Issues, 46*, 27–46.

Bandura, A. (1999). Moral disengagement in the perpetuation of inhumanities. *Personality and Social Psychology Review, 3*, 193–209.

Bandura, A. (2002). Selective moral disengagement in the exercise of moral agency. *Journal of Moral Education, 31*, 101–119.

Barsade, S. G. (2002). The ripple effect: Emotional contagion and its influence on group behavior. *Administrative Science Quarterly, 47*, 644–675.

Barsky, A. (2004). *The ethical cost of assigned performance goals.* Unpublished dissertation, Tulane University, New Orleans.

Batson, C. D., Kobrynowicz, D., Dinnerstein, J. L., Kampf, H. C., & Wilson, A. D. (1997). In a very different voice: Unmasking moral hypocrisy. *Journal of Personality and Social Psychology, 72*, 1335–1348.

Batson, C. D., Thompson, E. R., Seuferling, G., Whitney, H., & Strongman, J. A. (1999). Moral hypocrisy: Appearing moral to oneself without being so. *Journal of Personality and Social Psychology, 77*, 525–537.

Baucus, M. S. (1989). Why firms do it and what happens to them: A reexamination of the theory of corporate behavior. In L. E. Preston (Ed.), *Research in corporate social performance and policy* (Vol. 11, pp. 93–118). Greenwich, CT: JAI Press.

Baucus, M. S. (1994). Pressure, opportunity and predisposition: A multivariate model of corporate illegality. *Journal of Management, 20*, 699–721.

Baumeister, R. F., & Leary, M. R. (1995). The need to belong: Desire for interpersonal attachments as a fundamental human motivation. *Psychological Bulletin, 117,* 497–529.

Baumhart, R. C. (1961). How ethical are businessmen? *Harvard Business Review, 39*(4), 6–176.

Bennett, R. J., & Robinson, S. L. (2003). The past, present, and future of workplace deviance research. In J. Greenberg (Ed.), *Organizational behavior: The state of the science* (2nd ed., pp. 247–281). Mahwah, NJ: Lawrence Erlbaum.

Benson, M. L. (1985). Denying the guilty mind: Accounting for involvement in a white-collar crime. *Criminology, 23,* 583–607.

Berelson, B., & Freedman, R. (1964). A study in fertility control. *Scientific American, 210*(5), 29–37.

Bergen, D. L. (2003). *War and genocide: A concise history of the Holocaust.* Lanham, MD: Rowman & Littlefield.

Berman, D. K., Angwin, J., & Cummins, C. (2002, 23 December). What's wrong? Tricks of the trade: As market bubble neared end, bogus swaps provided a lift. *Wall Street Journal,* p. A1.

Bettenhausen, K., & Murnighan, J. K. (1985). The emergence of norms in competitive decision-making groups. *Administrative Science Quarterly, 30,* 350–372.

Bloch, H. A., & Geis, G. (1962). *Man, crime, and society: The forms of criminal behavior.* New York: Random House.

Bratton, W. (1998). *Turnaround: How America's top cop reversed the crime epidemic.* New York: Random House.

Brenner, S. N., & Molander, E. A. (1977). Is the ethics of business changing? *Harvard Business Review, 55*(1), 57–71.

Brief, A. P., Buttram, R. T., & Dukerich, J. M. (2001). Collective corruption in the corporate world: Toward a process model. In M. E. Turner (Ed.), *Groups at work: Theory and research* (pp. 471–499). Mahwah, NJ: Erlbaum.

Brockner, J. (1992). The escalation of commitment to a failing course of action: Toward theoretical progress. *Academy of Management Review, 17,* 39–61.

Bromiley, P., & Marcus, A. (1989). The deterrent to dubious corporate behavior: Profitability, probability and safety recalls. *Strategic Management Journal, 10,* 233–250.

Cain, D. M., Loewenstein, G., & Moore, D. A. (2005). Coming clean but playing dirtier: The shortcomings of disclosure as a solution of conflicts of interest. In D. A. Moore, D. M. Cain, G. Loewenstein & M. H. Bazerman (Eds.), *Conflicts of interest: Challenges and solutions in business, law, medicine, and public policy* (pp. 104–125). New York: Cambridge University Press.

Christakis, N. A., & Fowler, J. H. (2007). The spread of obesity in a large social network over 32 Years. *New England Journal of Medicine, 357,* 370–379.

Chugh, D., Bazerman, M. H., & Banaji, M. R. (2005). Bounded ethicality as a psychological barrier to recognizing conflicts of interest. In D. A. Moore, D. M. Cain, G. Loewenstein & M. H. Bazerman (Eds.), *Conflicts of interest: Challenges and solutions in business, law, medicine, and public policy* (pp. 74–95). New York: Cambridge University Press.

Cialdini, R. B. (1984). *Influence: The psychology of persuasion.* New York: William Morrow.

Cialdini, R. B., Vincent, J. E., Lewis, S. K., Catalan, J., Wheeler, D., & Darby, B. L. (1975). Reciprocal concessions procedure for inducing compliance: The door-in-the-face technique. *Journal of Personality and Social Psychology, 31*, 206–215.

Cleveland, H. H., & Wiebe, R. P. (2003). The moderation of adolescent–to–peer similarity in tobacco and alcohol use by school levels of substance use. *Child Development, 74*, 279–297.

Cochran, P. L., & Nigh, D. (1987). Illegal corporate behavior and the question of moral agency: An empirical examination. In W. C. Frederick (Ed.), *Research in corporate social performance and policy* (Vol. 9, pp. 73–91). Greenwich, CT: JAI Press.

Coleman, J. S. (1990). *Foundations of social theory.* Cambridge, MA: Harvard University Press.

Coleman, J. S. (1996). The asymmetric society: Organizational actors, corporate power, and the irrelevance of persons. In M. D. Ermann & R. J. Lundman (Eds.), *Corporate and governmental deviance: Problems of organizational behavior in contemporary society* (5th ed., pp. 51–60). New York: Oxford University Press.

Coleman, J. S., Katz, E., & Menzel, H. (1957). The diffusion of innovation among physicians. *Sociometry, 20*, 253–270.

Coleman, J. S., Katz, E., & Menzel, H. (1966). *Medical innovation: A diffusion study.* New York: Bobbs-Merrill.

Cressey, D. R. (1953). *Other people's money: A study in the social psychology of embezzlement.* Glencoe, IL: The Free Press.

Dalton, M. (1959). *Men who manage: Fusions of feeling and theory in administration.* New York: Wiley.

Dana, J., & Loewenstein, G. (2003). A social science perspective on gifts to physicians from industry. *Journal of the American Medical Association, 290*, 252–255.

Darley, J. M. (1992). Social organization for the production of evil. *Psychological Inquiry, 3*, 199–218.

Darley, J. M. (2005). The cognitive and social psychology of contagious organizational corruption. *Brooklyn Law Review, 70*, 1177–1194.

De Cremer, D., & van Dijk, E. (2005). when and why leaders put themselves first: Leader behavior in resource allocations as a function of feeling entitled. *European Journal of Social Psychology, 35*, 553–563.

Diekmann, K. A., Samuels, S. M., Ross, L., & Bazerman, M. H. (1997). Self-interest and fairness in problems of resource allocation: Allocators versus recipients. *Journal of Personality and Social Psychology, 72*, 1061–1074.

Dillard, J. P., Hunter, J. E., & Burgoon, M. (1984). Sequential-request persuasive strategies: Meta-analysis of foot-in-the-door and door-in-the-face. *Human Communication Research, 10*, 461–488.

Douglas, J. D. (1977). *Official deviance: Readings in malfeasance, misfeasance, and other forms of corruption.* New York: Lippincott.

Eichenwald, K. (1995). *Serpent on the rock.* New York: HarperBusiness.

Ermann, M. D., & Lundman, R. J. (1996). Corporate and governmental deviance: Origins, patterns and reactions. In M. D. Ermann & R. J. Lundman (Eds.), *Corporate and governmental deviance: problems of organizational behavior in contemporary society* (5th ed., pp. 3–44). New York: Oxford University Press.

Feinberg, W. E., & Johnson, N. R. (1988). „Outside agitators" and crowds: Results from a computer simulation model *Social Forces, 67*, 398–423.

Ferraro, F., Pfeffer, J., & Sutton, R. I. (2005). Economics language and assumptions: How theories can become self-fulfilling. *Academy of Management Review, 30*, 8–24.

Ferrell, O. C., & Gresham, L. G. (1985). A contingency framewoprk for understanding ethical decision-making in marketing. *Journal of Marketing, 49*, 87–96.

Finney, H. C., & Lesieur, H. R. (1982). A contingency theory of organizational crime. In S. B. Bacharach (Ed.), *Research in the sociology of organizations* (Vol. 1, pp. 255–299). Greenwich, CT: JAI Press.

Freedman, J. L., & Fraser, S. C. (1966). Compliance without pressure: The foot-in-the-door technique. *Journal of Personality and Social Psychology, 4*, 196–202.

Gauthier-Villars, D., & Mollenkamp, C. (2008, February 2). How to lose $7.2 billion: A trader's tale. *Wall Street Journal*, pp. A1-A7.

Geis, G. (1962). Toward a delineation of white-collar offenses. *Sociological Inquiry, 32*(2), 160–171.

Gino, F., & Bazerman, M. H. (2007). Slippery slopes and misconduct: The effect of gradual degradation on the failure to notice others' unethical behavior. *Harvard Working Paper No. 06-007*.

Gioia, D. A. (1992). Pinto fires and personal ethics: A script analysis of missed opportunities. *Journal of Business Ethics, 11*, 379–389.

Gladwell, M. (1996, June 3). The tipping point. *The New Yorker, 32*–39.

Gourevitch, P., & Morris, E. (2008, March 24). Exposure: The woman behind the camera at Abu Ghraib. *The New Yorker, 44*–57.

Gow, D. (2008, March 21). Rogue traders leave Credit Suisse's credibility battered. *The Guardian*, p. 35.

Granovetter, M. (1978). Threshold models of collective behavior. *American Journal of Sociology, 83*, 1420–1443.

Granovetter, M. (1985). Economic action and social structure: The problem of embeddedness. *American Journal of Sociology, 91*, 481–510.

Gross, E. (1978). Organizational crime: A theoretical perspective. *Studies in Symbolic Interaction, 1*, 55–85.

Gross, E. (1980). Organizational structure and organizational crime. In G. Geis & E. Stotland (Eds.), *White collar crime: Theory and research* (pp. 52–76). Beverly Hills, CA: Sage.

Hamblin, R. L., Miller, J. L. L., & Saxton, D. E. (1979). Modeling use diffusion. *Social Forces, 57*, 799–811.

Heffernan, W. C., & Kleinig, J. (2004). *Private and public corruption*. Lanham, MD: Rowman & Littlefield.

Hersh, S. M. (2004). *Chain of command : The road from 9/11 to Abu Ghraib*. New York: HarperCollins.

Hogg, M. A., & Turner, J. C. (1987). Social identity and conformity: A theory of referent informational influence. In W. Doise & S. Moscovici (Eds.), *Current issues in European social psychology* (Vol. 2, pp. 139–182). Cambridge, UK: Cambridge University Press.

Isenberg, D. J. (1986). Group polarization: A critical review and meta-analysis. *Journal of Personality and Social Psychology, 50*, 1141–1151.

Janis, I. L. (1972). *Victims of groupthink.* Boston: Houghton Mifflin

Janis, I. L. (1983). *Groupthink: Psychological studies of policy decisions and fiascoes* (2nd ed.). Boston: Houghton Mifflin.

Johns, G. (1999). A multi-level theory of self-serving behaviour in and by organizations. *Research in Organizational Behavior, 21,* 1–38.

Johnson, N. R., & Feinberg, W. E. (1977). A computer simulation of the emergence of consensus in crowds *American Sociological Review, 42,* 505–521.

Johnson, R. (1998). *Death work: A study of the modern execution process* (2nd ed.). Belmont, CA: Wadsworth.

Jones, G. E., & Kavanagh, M. J. (1996). An experimental examination of the effects of individual and situational factors on unethical behavioral intentions in the workplace *Journal of Business Ethics 15,* 511–523.

Jones, T. M., & Ryan, L. V. (1997). The link between ethical judgment and action in organizations: A moral approbation approach. *Organization Science, 8,* 663–680.

Jong-sung, Y., & Khagram, S. (2005). A comparative study of inequality and corruption. *American Sociological Review, 70,* 136–157.

Kahneman, D. (2003a). Maps of bounded rationality: Psychology for behavioral economics. *American Economic Review, 93,* 1449–1475.

Kahneman, D. (2003b). A perspective on judgment and choice: Mapping bounded rationality. *American Psychologist, 58,* 697–720.

Kahneman, D., & Tversky, A. (1979). Prospect theory: An analysis of decisions under risk. *Econometrica, 47,* 263–291.

Kahneman, D., & Tversky, A. (Eds.). (2000). *Choices, values, and frames.* Cambridge, UK: Cambridge University Press.

Kelman, H. C. (1973). Violence without moral restraint: Reflections on the dehumanization of victims and victimizers. *Journal of Social Issues, 29,* 25–61.

Kelman, H. C., & Hamilton, V. L. (1989). *Crimes of obedience.* New Haven, CT: Yale University Press.

Kleinig, J., & Heffernan, W. C. (2004). The corruptibility of corruption. In W. C. Heffernan & J. Kleinig (Eds.), *Private and public corruption* (pp. 3–22). Lanham, MD: Rowman & Littlefield.

Ku, G., Malhotra, D., & Murnighan, J. K. (2005). Towards a competitive arousal model of decision-making: A study of auction fever in live and Internet auctions. *Organizational Behavior and Human Decision Processes, 96,* 89–103.

Kurzban, R., & Leary, M. R. (2001). Evolutionary origins of stigmatization: The functions of social exclusion. *Psychological Bulletin, 127,* 187–208.

Leeson, N. (1996). *Rogue trader: How I brought down Barings Bank and shook the financial world.* Boston: Little Brown.

Levin, D. T. (2002). Change blindness as visual metacognition. *Journal of Consciousness Studies 9*(5–6), 111–130.

Levitt, S. D., & Dubner, S. J. (2005). *Freakonomics: A rogue economist explores the hidden side of everything.* New York: HarperCollins.

Levy, D. A., & Nail, P. R. (1993). Contagion: A theoretical and empirical review and reconceptualization. *Genetic, Social & General Psychology Monographs, 119,* 235–283.

Lewis, M. (1989). *Liar's poker.* New York: Penguin.

Lifton, R. J. (1986). *The Nazi doctors.* New York: Basic Books.

Locke, E. A., & Latham, G. P. (2002). Building a practically useful theory of goal setting and task motivation: A 35-year odyssey. *American Psychologist, 57*, 705–717.

Mackie, D. M., & Cooper, J. (1984). Attitude polarization: The effects of group membership. *Journal of Personality and Social Psychology, 46*, 575–585.

MacLean, T. (2001). Thick as thieves: A social embedded model of rule breaking in organizations. *Business and Society, 40*, 167–196.

Macy, M. W. (1991). Chains of cooperation: Threshold effects in collective action. *American Sociological Review, 56*, 730–747.

Maremont, M. (1996, September 16). Anatomy of a fraud. *BusinessWeek*, 90–94.

Mars, G. (1974). Dock pilferage: A case study in occupational theft. In P. Rock & M. McIntosh (Eds.), *Deviance and social control* (pp. 209–228). London: Tavistock Institute.

Mars, G. (1982). *Cheats at work: An anthropology of workplace crime.* London: George Allen & Unwin.

Matza, D. (1964). *Delinquency and drift.* New York: John Wiley & Sons.

McLean, B., & Elkind, P. (2003). *The smartest guys in the room: The amazing rise and scandalous fall of Enron.* New York: Portfolio.

Mercy, J. A., Kresnow, M.-j., O'Carroll, P. W., Lee, R. K., Powell, K. E., Potter, L. B., et al. (2001). Is suicide contagious? A study of the relation between exposure to the suicidal behavior of others and nearly lethal suicide attempts. *American Journal of Epidemiology, 154*, 120–127.

Messick, D. M. (1999). Alternative logics for decision making in social settings. *Journal of Economic Behavior and Organization, 39*, 11–28.

Milgram, S. (1963). Behavioral study of obedience. *Journal of Abnormal and Social Psychology, 67*, 371–378.

Milgram, S. (1974). *Obedience to authority: An experimental view.* New York: Harper & Row.

Miller, D. T. (1999). The norm of self-interest. *American Psychologist, 54*, 1053–1060.

Miller, S., Roberts, P., & Spence, E. (2004). *Corruption and anti-corruption.* Upper Saddle River, NJ: Pearson Education.

Mitchell, L. E. (2001). *Corporate irresponsibility: America's newest export.* New Haven: Yale University Press.

Moon, H. (2001). The two faces of consientiousness: Duty and achievement striving in escalation of commitment dilemmas. *Journal of Applied Psychology, 86*, 533–540.

Moore, D. A., & Loewenstein, G. (2004). Self-interest, automaticity, and the psychology of conflict of interest. *Social Justice Research, 17*, 189–202.

Moore, D. A., Tetlock, P. E., Tanlu, L., & Bazerman, M. H. (2006). Conflicts of interest and the case of auditor independence: Moral seduction and strategic issue cycling. *Academy of Management Review, 31*, 10–29.

Moscovici, S., & Zavalloni, M. (1969). The group as a polaraizer of attitudes. *Journal of Personality and Social Psychology, 12*, 125–135.

Needleman, M. L., & Needleman, C. (1979). Organizational crime: Two models of criminogenesis. *Sociological Quarterly, 20*(Autumn), 517–528.

Oliver, P. E., & Marwell, G. (1988). The paradox of group size in collective action: A theory of critical mass, II. *American Sociological Review, 53*, 1–8.

Oliver, P. E., & Myers, D. J. (2002). Formal models in studying collective action and social movements. In B. Klandermans & S. Staggenborg (Eds.), *Methods of Social Movement Research* (pp. 32–61). Minneapolis: University of Minnesota Press.

Osofsky, M. J., Bandura, A., & Zimbardo, P. G. (2005). The role of moral disengagement in the execution process. *Law and Human Behavior, 29*, 371–393.

Pfarrer, M. D., DeCelles, K. A., Smith, K. G., & Taylor, M. S. (2008). After the fall: Reintegrating the corrupt organization. *Academy of Management Review, 33*, 730–749.

Picker, R. C. (1997). Simple games in a complex world: A generative approach to the adoption of norms. *University of Chicago Law Review, 64*, 1225–1288.

Pinto, J., Leana, C. R., & Pil, F. K. (2008). Corrupt organizations of organizations of corrupt individuals? Two types of organization-level corruption. *Academy of Management Review, 33*, 685–709.

Pitcher, B. L., Hamblin, R. L., & Miller, J. L. L. (1978). The diffusion of collective violence. *American Sociological Review, 43*, 23–35.

Pliner, P., Hart, H., Kohl, J., & Saari, D. (1974). Compliance without pressure: Some further data on the foot-in-the-door technique. *Journal of Experimental Social Psychology, 10*, 17–22.

Ponemon, L. A. (1992). Ethical reasoning and selection-socialization in accounting. *Accounting, Organizations and Society, 17*, 239–258.

Quinney, E. R. (1964). The study of white collar crime: Toward a reorientation in theory and research. *Journal of Criminal Law, Criminology, and Police Science, 55*(2), 208–214.

Ritzer, G. (2000). *Classical sociological theory* (3rd ed.). Boston: McGraw-Hill.

Robinson, S. L., & Greenberg, J. (1998). Employees behaving badly: Dimensions, determinants, and dilemmas in the study of workplace deviance. In C. L. Cooper & D. M. Rousseau (Eds.), *Trends in Organizational Behavior* (Vol. 5, pp. 1–30). Chichester, England, UK: John Wiley & Son.

Rogers, E. M. (2003). *Diffusion of innovations* (5th ed.). New York: The Free Press.

Ross, J. (1997). [Review of the book Rogue trader: How I brought down Barings Bank and Shook the Financial World]. *Academy of Management Review, 22*, 1006–1010.

Ross, J., & Staw, B. M. (1993). Organizational escalation and exit: Lessons from the Shoreham nuclear power plant. *Academy of Management Journal, 36*, 701–732.

Ryan, B., & Cross, N. C. (1943). The diffusion of hybrid seed corn in two Iowa communities. *Rural Sociology, 8*, 15–24.

Saks, A. M., & Ashforth, B. E. (1997). Organizational socialization: Making sense of the past and present as a prologue for the future. *Journal of Vocational Behavior, 51*, 234–279.

Scherer, M., & Benjamin, M. (2006). The Abu Ghraib files. *Salon.com*. Retrieved July 9, 2008 from http://www.salon.com/news/abu_ghraib/2006/03/14/introduction/index.html

Schweitzer, M. E., Ordóñez, L., & Douma, B. (2004). Goal setting as a motivator of unethical behavior. *Academy of Management Journal, 47*, 422–432.

Sedikides, C., & Strube, M. J. (1997). Self-evaluation: To thine own self be good, to thine own self be sure, to thine own self be true, and to thine own self be better. *Advances in experimental social psychology, 29*, 209–269.

Shah, J. Y., Friedman, R., & Kruglanski, A. W. (2002). Forgetting all else: On the antecedents and consequences of goal shielding. *Journal of Personality and Social Psychology, 83*, 1261–1280.

Shover, N., & Bryant, K. M. (1993). Theoretical explanations of corporate crime. In M. B. Blankenship (Ed.), *Understanding corporate criminality* (pp. 141–176). New York: Garland.

Simon, D. R. (1999). *Elite deviance* (7th ed.). Boston, MA: Allyn & Bacon.

Sivanathan, N. (2009). *Scurrilous competitors: Risk-takers, bribers & saboteurs in promotion tournaments.* Unpublished dissertation, Northwestern University, Evanston, IL.

Sonenshein, S. (2007). The role of construction, intuition, and justification in responding to ethical issues at work: The sensemaking-intuition model. *Academy of Management Review, 32*, 1022–1040.

Staw, B. M. (1976). Knee deep in the big muddy: A study of escalating commitment to a chosen course of action. *Organizational Behavior and Human Decision Processes, 16*, 27–44.

Staw, B. M. (1981). The escalation of commitment to a course of action. *Academy of Management Review, 6*, 577–587.

Staw, B. M. (1997). The escalation of commitment: An update and appraisal. In Z. Shapira (Ed.), *Organizational decision making* (pp. 191–215). Cambridge, UK: Cambridge University Press.

Staw, B. M., Barsade, S. G., & Koput, K. W. (1997). Escalation at the credit window : A longitudinal study of bank executives' recognition and write-off of problem loans. *Journal of Applied Psychology, 82*, 130–142.

Staw, B. M., & Ross, J. (1987). Behavior in escalation situations: Antecedents, prototypes, and solutions. *Research in Organizational Behavior, 9*, 39–78.

Staw, B. M., & Ross, J. (1989). Understanding behavior in escalation situations. *Science, 246*, 216–220.

Strack, F., & Mussweiler, T. (1997). Explaining the enigmatic anchoring effect: Mechanisms of selective accessibility. *Journal of Personality and Social Psychology, 73*, 437–446.

Strang, D., & Soule, S. A. (1998). Diffusion in organizations and social movements: From hybrid corn to poison pills. *Annual Review of Sociology, 24*, 265–290.

Street, M. D., Robertson, C., & Geiger, S. W. (1997). Ethical decision making: The effects of escalating commitment. *Journal of Business Ethics, 16*(11), 1153–1161.

Street, M. D., & Street, V. (2006). The effects of escalating commitment on ethical decision making. *Journal of Business Ethics, 64*(4), 343–356.

Sutherland, E. H. (1939). *Principles of criminology* (Rev. ed.). New York: J. P. Lippincott.

Sutherland, E. H. (1983). *White collar crime: the uncut version* (Rev. ed.). New Haven: Yale University Press. (Originally published in 1949)

Szwajkowski, E. (1985). Organizational illegality: Theoretical integration and illustrative application. *Academy of Management Review, 10*, 558–567.

Tenbrunsel, A. E. (1998). Misrepresentation and expectations of misrepresentation in an ethical dilemma: The role of incentives and temptation. *Academy of Management Journal, 41*, 330–339.

Tenbrunsel, A. E., & Messick, D. M. (1999). Sanctioning systems, decision frames, and cooperation. *Administrative Science Quarterly, 44*, 684–707.

Tenbrunsel, A. E., & Messick, D. M. (2004). Ethical fading: The role of self-deception in unethical behaviour. *Social Justice Research, 17*(2), 223–236.

Tenbrunsel, A. E., & Smith-Crowe, K. (in press). Ethical decision making: Where we've been and where we're going. *Academy of Management Annals.*

Tetlock, P. E., & Lerner, J. (1999). The social contingency model: Identifying empirical and normative boundary conditions on the error-and-bias portrait of human nature. In S. Chaiken & Y. Trope (Eds.), *Dual-process theories in social psychology* (pp. 571–585). New York: Guildford Press.

Tetlock, P. E., Skitka, L., & Boettger, R. (1989). Social and cognitive strategies for coping with accountability: Conformity, complexity, and bolstering. *Journal of Personality and Social Psychology, 57*, 632–640.

Thorson, J., & Biederman-Thorson, M. (1974). Distributed relaxation processes in sensory adaptation. *Science, 183*, 161–172.

Treviño, L. K. (1986). Ethical decision-making in organizations: A person-situation interactionist model. *Academy of Management Review, 11*, 601–617.

Treviño, L. K., Weaver, G. R., & Reynolds, S. J. (2006). Behavioral ethics in organizations: A review. *Journal of Management, 32*, 951–990.

Treviño, L. K., & Youngblood, S. A. (1990). Bad apples in bad barrels: A causal analysis of ethical decisionmaking behavior. *Journal of Applied Psychology, 75*, 378–385.

Turner, J. C., Hogg, M. A., Oakes, P. J., Reicher, S. D., & Wetherell, M. S. (Eds.). (1987). *Rediscovering the social group: A self-categorization theory.* New York: Basil Blackwell.

Tversky, A., & Kahneman, D. (1981). The framing of decisions and the psychology of choice. *Science, 211*, 452–458.

Tversky, A., & Kahneman, D. (1992). Advances in prospect theory: Cumulative representation of uncertainty. *Journal of Risk and Uncertainty, 5*, 297–323.

Tversky, A., & Wakker, P. (1995). Risk attitudes and decision weights. *Econometrica, 63*, 1255–1280.

Vandivier, K. (1996). Why should by conscience bother me? Hiding aircraft brake hazards. In M. D. Ermann & R. J. Lundman (Eds.), *Corporate and governmental deviance: Problems of organizational behavior in contemporary society* (5th ed., pp. 118–138). New York: Oxford University Press.

Van Maanen, J. (1976). Breaking in: Socialization to work. In R. Dubin (Ed.), *Handbook of work, organization, and society* (pp. 67–130). Chicago: Rand McNally.

Vaughan, D. (1996). *The Challenger launch decision: Risky technology, culture, and deviance at NASA.* University of Chicago Press.

Venable, V. (1945). *Human nature: A Marxian view.* New York: Knopf.

Wazana, A. (2000). Physicians and the pharmaceutical industry: Is a gift ever just a gift? *Journal of the American Medical Association, 283*, 373–380.

Weber, J. M., Kopelman, S., & Messick, D. M. (2004). A conceptual review of decision making in social dilemmas: Applying a logic of appropriateness. *Personality and Social Psychology Review, 8*, 281–307.

Wheeler, L. (1966). Toward a theory of behavioral contagion. *Psychological Review, 73*, 179–192.

Williams, R. (2000). Introduction. In R. Williams (Ed.), *Explaining corruption* (Vol. 1, pp. ix–xvi). Cheltenham, UK: Edward Elgar.

Wilson, D. S., Near, D., & Miller, R. R. (1996). Machiavellianism: A synthesis of the evolutionary and psychological literatures. *Psychological Bulletin, 119*, 285–299.

Wilson, J. Q., & Kelling, G. L. (1982). Broken windows: The police and neighborhood safety. *The Atlantic, 249*(3), 29–38.

Winnett, R. (2008a, March 22). London traders sacked in £1.4 billion bank fraud. *The Daily Telegraph.*

Winnett, R. (2008b, March 21). Revealed: The dirty tricks of rogue traders. *The Daily Telegraph.*

Zey-Ferrell, M., & Ferrell, O. C. (1982). Role-set configuration and opportunity as predictors of unethical behaviour in organizations. *Human Relations, 35*, 587–604.

Zey-Ferrell, M., Weaver, K. M., & Ferrell, O. C. (1979). Predicting unethical behavior among marketing practitioners. *Human Relations, 32*, 557–569.

PART III

PROCESSES WITHIN THE INDIVIDUAL
AND ETHICAL BEHAVIOR

CHAPTER 4

MORAL SELF-REGULATION

Licensing and Compensation

Chen-Bo Zhong
University of Toronto

Katie A. Liljenquist
Brigham Young University

Daylian M. Cain
Yale University

People navigate moral choices on a daily basis. A day's choice might begin when a coffee barista inadvertently returns too much change, continue with noticing (while comfortably seated) a senior citizen standing on the crowded bus at the beginning of the long ride to work, and escalate to being asked to stretch the truth to cover for a tardy colleague. Despite the diversity of circumstances such as these, past moral choice can affect current choices, which then influence future choices. For example, a customer who silently pockets the extra coffee change may subsequently be more inclined to give up his seat to the senior citizen; this altruistic act may later license lying for his late co-worker.

Psychological Perspectives on Ethical Behavior and Decision Making, pages 75–89
Copyright © 2009 by Information Age Publishing
All rights of reproduction in any form reserved.

However, examining people's decisions within the context of their recent behavioral history is largely absent in existing theories of ethical decision making, which tend to take a singular, episodic approach to explaining moral behavior. The moral development model (Kohlberg, 1981), for instance, suggests that moral behavior is determined by the sophistication (or stage) of a person's moral reasoning. Although individuals who have reached advanced stages may occasionally reason at a lower stage, the central tenet of Kohlberg's model is that people at more developed stages make superior moral decisions than those at earlier stages (Gibbs, Basinger, & Fuller, 1992; Rest & Navarez, 1994). Thus, Kohlberg's model predicts consistency in moral behavior over time.

Other studies focus on situational variations in addition to moral characteristics or traits. Rest (1986), for example, divides ethical decision making into four discrete steps—awareness, judgment, intention, and behavior and the success of one stage does not imply the success of subsequent stages. A decision maker may possess moral judgment but fail to establish moral intent, hence failing to engage in ethical behavior. Thus, behavioral discrepancies may be caused by situational factors such as job context, incentive structures, organizational culture (Ferrell, Gresham, & Fraedrich, 1989; Treviño, 1986), or social norms (De Cremer & van Dijk, 2008); others may stem from individual differences in moral engagement (see Bandura, Barbaranelli, Caprara, & Pastorelli, 1996). Additionally, good people sometimes engage in morally questionable acts simply because they do not recognize the moral implications of their actions (Bazerman & Moore, 2008; Jones, 1991; Murnighan, Cantelon, & Elyashiv, 2001). These extensions provide important qualifications to the correspondence between moral characteristics and moral behavior by recognizing the moderating role of the situation in determining behavior. Each of these approaches acknowledges that individuals with certain moral characteristics may not behave consistently across different situations; however, they attribute inconsistencies to exogenous factors such as situational constraints rather than to the influence of the individual's previous choices. From these perspectives, moral behaviors are examined outside the temporal context of one's behavioral history.

Contrary to the above positions, we consider an individual's behavioral history and how prior decisions affect subsequent choices. Prior decisions influence which attributes are highlighted in subsequent choices, how they are weighted, and which option is ultimately chosen (e.g., Dhar & Simonson, 1992; Drolet, 2002; Simonson & Tversky, 1992). Many studies have shown that how options are "bracketed" highlights concerns not salient when considering choices in isolation (for review, see: Read, Loewenstein, & Rabin, 1999). For example, Simonson (1990) asked participants to choose between audio tracks for listening; participants tended to choose low-variety sets when picking the next song after the current song ended. However, participants were more inclined to choose high-variety sets when making all song choices up front, demonstrating a difference between sequential vs. simultaneous choice. Dhar and Simonson (1999) argue that consumers try to "balance" their choices. For example, people usually prefer an inexpensive cigar before a meal and an expensive cigar afterwards, because ending a meal with an expensive cigar is consistent with a preference for improvement (Ross & Simonson, 1991; Loewenstein & Prelec, 1993). If people have smoked an expensive cigar prior to a meal, they will opt for an inexpensive one afterwards to balance against their previous choice (Dhar & Simonson, 1999).

People seek balance in ethical decisions as well. Khan and Dhar (2006) found that people donated less money to charity if they had previously committed to help a foreign student in the future. Similarly, Monin and Miller showed that past virtuous behaviors licensed questionable actions (2001). Monin and Miller asked participants to make two consecutive hiring decisions. The first required participants to choose among five applicants for a position in a large consulting firm: In one condition, a man was the obviously superior applicant, whereas in the other, a woman was clearly the better choice. Most chose the strongest applicant, regardless of gender. The second hiring decision required participants to choose a candidate for a stereotypically male job (e.g., foreman). Interestingly, the first decision influenced the second, even though participants saw no connection between them: They were more likely to favor a male applicant in the second decision if they had picked a woman in the first hiring decision. The authors argue that the act of choosing a female applicant in the first task (thereby establishing "moral credentials") buffered participants from worries about appearing sexist in the second task and, hence, licensed their prejudicial decision.

This type of "moral bracketing" highlights the importance of considering behavioral histories to understand how people regulate their moral choices. The previously discussed studies by Khan and Dhar (2006) and Monin and Miller (2001) examined contexts in which sequential behaviors occurred in the same domain (i.e., both decisions related to either helping behavior or prejudice). In this chapter, we place ethical decision making in the context of one's behavioral history but do so regardless of whether the behaviors reside in the same domain. Based on moral-identity theory and the self-regulatory view of self-knowledge, we break down moral regulation into two distinct mechanisms—moral licensing and moral compensation. We introduce the process of moral self-regulation, followed by a review of research that reveals licensing and compensation phenomena, and conclude with the implications for future research of an "equilibrium" approach to moral decision-making.

MORAL SELF-REGULATION

Although individuals differ in the extent to which morality is central to their self-concept, most people see themselves as more ethical than others (Tenbrunsel, 1998; Zhong & Liljenquist, 2008). Individuals tend to conclude that self-interested outcomes are not only desirable but morally justifiable (Epley & Caruso, 2004). For example, people who were randomly assigned to the role of plaintiff or defendant in a hypothetical court case differed in their perceptions of a fair settlement by nearly $18,000 in a self-serving direction (Loewenstein, Issacharoff, Camerer, & Babcock, 1993). Furthermore, the process of justifying self-serving outcomes does not necessarily require conscious attention or cognitive effort (Epley & Caruso, 2004).

The desired "moral self" not only motivates goal achievement, but also serves as a reference point against which discrepancies between the desired self and the actual self can be monitored or evaluated (Higgins, 1996). Thus, people may ask themselves, "Am I a moral person?" and attempt to answer that question by comparing their actual behavior to their moral ideals, motivating a bolstering of the self (compensation) when their actual behavior compares poorly, or allowing them to slack off in the moral domain (licensing) when their actual behavior compares well.

People tend to experience emotional distress when they conclude that they are not living up to their moral aspirations (Higgins, 1987) and are more likely to engage in moral behaviors to compensate for their inadequacies to rebalance the moral scale. Whether from a more subjective transgression such as lying (Shaffer, 1975) or their guilt stems from a clear moral transgression such as delivering excessively harsh criticism (Noel, 1973), few can escape their consciences, which prick long after the crime was committed (Ring, Wallston, & Corey, 1970). In particular, guilt lingers longest when individuals cannot blame their behavior on external incentives (Carlsmith, Collins, & Helmreich, 1966) or situational constraints (Calder, Ross, & Insko, 1973). Of course, guilt may not always translate into compensatory behaviors since individuals may distort their perceptions and rationalize that what they have done was not so morally wrong (Bandura et al., 1996).

On the other hand, some may decide that their actual selves have matched or even exceeded their ideal selves. This can reverse the compensatory mechanism, producing a sense of entitlement to some moral laxity. Supportive of this, the implicit-goal-priming literature (Forster, Liberman, & Higgins, 2005) has shown that once a goal has been reached, activation of goal-related constructs wanes. Therefore, individuals who have validated or exceeded their ideal moral selves may experience a respite from moral regulatory forces and take ethical liberties in subsequent situations.

The motivational force of moral regulation could be compared to a rubber band. When self-perception deviates from the ideal moral image, the band is stretched and produces the greatest motivational force. This force causes people to refrain from further transgressing the bounds of the moral self. However, when self-perception matches or exceeds the moral self, the band "relaxes," exerting less restraint on moral choice and licensing immoral behavior until it is stretched to a point where moral deviations signaling a new threat to the self, and the compensatory mechanism is once again activated (see also Zhong, Ku, Lount, & Murnighan, 2008). With moral compensation and moral licensing, it is not enough to know a person's moral identity, moral reasoning, or situational variables to predict moral behavior. What people do is inevitably affected by their current "moral tension." If there is sufficient slack in the moral band, ethically questionable choices are more likely to be made. What people have done in the past affects how much "room" their moral behavior will have in the future. Thus, we must consider people's behavioral histories to understand the influences on their ethical decisions and the complex processes that allow seemingly "good" people to make unsavory choices yet still emerge with their sense of morality intact.

Moral Compensation

Unethical acts pose direct threats to one's moral self, and the emotional repercussions are both uncomfortable and enduring (Cialdini, Darby, & Vincent, 1973; Klass, 1978). As individuals seek to escape moral self-censure, the negative emotions spawned by transgression motivates protective cognitions and behaviors (Bandura et al., 1996). For example, Klass (1978) noted that, although individuals are emotionally plagued by unethical choices, there is no evidence that their overall self-worth suffers as a result. The resilience of self-esteem in the face of transgressions is arguably due to the great lengths taken, consciously and unconsciously, to protect one's moral image.

Much research on how people respond to immoral behavior focuses on cognitive distortion and rationalization, which spare transgressors self-sanction by allowing them to disengage morally from behaviors that threaten their self-esteem. Bandura et al. (1996) examined various forms of moral disengagement in children who had misbehaved, such as diffusion of responsibility, dehumanizing the victim, moral justification, euphemistic relabeling, and advantageous comparisons. Exploring the potency of moral justification and advantageous comparisons, Sagarin, Rhoads, and Cialdini (1998) found that individuals who tell damaging lies employ "an ego-protective false consensus mechanism . . . a normalizing belief in others' dishonesty." By derogating the target's integrity, participants in their study were able to simultaneously normalize their own unscrupulous behavior and generate a less-threatening social comparison. In an investigation of moral disengagement in the aftermath of the 9/11 attack, McAlister, Bandura, and Owen (2006) noted the prevalence of euphemistic relabeling in the military, citing phrases such as "servicing the target" (bombing missions) or "collateral damage" (unintended civilian deaths).

However, distortions and euphemisms can only do so much to shield against moral scrutiny; when individuals can no longer squelch a threat to their moral identity, direct restitution is an obvious option for absolution. Liars can confess their deception; thieves can return stolen goods. For example, feminists who were induced to display anti-feminist behaviors in a gender-role stereotyping task were more likely subsequently to assert their feminist beliefs (Sherman & Gorkin, 1980). In another example, Ramanathan and Williams (2007) examined penance among indulgent consumers. They found that consumers attempt to "launder" the negative emotions resulting from overindulgence by subsequently making more utilitarian (versus hedonic) consumption choices, thereby restoring a self-view of prudence and restraint. Direct behavioral compensation such as this is well understood by researchers and lay people alike.

What is much less understood, however, are the diverse forms of behaviors that can psychologically compensate for moral transgression and the lack of conceptual overlap required between the compensatory behavior and the transgression. Carlsmith and Gross (1969), for example, noted that compliance with requests for help increases after moral values have been violated, even when such compliance in no way rectifies the previous damage. Similarly, inflicting punishment upon oneself also represents a path to redemption. Wallington (1973) found that people who violate moral rules will actively cause themselves to suffer in other domains. In an ostensible test of perceptual sensitivity, participants were asked to administer electric shocks to themselves. Those who had previously been induced to lie to the experimenter delivered more severe shocks to themselves than those who had not lied.

Underlying these compensatory behaviors is the basic need to affirm one's central values. According to Wicklund and Gollwitzer's (1981) self-completion theory, we each have ways of defining ourselves, and when an aspect of our self-definition is inadequate or threatened, we engage in activities that complete the definition (e.g., an athlete who receives criticism from his coach may put in additional training). To the extent that a person's moral identity consists of diverse traits such as honesty, compassion, and diligence (Aquino & Reed, 2002), moral self-completion may involve any subset of those traits. Thus, an individual whose moral self is threatened by dishonesty may volunteer in a soup kitchen as compensation. Similarly, we should not be surprised to discover that a disingenuous politician may be the most dedicated of blood donors, or that a tax evader may be the most generous of philanthropists. Such examples are consistent with self-affirmation theory (Steele, 1988) as well as Tesser's (2001) work on the plasticity of self-defense that documents remarkable flexibility in how individuals respond to threats and repair identity. Of course, it is more effective to compensate in a manner that is consistent with the threat, (e.g., those experiencing cognitive dissonance after a hypocritical act would rather reduce dissonance by directly amending the inconsistent behavior than by affirming themselves in another domain, Stone, Wiegand, Cooper, & Aronson, 1997); nevertheless, alternative routes can be equally effective when a direct route is not available or is too costly.

The strongest evidence for moral-compensatory motivation comes from moral-cleansing theory (Tetlock, Kristel, Elson, Green, & Lerner, 2000), which suggests that when individuals violate their own values, they are likely to engage in moral cleansing that reaffirms their values and loyalties. Moral cleansing is much broader than direct restitution; it can include any activities that affirm one's core values rather than just behaviors that directly repair the damage caused by the transgression. Thus, when social liberals discovered that the formula they devised for insurance premiums was based on the racial composition of the neighborhood, they not only directly compensated for their moral infraction (i.e., by revising their premium estimates), they also expressed interest in attending African American cultural events and racial-equality rallies (Tetlock et al., 2000). Interestingly, one does not have to be personally implicated in a moral violation to experience a threat to one's moral identity. Exposure to others' moral infractions is sufficient to instill a sense of contamination (Tetlock et al., 2000). For example, participants who read about someone endorsing reprehensible behavior felt morally defiled and were more likely to volunteer for a campaign against the behavior.

While Tetlock's work dealt with cleansing that was strictly symbolic, other researchers have identified a literal version of moral cleansing that pushes the envelope of compensatory methods. In their work on the "Macbeth effect," Zhong and Liljenquist (2006) explored the possibility that moral violations could engender feelings of physical contamination, in which case physical cleansing could serve as a surrogate for moral purification and allow individuals to literally cleanse their consciences. By manipulating exposure to unethical behavior in multiple ways, the authors determined that moral threats activate one's need to cleanse physically. This was demonstrated through concept accessibility, attitudinal preferences for household cleansing products, and actual behavioral choices. In one experiment, participants who had recalled either an ethical or an unethical deed from their past were given the opportunity to choose between two free gifts—a pencil or sanitizing hand wipes. Those whose moral identity had been threatened by the unethical memory were twice as likely to choose the hand wipes as those who had recalled an ethical deed. In a subsequent experiment, Zhong and Liljenquist (2006) tested whether physical cleansing actually alleviates pangs of guilt and restores moral self-image. Participants were asked to write about an unethical behavior they had committed. Afterwards, half of the participants were given the opportunity to sanitize their hands with an antiseptic wipe. Those who cleansed their hands experienced a reduction in moral emotions (e.g., regret and guilt) and were significantly less likely to engage in compensatory behaviors (volunteering to participate in a study for free) than those who were not given the opportunity to physically cleanse themselves. In this sense, physical cleansing washed away moral sins by reducing the dissonance inflicted by the recall of unethical behavior.

Thus, the literature on moral compensation confirms our view of moral regulation: Threats to an individual's moral image induces compensatory behaviors to repair the moral self. What is more important, however, is that those compensatory behaviors do not always repair the damage caused to others by the initial transgression. Instead, morality threats and feelings of guilt can also be mitigated by symbolic compensation such as minor self-punishment or even a hand washing. These recent studies expand the scope of moral cleansing and provide compelling support for the general efficacy of indirect and symbolic moral restitution.

Moral Licensing

Prior behavior motivates moral compensation, but it can also license subsequent actions that are morally questionable. Strahilevitz and Myers (1998) showed that promising to donate to charity made consumers' subsequent choices more frivolous. Kivetz and Simonson (2002) showed that the more effort a customer-loyalty program required, the more customers preferred luxury rewards over necessity rewards, suggesting that past effort justifies future extravagance. Other research predicts that seeing current self-control choices in terms of a series of future self-control choices will increase self-control (Benabou & Tirole, 2004; Loewenstein & Prelec, 1991); however, if one is overly optimistic about one's future self-control, such optimism can license current indulgences (e.g., "I can spend today, since I will save tomorrow."). The goal-achievement literature contains similar examples. Fischbach and Dhar (2005) demonstrate that pursuit of higher-order goals (e.g., exercising) can license the pursuit of lower-order and more tempting goals (e.g., snacking).

In their work on conflicts of interest, Cain and his colleagues (Cain, Loewenstein, & Moore, 2005; 2009; Moore, Cain, Loewenstein, & Bazerman, 2005; Cain, 2006) argue that the seemingly forthright act of disclosing one's conflict of interest can license giving worse advice (i.e., advice biased towards the advisor's self-interest and further from objective truth). Prior disclosure, the authors claim, leads advisors to feel that the audience has been warned, thereby rationalizing that disclosure makes it okay to give biased advice. For example, suppose "Jim" is offering house-buying advice to a new arrival in town. The house in question has been appraised at $200,000, and Jim knows this. Jim values telling the truth, but he has a conflict of interest when it comes to the home's value: Jim's favorite cousin owns this house. If Jim does not disclose his conflict of interest and succumbs (intentionally or unintentionally) to his self-interest, Jim might inflate the home's value. No surprise there. And, not surprisingly, the potential buyer may not suspect foul play and may anchor his estimate of the home's value on the inflated figure provided by Jim. What is surprising, however, is that Cain and colleagues' research suggests that if Jim discloses his conflict of interest (i.e., warns the prospective buyer that his cousin owns the house), Jim will be more inclined to exaggerate the value of the house because he feels less responsible for telling the truth. Alerted by the disclosure, the advisee will discount the advice when warned, but not enough to counteract the increased bias in the advice; in their studies, Cain and his colleagues find that the audience is ironically worse off for having been cautioned against the conflict of interest. It seems that disclosure might warn an audience to cover its ears, but it may also license conflicted advisors to yell even louder.

It is as if prior good acts earn points in a mental account that subsequent immoral acts can spend. Indeed, Khan and Dhar (2006) show that prior choices that boost the self-concept tend to license self-indulgence; they also show that indulgence diminishes if the prior good acts are attributed to an external motive. An alternative explanation also exists: Prior good acts can cast a positive light on subsequent acts, regardless of the motivation behind the prior acts (Monin & Miller, 2001). This is the sort of license people seek when prefacing a racist joke by saying that their best friend belongs to the same race that they are ridiculing. It is not as if having friends of a certain race earns "points" that can be spent by uttering racist jokes; rather, one hopes that, because of one's diverse social connections, the joke cannot be construed as evidence that the teller is racist. In both cases, however, individuals' prior behavior licenses subsequent actions, highlighting the need to examine behavioral histories to understand moral regulatory mechanisms.

FURTHER CONSIDERATIONS

Conscious versus Unconscious

The idea that individuals construct their moral images based on recent or salient behaviors seems to contradict research on self-esteem which shows no evidence that engaging in unethical behaviors reduces self-esteem. Researchers have found that previous dishonesty does not dampen the favorability of self-descriptions (Wallington, 1973), that rewards obtained by lying have no impact on the self-esteem of liars (Cooper & Duncan, 1971), and that aggressive behavior (Okel & Mosher, 1968) and inflicting harm on others (Glass & Wood, 1969) does not tarnish self-evaluations. One possible explanation is that self-esteem is a composite measure that captures many different aspects of the self. When the moral aspect is lacking, people can easily make up for it on other dimensions (e.g., "I may have lied, but I am a worthy person because I am very smart [and/or because of the good things I did or am about to do]"). This highlights an important point: While individuals may be motivated to engage in compensatory behaviors, this may not be conscious. For example, Khan and Dhar (2006) found that people donated less money to charity after expressing a decision to help a foreign student in the future, but generally failed to acknowledge that these future intentions had affected their charitable donations. Such findings suggests that moral balancing may occur below the level of conscious awareness.

Consistency versus Deviation

The central tenet of our chapter is that moral regulation is a dynamic process that involves the interplay of the perceived moral self and ideal moral self. Unlike traditional research that predicts consistency in moral behavior based on traits or tendencies such as moral identity and moral disengagement, our model predicts a dynamic equilibrium: An initial immoral act may produce future moral behaviors and vice versa. This leads to the question of when we can expect consistency and when we will observe the ups and downs of a dynamic equilibrium (Zhong, Ku, Lount, & Murnighan, 2008).

We speculate that the tendency to be consistent rather than fluctuate (as in our model) may be partly dependent on how central morality is to one's self-definition. For individuals who place morality at the very core of their self-concept, we may expect greater consistency over time. Those individuals may scrupulously monitor their behavior according to their moral standards and hence display less deviation from their moral ideal compared to others. Damon and Hart (1992), for example, state that, "there are both theoretical and empirical reasons to believe that the centrality of morality to self may be the single most powerful determiner of concordance between moral judgment and conduct." Given this, we might also expect consistency from people who have self-interest at their core. Taken to the extreme, imagine people completely self-interested; free from moral regulation, their behaviors would be entirely driven by their own benefits, and they would be consistently selfish. Finally, there is a wide band of people who fall somewhere in the middle—those who value morality but for whom moral living is not a core component of their identity. Among these individuals, moral regulation may predict inconsistency, driving individuals to compensate for sins of the past when their morality is threatened and license indiscretions when moral regulatory forces relax. Of course, even within this middle band of people, there will still be some degree of consistency as individual differences inevitably account for some of the variance in moral behavior, but our perspective of moral decision-making predicts far less consistency than models that ignore behavioral history.

CONCLUSIONS

Moral regulation is a complex process; when we are perplexed by others' seemingly incongruous behavior, we should step back and consider their actions in the context of their behavioral history. The sequence of ethical decisions that comprise each individual's behavioral history is a critical predictor of moral behavior. Seeming altruism may spring from past misdeeds, while transgressions may ironically be rooted in bygone virtues. The dynamic nature of moral regulation means that people can find themselves most vulnerable to temptation at the very moment they believe they have achieved their moral ideals. Thus, it is not just bad apples who make rotten choices in life; as the ethical pendulum swings, even the best among us are unlikely to chart an undeviating course of virtue. However, the alternating mechanisms of moral compensation and licensing may establish a dynamic equilibrium around which moral behaviors can be predicted.

REFERENCES

Aquino, K., & Reed, A. (2002). The self-importance of moral identity. *Journal of Personality and Social Psychology, 83,* 1423–1440.

Bandura, A., Barbaranelli, C., Caprara, G., & Pastorelli, C. (1996). Mechanisms of moral disengagement in the exercise of moral agency. *Journal of Personality and Social Psychology, 71,* 364–374.

Bazerman, M., & Moore, D. A. (2008). *Judgment in managerial decision making.* 7th ed. Hoboken, NJ: Wiley.

Bénabou, R., & Tirole, J. (2004). Willpower and personal rules. *Journal of Political Economy, 112*(4), 848–886.

Cain, D. M. (2006). *Regulating behavior off the books.* In B. Mannix, M. Neale, & A. Tenbrunsel (Eds), Research on managing groups and teams: Ethics and groups (8), Greenwich, CT: JAI Press.

Cain, D. M., Loewenstein, G., & Moore, D. A. (2005). The dirt on coming clean: The perverse effects of disclosing conflicts of interest. *Journal of Legal Studies, 34,* 1–25.

Cain, D. M., Loewenstein, G., & Moore, D. A. (2009). *The price is wrong: Consumer protection and the failure of disclosure.* An empirical study demonstrating the failure of disclosure as a response to conflicts of interest. Manuscript in preparation.

Calder, B. J., Ross, M., & Insko, C. (1973). Attitude change and attitude attribution: Effects of incentive, choice, and consequences. *Journal of Personality and Social Psychology, 25,* 84–99.

Carlsmith, J. M., & Gross, A. E. (1969). Some effects of guilt on compliance. *Journal of Personality and Social Psychology, 11,* 232–239.

Calsmith, J. M., Collins, B. E., & Helmreich, R. I. (1966). Studies in forced compliance I: the effect of pressure for compliance on attitude change produced by face-to-face role playing and anonymous essay writing. *Journal of Personality and Social Psychology, 4,* 1–13.

Cialdini, R. B., Darby, B. L., & Vincent, J. E. (1973). Transgression and altruism: A case for hedonism. *Journal of Experimental Social Psychology, 9,* 502–516.

Cooper, J., & Duncan, B. (1971). Cognitive dissonance as a function of self-esteem and logical inconsistency. *Journal of Personality, 39,* 289–302.

Damon, W., & Hart, D. (1992). Self-understanding and its role in social and moral development. In M. Bornstein, & M. E. Lamb (Eds.), *Developmental psychology: An advanced textbook* (3rd ed., pp. 421–464). Hillsdale, NJ: Erlbaum.

De Cremer, D., & van Dijk, E. (2008). Leader-follower effects in resource dilemmas: The roles of leadership selection and social responsibility. *Group Processes and Intergroup Relations, 11,* 355–369.

Dhar, R., & Simonson, I. (1992). The Effect of the focus of comparison on consumer preferences. *Journal of Marketing Research, 29:* 430–440.

Dhar, R., & Simonson, I. (1999). Making complementary choices in consumption episodes: Highlighting versus balancing. *Journal of Marketing Research, 36,* 29–44.

Drolet, A. (2002). Inherent rule variability in consumer choice: Changing rules for change's sake. *Journal of Consumer Research, 29,* 293–305.

Epley, N., & Caruso, E. M. (2004). Egocentric ethics. *Social Justice Research, 17,* 171–187.

Ferrell, O. C., Gresham, L. G., & Fraedrich, J. (1989). A synthesis of ethical decision models for marketing. *Journal of Macromarketing, 9,* 55–64.

Forster, J., Liberman, N., & Higgins, E. T. (2005). Accessibility from active and fulfilled goals. *Journal of Experimental Social Psychology, 41,* 220–239.

Gibbs, J. C., Basinger, K. S., & Fuller, D. (1992). *Moral maturity: Measuring the development of sociomoral reflection.* Hillsdale, NJ: Erlbaum.

Glass, D. C., & Wood, J. D. (1969). The control of aggression by self-esteem and dissonance. In P. G. Zimbardo (Ed.), *The cognitive control of motivation.* Glenview, IL: Scott Foresman.

Higgins, E. T. (1987). Self-discrepancy: A theory relating self and affect. *Psychological Review, 94,* 319- 340.

Higgins, E. T. (1996). The "self digest": Self-knowledge serving self-regulatory functions. *Journal of Personality and Social Psychology, 71,* 1062–1083.

Jones, T. M. (1991). Ethical decision making by individuals in organizations: An issue-contingent model. *Academy of Management Review, 16,* 366–395.

Khan, U., & Dhar, R. (2006). Licensing effect in consumer choice. *Journal of Marketing Research,* 43: 259–266.

Kivetz, R., & Simonson, I. (2002). Earning the right to indulge: Effort as a determinant of customer preferences towards frequency program rewards. *Journal of Marketing Research, 39,* 155–170.

Klass, E. T. (1978). Psychological effects of immoral actions: The experimental evidence. *Psychological Bulletin, 85,* 756–771.

Kohlberg, L. (1981). *Essays on Moral Development, Vol. I: The Philosophy of Moral Development.* San Francisco: Harper & Row.

Loewenstein, G., Issacharoff, S., Camerer, C., & Babcock, L. (1993). Self-serving assessments of fairness and pretrial bargaining. *Journal of Legal Studies, 22,* 135–159.

Loewenstein, G., & Prelec, D. (1991). Negative time preference. *American Economic Review, 81*(2), 347–352.

Loewenstein, G., & Prelec, D. (1993). Preferences for sequences of outcomes. *Psychological Review, 100,* 91–108.

McAlister, A. J., Bandura, A., & Owen, S. V. (2006). Mechanisms of moral disengagement in support of military force: The impact of September 11. *Journal of Social and Clinical Psychology, 25,* 141–165.

Monin, B., & Miller, D. T. (2001). Moral credentials and the expression of prejudice. *Journal of Personality and Social Psychology, 81*(1), 33–43.

Moore, D. A., Cain, D. M., Lowenstein, G., & Bazerman, M. (Eds.). (2005). *Conflicts of interest: Problems and solutions from law, medicine and organizational settings.* Cambridge, MA: Cambridge University Press.

Murnighan, J. K., Cantelon, D. A., & Elyashiv, T. (2001). Bounded personal ethics and the tap dance of real estate agency. In J. A. Wagner III, J. M. Bartunek, & K. D. Elsbach (Eds.), *Advances in qualitative organizational research, 3,* (pp. 1–40). New York: Elsevier/JAI.

Noel, R. C. (1973). Transgression-compliance: A failure to confirm. *Journal of Personality and Social Psychology, 27,* 151–153.

Okel, E., & Mosher, D. L. (1968). Changes in affective states as a function of guilt over aggressive behavior. *Journal of Consulting and Clinical Psychology, 32,* 265–270.

Ramanathan, S., & Williams, P. (2007). Immediate and delayed emotional consequences of indulgence: The moderating influence of personality type on mixed emotions. *Journal of Consumer Research, 34,* 212–223.

Read, D., Loewenstein, G., & Rabin, M. (1999). Choice bracketing. *Journal of Risk and Uncertainty, 19,* 171–197.

Rest, J. R. (1986). *Moral development: Advances in research and theory.* New York: Prae-ger.

Rest, J. R., & Navarez, D. (1994). *Moral development in the professions: Psychology and applied ethics.* Hillsdale, NJ: Erlbaum.

Ring, K., Wallston, K., & Corey, M. (1970). Mode of debriefing as a factor affecting subjective reactions to a Milgram-type obedience situation. *Representative Research in Social Psychology, 1,* 67–85.

Ross, W. T., & Simonson, I. (1991). Evaluations of pairs of experiences: A preference for happy endings. *Journal of Behavioral Decision Making, 4,* 273–282.

Sagarin, B. J., Rhoads, K., & Cialdini, R. B. (1998). Deceiver's distrust: Denigration as a consequence of undiscovered deception. *Personality and Social Psychology Bulletin, 24,* 1167–1176.

Shaffer, D. R. (1975). Some effects of consonant and dissonant attitudinal advocacy on initial attitude salience and attitude change. *Journal of Personality and Social Psychology, 32,* 160–168.

Sherman, S. J., & Gorkin, L. (1980). Attitudes bolstering when behavior is incon-sistent with central attitudes, *Journal of Experimental Social Psychology, 16,* 388–403.

Simonson, I. (1990). The effect of purchase quantity and timing on variety seeking behavior. *Journal of Marketing Research, 27,* 150–162.

Simonson, I., & Tversky, A. (1992). Choice in context: Tradeoff contrast and ex-tremeness aversion. *Journal of Marketing Research, 29,* 281–295.

Steele, C. M. (1988). The psychology of self-affirmation: Sustaining the integrity of the self. In L. Berkowitz (Ed.), *Advances in experimental social psychology* (Vol. 21, pp. 261–302). New York: Academic Press.

Stone, J., Wiegand, A. W., Cooper, J., & Aronson, E. (1997). When exemplification fails: Hypocrisy and the motive for self-integrity. *Journal of Personality and Social Psychology, 72,* 54–65.

Strahilevitz, M., & Myers, J. G. (1998). Donations to charity as purchase incentives: How well they work may depend on what you are trying to sell. *Journal of Consumer Research, 24,* 434–446.

Tenbrunsel, A. (1998). Misrepresentation and expectations of misrepresentation in an ethical dilemma: The role of incentives and temptation. *Academy of Management Journal, 41,* 330–339.

Tesser, A. (2001). On the plasticity of self-defense. *Current Directions in Psychological Science, 10,* 66–69.

Tetlock, P. E., Kristel, O., Elson, B., Green, M., & Lerner, J. (2000). The psychol-ogy of the unthinkable: Taboo trade-offs, forbidden base rates, and heretical counterfactuals. *Journal of Personality and Social Psychology, 78,* 853–870.

Treviño, L. K. (1986). Ethical decision making in organizations: A person-situation interactionist model. *Academy of Management Review, 11,* 601–617.

Wallington, S. A. (1973). Consequences of transgression: Self-punishment and de-pression. *Journal of Personality and Social Psychology, 28,* 1–7.

Wicklund, R. A., & Gollwitzer, P. M. (1981). Symbolic self-completion, attempted influence, and self-deprecation. *Basic and Applied Social Psychology, 2,* 89–114.

Zhong, C. B., Ku, G., Lount, R., & Murnighan, J. K. (2008). *Compensatory ethics.* Un-published manuscript.

Zhong, C. B., & Liljenquist, K. A. (2006). Washing away your sins: Threatened morality and physical cleansing. *Science, 313,* 1451–52.

Zhong, C. B., & Liljenquist, K. A. (2009). *Morality and Hygiene.* Unpublished Manuscript.

CHAPTER 5

ETHICAL STANDARDS IN GAIN VERSUS LOSS FRAMES

Jessica S. Cameron
Dale T. Miller
Stanford University

The American media's coverage of the current drug controversy in major league baseball has understandably focused on superstars such as Mark McGwire, Barry Bonds, and Roger Clemens. But lesser players have also been implicated in the story. One of these is Bobby Estalella, a journeyman who played in the major leagues for nine seasons, beginning in 1996.[1] Over those nine years, his overall batting average was a mere .216. Estalella was primarily a backup catcher who occasionally seemed on the verge of a breakthrough, but who mainly teetered between making it big, getting traded, and being sent back down to the minors. In his nine years in the majors, Estalella played for a total of six major league teams, never spending more than three years with a single one.

What makes Bobby Estalella worthy of discussion here is less his major league record than his appearance in the Mitchell Report (2007), the prod-

---

Psychological Perspectives on Ethical Behavior and Decision Making, pages 91–106

uct of an investigation led by former U.S. Senator George Mitchell into the use of performance enhancing drugs in baseball. According to this report, and to Estalella's own testimony three years earlier (Williams & Fainaru-Wada, 2004), Estalella in 2002 used a variety of substances – including human growth hormone and a steroid known as "the clear"—while recovering from shoulder surgery. His use of these substances was widely known, if unproven; a scout for the Los Angeles Dodgers noted that a member of her organization called Estalella "a poster boy for the chemicals" (p. 131).

Without testimony from Bobby Estalella himself, we can only speculate as to the circumstances that led him to allegedly use performance enhancing substances. But we can consider two possible narratives, and see how sympathetic each one makes him seem.

Narrative 1: Imagine that in 2002 Estalella got greedy. He was tired of being a backup catcher, and decided that he wanted to make it big—and after undergoing shoulder surgery, steroids presented the best chance he had of doing that.

Narrative 2: Imagine that in 2002 Estalella got desperate. He was tired of being in constant danger of being sent down to the minor leagues, and wanted to protect his position in the majors—and after undergoing shoulder surgery, steroids presented the best chance he had of doing that.

Although using performance enhancing substances is difficult to justify, we suspect that most people would find it even harder to justify in the former narrative than in the latter. In general, the media and the realm of public opinion are harder on people who seem to accomplish amazing things as a result of cheating; consider the relative numbers of column inches written on the players named in the opening paragraph and on Estalella. Taking shortcuts to avoid losing ground simply seems more understandable, if not more forgivable.

We know that losses are particularly aversive (Kahneman & Tversky, 1979), and in this chapter we will review evidence that the desire to avoid them can justify and motivate unethical behavior. First we will review the impact that small changes in framing can have on ethical behavior, looking specifically at the power of loss aversion and at the self-interested and unethical behaviors that loss framings can elicit. Next, we will explore the idea that loss framings have the impact they do because they highlight the discrepancy between what people have earned and what they think they deserve. Finally, we will discuss some real-world implications of the role of loss framings in unethical behavior.

THE GENERAL POWER OF FRAMING

Putting a different spin on a situation, or changing how we frame it, can change how we interpret that situation. Changes in framing can also lead us to act in ways that we would not under differently framed circumstances. In particular, shifts in how we frame situations have the power to elicit—or at least to remove psychological barriers against—cheating. People who are more focused on winning than on cooperating in a prisoner's dilemma game are not only more competitive, but also more likely to deceive their opponents about their intentions in order to achieve an even bigger win (Schweitzer, DeChurch, & Gibson, 2005). Similarly, framing successful performance on a task as achieving a specific goal makes people more likely to misrepresent their performance in order to "meet" that goal (Schweitzer, Ordóñez, & Douma, 2004). Simple shifts in framing can also change how we judge other people's unethical acts. For example, people judge a deceptive action by a company less harshly if they read that the organization's ethical record is better than that of one-third of its competitors than if they read that it is worse than that of two-thirds (and obviously, these two pieces of information are equivalent; Dunegan, 1996).

In this chapter, we propose that trying to avoid a loss will not only elicit more sympathetic evaluations of unethical behavior, as in the example of Bobby Estalella above, but will also elicit more unethical behavior than will trying to secure a win. At the root of this idea is the psychology of loss aversion.

THE SPECIFIC POWER OF A LOSS FRAMING

Kahneman and Tversky first outlined the concept of loss aversion as a component of prospect theory (1979). Prospect theory was developed to explain departures from rationality in economic decision making. These researchers proposed that, in contrast to accepted economic theory (Friedman & Savage, 1948), people do not rationally evaluate gambles such as lotteries and insurance policies on the basis of what the impact on their total wealth would be. Instead, individuals are particularly sensitive to relative changes in wealth—and thus behave differently if they are faced with possible gains or with potential losses. Specifically, people are risk-averse when it comes to securing gains, but risk-seeking when trying to avoid losses.

An Example of Loss Aversion

Using a rational economic analysis, one should evaluate the following two scenarios the same way:

> **Scenario 1.** You have been given $0. Choose between
> A) a 20% chance of earning $1000 (and an 80% chance of earning $0), and
> B) a 100% chance of earning $200.
>
> **Scenario 2.** You have been given $1000. Choose between
> A) a 20% chance of losing $0 (and an 80% chance of losing $1000), and
> B) a 100% chance of losing $800.

In both scenarios, choosing option A will leave a person with a 20% chance of walking away with $1000 and an 80% chance of walking away with nothing, while choosing option B will always mean a sure gain of $200 over the starting point. The only difference between these scenarios is in their framing; scenario 1 is presented as a gain relative to a reference point of $0, while scenario 2 is presented as a loss relative to a reference point of $1000. All four options have expected values of $200—so assuming rationality, choices should depend on individuals' tolerance for financial risk, determined perhaps by what $1000 means to them given their overall net worth (Friedman & Savage, 1948; Markowitz, 1952).

However, when Kahneman and Tversky (1979) presented people with similar scenarios, they confirmed that rationality is an unreasonable assumption to make. In fact, framing makes a great deal of difference, and it turns out that people's evaluation of these scenarios depends largely on whether the options are framed as relative losses or as relative gains. Given scenario 1, most would choose option B, the sure gain of $200—but given scenario 2, most would make the opposite choice, preferring option A and the chance of losing nothing. We will take a greater risk to avoid a certain loss than to pursue an equivalent gain, and this subjective distinction has implications for many of the economic choices we make (Kahneman & Tversky, 1984).

We are interested in whether the risks we will take with material goods can extend to our reputations as well. Given that people will take risks to avoid certain loss, we propose that those risks may include behaviors that, if detected, would bring the actor punishment or censure. Specifically, we are interested in cases in which loss aversion may facilitate—or even encourage—self-interested and unethical behavior. Past research has made the connection between loss aversion and self-interested behavior, while our own research offers evidence that potential losses can in fact motivate patently unethical acts as well.

LOSS AVERSION PROMOTES SELF-INTERESTED BEHAVIOR

Brewer and Kramer (1986) first showed that loss framings make us more selfish, by pitting economic games known as the commons dilemma and the public goods dilemma against each other. In a commons dilemma, participants have to decide in a series of rounds how much they would take, or gain, from a common pool, balancing their desire to obtain as much of the resource as possible with their need to keep the common pool large enough to sustain themselves and the other participants for a long time. In a public goods dilemma, participants have the same considerations, but they have to decide how much they would give, or lose, to a common pool. Brewer and Kramer told commons dilemma participants that they could take up to 25 units per round, and told public goods dilemma participants that they would start each round with 25 units from the pool and could give back as many of them as they wished—making the stakes the same, but the framing different. They found that participants who had to give up resources behaved more selfishly, keeping more resources for themselves than participants who had to take from the common pool. The loss framing of the public goods dilemma elicited more self-interested behavior from participants.

In an intriguing replication of Brewer and Kramer's work, McCusker and Carnevale (1995) found that in a public goods dilemma, offering participants rewards for generosity reduced their selfishness and made them more cooperative. Interestingly, they suggest that the reward may have had this effect not by making participants more civic minded, but rather by switching their attention—and their competitive efforts—to obtaining the reward. De Dreu and McCusker (1997) gave participants a different opportunity to appear cooperative while really being self-interested. They gave participants in social dilemmas a pro-social orientation by basing the participants' payments on both their own and their opponent's earnings, and found that these individuals were more generous in public goods dilemmas (loss framing) than in commons dilemmas (gain framing). However, in this scenario generosity is not altruism; a participant who tries to maximize the earnings of both parties is indeed behaving in a self-interested manner. These findings suggest that people trying to avoid a loss may engage in behaviors that, while cooperative on the surface, reveal a high degree of competitiveness when considered more carefully. Trying to avoid a loss can make us act in creatively self-interested ways.

In De Dreu and McCusker's (1997) example, being self-interested worked to both parties' benefit—but at other times, the self-interest spurred by a loss framing can operate to the detriment of all involved. Neale and Bazerman (1985) had participants complete a negotiation task with an experimental confederate, and instructed them to either try to make minimal concessions to the other side, thus minimizing their losses, or to try to maximize the other side's concessions, thus maximizing their gains. Negotiators who were put in a loss frame established higher minimum outcomes that they would accept and made fewer concessions to their opponents, and their negotiations resulted in less successful outcomes for both sides. These participants appeared to be more determined to avoid a loss than to secure a win—and that determination proved to be counterproductive.

Loss aversion not only leads people to behave in more self-interested ways, it can also establish an excuse for their behavior. Kahneman and his colleagues found that people recognize that loss aversion provides a justification for corporate actions. If their participants learned that a company had raised prices in order to compensate for financial losses, they found that acceptable, but if they learned that a company had raised prices in order to attain even greater profits, they judged that action to be unfair (Kahneman, Knetsch, & Thaler, 1986). When we judge whether an individual or an organization's behavior is fair or unfair, ethical or unethical, we take into account what we know of their motivations (see also Jensen, Arnett, Feldman, & Cauffman, 2002).

LOSS AVERSION PROMOTES UNETHICAL BEHAVIOR

We have reviewed evidence that loss framing changes our tolerance for our own and others' self-interested behavior. We know that we will go to greater lengths to avoid a loss than to secure a gain—but just how far will we go? Will a loss framing make us relax our moral standards, and act in unethical ways? Given the evidence that loss framings make participants act more selfishly and competitively in order to avoid that loss, and that participants who approach a social dilemma more competitively are more likely to deceive their opponents to obtain a favorable outcome for themselves (Schweitzer, DeChurch, & Gibson, 2005), it would make sense that loss framings would also make individuals more likely to cheat in order to succeed—if given the opportunity.

AN EXPERIMENT: CHEATING TO WIN VERSUS CHEATING NOT TO LOSE

In order to investigate this possibility, we (Cameron, Miller, & Monin, 2008) created a situation where participants had to work to complete a difficult task. We made money a motivator in one of two ways. Participants in this study were told either that they would earn money for performing well on the task, or that they would avoid losing money by performing well. Our hypothesis was that participants given the latter, loss framing would be particularly motivated to do well—and that if their ability to do well honestly was thwarted, they would be more likely to resort to unethical tactics in order to succeed.

Procedure

The difficult task required solving a series of anagrams. When they came into the lab, participants were given a booklet containing nine, six-letter anagrams. They then learned that on top of a $1 bonus just for coming in, each anagram was worth $1—and if they solved all of them, they could earn as much as $10 for only fifteen minutes of their time. The catch was that participants needed to solve the anagrams in order, because once they missed one, they wouldn't be paid for any of the anagrams that came after it. Thus, a subject who only solved the first anagram and a subject who solved every anagram but the second one would both be paid the same amount: $2.[2]

What made this task difficult was that two of the anagrams were essentially unsolvable. Most of the anagrams in this study were quite simple to solve (one example of an easy anagram was ELLOWY), but these two were fiendishly hard. Their difficulty came not from the arrangement of the letters, but from the obscurity of the words; pretesting revealed that no participants could solve, or even knew the meanings of, the difficult words we used. We planted these impossible anagrams in the second and seventh positions in the booklet—thus guaranteeing that earning more than $2 would be a real challenge. We assumed that few, if any, participants in this study would know these words—and on the off chance that a small number of participants did recognize them, we would expect those wordsmiths to be equally divided between the two conditions.

Our two conditions in this study, a gain condition and a loss condition, were distinguished by a subtle manipulation: a difference in how the payment structure was described to participants. We told participants in the gain condition that they were starting with $1 and that they would earn $1 for each anagram they solved in order. In contrast, we told participants in the loss condition that they were starting with $10 and that they would lose $1 for each anagram that they failed to solve, including any that followed the last anagram they were able to solve in order. We emphasized these messages about the payment, by counting out dollar bills in front of the participants and by leaving the appropriate "base pay" ($1 or $10) on the table in front of them. So from the beginning, participants were aware that they were trying either to gain or to not lose money.

Considering what we know about people's aversion to losing money, one might expect participants given a loss framing to try harder and to persist longer at completing this task, and to ultimately be more successful. However, the nature of the anagrams did not give participants that opportunity—honest effort wouldn't help them solve the unsolvable second or seventh anagrams. Failing to solve the second anagram meant that a participant could not earn more than $2, while failing to solve the seventh limited earnings to $7. Consequently, honest participants could only earn $2. Participants could earn up to $7 by cheating once, on that early impossible anagram. In order to earn $8 or more, a participant would have to cheat twice, by claiming to have solved both impossible anagrams. Our participants, of course, did not know that the second and seventh anagrams were unsolvable for everyone—merely that they were unsolvable for them personally.

In order to increase the temptation to be dishonest—or, more precisely, to remove any barriers preventing dishonesty—we incorporated a few additional features into the study to make our participants believe that we would not be able to detect their cheating (Mazar, Amir, & Ariely, 2008). First, participants were asked to mark the anagrams that they were able to solve on a tracking sheet separate from the anagrams themselves, and were told that we would base their payment solely on what they wrote on the sheet. This requirement meant that participants did not have to worry that we would check over any questionable (or nonexistent) answers they may have arrived at. Second, the experimenter interrupted participants a few minutes before their time was up, and told them that he needed to go and set up for another subject down the hall. He asked participants to do him a favor and "just pay [themselves]"—either by taking additional money out of an envelope on the table in the gain condition, or by leaving any money that they did not earn in a similar envelope in the loss condition—and to leave only their tracking sheet in the room. With both of these measures in place, participants could easily misrepresent their performance, both on paper and in the amount of money they took.

We were most interested in what our loss and gain participants would do when confronted with both the impossible anagrams *and* the readily available opportunity to cheat. There were a few possibilities. Participants could honestly report their inability to solve either anagram. They could misrepresent their success, by telling us that they had solved one or both anagrams, even when they knew they hadn't. Or they could lower their threshold for success, by accepting answers as correct that on careful reflection were clearly wrong. Either of the latter two options would represent dishonesty, and either would result in participants' taking more than $2.

Results and Discussion

Overall, many of our participants chose to take the low road: 42% of study participants took more than $2. The cheaters were disproportionately in the loss condition; 53% of participants in this condition took more than $2, compared to only 30% of gain participants. Even more striking was the difference in the proportions of participants who effectively cheated twice, by taking more than $7. Fully 35% of loss participants cheated twice, which was nearly four times the rate of that level of cheating in the gain condition (9%). The average loss participant cheated .88 times, or more than twice as much as the average gain participant, who cheated only .39 times. Nearly all of these participants recorded that they had "solved" a number of anagrams that corresponded to the amount of money that they took.

Cheating is a Risky Decision

Loss aversion is a response to decision under risk, and the decision that participants made to cheat was not a safe one. In the anagram study, cheating was a gamble for our participants—it could have had consequences including embarrassment, censure, and forfeiture of not only the ill-gotten money, but of the whole $10 payment for the session. In this scenario the safest course of action, even if it meant only earning $2, was to be very conservative in reporting one's anagram solving success. Although it may involve the possibility of a false negative, being conservative would mean double checking answers, having a very high standard for success, and of course, not misrepresenting one's performance. Not all of our participants proved to be this careful. We found that participants who were faced with losing $8 were more willing to take the risk of cheating than participants who were faced with not earning $8. This result is consistent with previous findings regarding loss aversion.

WHY LOSS AVERSION FACILITATES CHEATING

However, confirming that our participants were more risk-seeking when they were trying to avoid losing money does not explain just what is it about a loss that leads people to lie, cheat and steal in order to avoid it. We propose that loss aversion had the impact that it did in our study because starting with $10 emphasized to our participants that they were entitled to more money than we were paying them. All of our participants were being paid just $2 (if they were honest) for solving, in most cases, a total of seven anagrams. But this discrepancy, we believe, was felt most powerfully in the loss condition. By highlighting the gap between how much our participants felt they deserved and how much we were telling them they deserved, the loss framing led participants to go to great and dishonest lengths to address this imbalance.

What made this discrepancy so salient is the fact that our loss participants started from a higher reference point than our gain participants. We started them off with $10, compared to just $1 in the gain condition. De Cremer and van Dijk (2005) have demonstrated that changing an individual's role in a group (e.g., from follower to leader) can make him or her feel entitled to a higher share of the group's common resource. Manipulating individuals' initial standing on a task appears to have had a similar effect; just as naming individuals as leaders serves to indicate that they are more valuable group members, our loss participants seem to have taken their initial payment of $10 as a cue to what their anagram solving abilities were worth. Then, once they were thwarted in earning that full amount, cheating was these participants' only recourse for getting what they believed they deserved.

A related possibility, which is not incompatible with our ideas about reference points and entitlement, is that the goal of avoiding a loss may have made cheating a more acceptable option. Participants in both conditions may very well have been tempted to cheat when faced with what they saw as an unfair situation—but a greater number of our loss-focused participants were licensed to do so. Given the special approbation our society reserves for those who cheat in order to get more than they deserve, as demonstrated in Kahneman et al.'s (1986) research into corporate justifications, the gain-focused participants may have been inhibited from similarly pursuing their own self-interest. With a greater sense of entitlement to their $10, loss participants had an easier time marshalling sufficient justifications for their cheating, and were thus more likely to engage in it. The relative decrease in cheating in the gain condition suggests that framing consequences as losses in a domain where cheating is possible may be the riskiest choice of all.

IMPLICATIONS OF THE LINK BETWEEN LOSS AVERSION AND CHEATING

If college students will cheat at some anagrams to avoid losing $8, one might expect that cheating will also occur in a variety of more meaningful situations, involving potential losses with much higher stakes. While we are certainly stopping short of claiming that loss aversion can explain all cheating, we do propose that it is an underappreciated contributor to many types of unethical behavior. The reference points against which we measure our performance can motivate cheating if we feel that we are falling short, and if we also believe that honest effort will not help us get what we think we deserve. Armed with the knowledge that setting goals establishes those goals as reference points (Heath, Larrick, & Wu, 1999), that reward structures can strengthen those goals (McCusker & Carnevale, 1995), and that having concrete goals can also encourage unethical behavior (Schweitzer, Ordóñez, & Douma, 2004), we can form a more complete picture of how loss aversion can contribute to unethical behavior—and begin to speculate about the institutional structures that may either encourage or discourage it. We will consider three specific domains where cheating is not only common, but may be influenced to some degree by loss aversion: getting through high school, billing hours to clients, and paying taxes.

Getting Through High School

The pressure to cheat begins for many of us in high school. The incidence of high school cheating has increased dramatically over the past few decades: for example, in 1969 only 34% of students reported that they had used a cheat sheet on a test, while by 1989 nearly 68% had (Schab, 1991). Evidence suggests that one reason for this rise in cheating is that students increasingly see dishonesty as a temporary strategy, not a character flaw. While in 1969, 72% of students thought that a cheater in school would grow up to be a cheater at work, by 1989 only 43% of students had the same belief (Schab, 1991). That finding implies that students' cheating in high school is pragmatic, employed to accomplish some short term goal. And a discussion of goals leads us to wonder whether students are using this strategy to get ahead—or to keep from falling behind.

A loss aversion perspective suggests that the latter may be a more potent explanation. Particularly among successful high school students, the competition to get into an elite college is increasingly seen as a zero-sum game (Pope, 2001). The rewards are highly tempting—but the opportunities to achieve them increasingly few, as rates of undergraduate admission at many American colleges and universities dip near or below 10% for the first time (Dillon, 2007). Unfortunately, if a student has a top-university-or-bust mindset, then any outcome short of that goal will feel like a failure. And it may be the desire to avoid this negative outcome, more than the desire to achieve a positive objective, that motivates students to take all manner of shortcuts to ensure that they are eligible for admission to the most elite schools. Accordingly, we would expect to see the highest rates of cheating among students who are determined to get into one single school, and lower rates among students with a more gain framed objective of getting into a school that will be a good fit for them.

An additional possibility for improvement on this front is suggested by research into the limits of ingroup favoritism. Mummendey et al. (1992) found that this bias is attenuated when consequences for the outgroup are presented as actual punishments rather than as the mere denial of advantages. Under these circumstances, a sense of fairness prevails—and might as well even in the seemingly zero-sum game of college applications. We predict that a student who thinks of cheating as an act of aggression, entailing losses for other students, will be less likely to cheat than a student who thinks primarily about the relative benefits to him or herself. If educators frame individual cheating in terms of the losses suffered by others, that shift could make these behaviors less acceptable overall.

Billing Hours to Clients

High school students may not believe that their cheating peers are destined to be cheating adults, but a role for loss framing in cheating can be found in professional life as well. Once they have finished school, many professionals earn a living that is contingent upon their meeting some annual performance goal. Let's consider the example of attorneys working at private law firms. For these lawyers, both base salary and year-end bonuses—as well as assurances of continued employment—are almost always contingent upon their working a minimum number of billable hours per year. The American Bar Association (ABA) issued a report on billable hours in 2002, in which it found that the vast majority of firms surveyed—more than 96%—had minimum billing hour requirements. The report points out a number of disadvantages of this system, not least among them that the prevailing requirement (among 80% of law firms) that attorneys will bill between 1750 and 2050 hours per year translates into an average 56 to 65 hour work week—or up to 13 hours per day—just to earn one's base salary in most firms.[3]

Focusing on a high standard for billable hours can make less directly profitable uses of time decline in importance. DeVoe and Pfeffer (2007) found that people who are paid an hourly wage (as opposed to an annual salary) are less likely to volunteer their time, presumably because they are accustomed to calculating the cost of every hour. Similarly, the ABA raises the concern that young attorneys who bill by the hour are not doing enough pro bono and other unbillable, community-oriented work.

Lawyers might not be actively doing good while they are trying to bill hours—but does the system of billable hours encourage them to behave badly? Using what we know about loss aversion, reference points and unethical behavior, we would argue that it does. If a young law firm associate's reference point is the number of billable hours required to collect a base salary, then not meeting that target may be seen as a loss—which is arguably adaptive, especially if one's job is at stake. However, we propose that billable hours become particularly problematic when a potential bonus, with its even more burdensome billable hour demands, is emphasized. If a bonus is offered, it is likely that an associate's reference point will not be his or her base salary, but rather the total amount represented by the salary plus the bonus. Not obtaining a bonus is then seen as a loss—and as we know, people will go to great lengths to avoid a loss. Although there is some evidence that viewing bonuses through a loss frame can motivate greater work effort and performance (Merriman & Deckop, 2007), we propose that it can also motivate more unethical work behaviors. Not surprisingly, the ABA (2002) documented that attorneys will often cut corners to meet onerous billable hour requirements, ranging from conducting unnecessary research to misrepresenting the number of hours they spend on assignments. This deception is necessary because attorneys at private firms face two problems: there is not always enough work to do to generate the required number of hours, and there are not always enough hours in the day to balance billing requirements, other work responsibilities, and a life away from work. With these constraints, certain shortcuts may well become inevitable.

The good news for the above two situations is that changes in framing can lower rates of cheating. Encouraging students to take a less goal-oriented, winner-take-all approach to the college application process could help bring rates of cheating back down to 1960s levels. Switching from a compensation system that relies solely on billable hours to one that incorporates other measures of quality, reducing the emphasis placed on bonuses, or even eliminating billable hour minimums altogether can move attorneys out of a loss framing and into one that makes cheating a less attractive option. The bad news is that institutional change can be slow—but of course, knowing where to begin changing is the first step.

To end this chapter on a positive note, let us contrast the above two examples—where loss aversion elicits increased unethical behavior—with the example of tax evasion.

Paying Taxes

Tax evasion is a costly problem in the United States. An estimated 15.0 to 16.6% of taxpayers are noncompliant in some way, to the tune of up to $298 million dollars in lost tax revenue per year (Internal Revenue Service, 2005). This percentage seems low, however, when we consider that with the low probability of detection of noncompliance, the rational thing to do is to cheat on one's taxes. In order to explain why noncompliance rates are not higher, economists have used prospect theory to explain tax evasion, proposing that over-withholding (as is generally done in the United States) increases compliance (Smith & Kinsey, 1987; Elffers & Hessing, 1997). They argue that tax compliance is the norm because most taxpayers can expect a refund come filing time—and because we are less likely to cheat in order to obtain a bigger refund (a gain) than we are to avoid making a larger payment (a loss), tax evasion is attenuated. In the United States, tax payment is one area in which the strategic application of a gain framing encourages more ethical behavior than we might see otherwise.

CONCLUSION

In this chapter, we have looked at the role that loss aversion plays in ethical judgments and behavior. Loss aversion can motivate increased competitiveness and self-interested behavior, can make us more forgiving of others' ethical lapses, and can lead us to commit unethical acts ourselves. There is more to unethical behavior than one single framing effect, but an understanding of how this tendency can influence our ethical decision making can and should inform how we structure our social, educational and professional institutions.

NOTES

1. The authors would like to thank Dan Tuller for providing this illustrative example.
2. Given that experiment pay rates at the time were generally around $20 per hour, $10 for only fifteen minutes was intended to seem generous—while we anticipated that participants would view $2 as a very small, if not insulting, payment for their time.
3. This range is a conservative estimate, assuming the common maxim that lawyers work up to three hours for every two that they bill (Yale Law School Career Development Office, 2007). We are also factoring in an estimated five weeks of holiday and vacation per year.

REFERENCES

American Bar Association (2002). *ABA Commission on Billable Hours Report 2001–2002.* Retrieved January 25, 2008, from www.abanet.org/careercounsel/billable/toolkit/bhcomplete.pdf

Brewer, M. B., & Kramer, R. M. (1986). Choice behavior in social dilemmas: Effects of social identity, group size and decision framing. *Journal of Personality and Social Psychology, 50,* 543–549.

Cameron, J. S., Miller, D. T., & Monin, B. (2008). *Deservingness and unethical behavior in loss and gain frames.* Unpublished manuscript.

De Cremer, D., & Van Dijk, E. (2005). When and why leaders put themselves first: Leader behaviour in resource allocations as a function of feeling entitled. *European Journal of Social Psychology, 35*, 553–563.

De Dreu, C. K. W., & McCusker, C. (1997). Gain-loss frames and cooperation in two-person social dilemmas: A transformational analysis. *Journal of Personality and Social Psychology, 72*, 1093–1106.

DeVoe, S. E., & Pfeffer, J. (2007). Hourly payment and volunteering: The effect of organizational practices on decisions about time use. *The Academy of Management Journal, 50*, 783–798.

Dillon, S. (2007, 4 April). A great year for Ivy League schools, but not so great for applicants to them. *The New York Times*, B7.

Dunegan, K. J. (1996). Fines, frames, and images: Examining formulation effects on punishment decisions. *Organizational Behavior and Human Decision Processes, 68*, 58–67.

Elffers, H., & Hessing, D. J. (1997). Influencing the prospects of tax evasion. *Journal of Economic Psychology, 18*, 289–304.

Friedman, M., & Savage, L. J. (1948). The utility analysis of choices involving risk. *The Journal of Political Economy, 56*, 279–304.

Heath, C., Larrick, R. P., & Wu, G. (1999). Goals as reference points. *Cognitive Psychology, 38*, 79–109.

Internal Revenue Service (2005). Tax gap facts and figures. Retrieved August 7, 2007 from http://www.irs.gov/pub/irs-utl/tax_gap_facts-figures.pdf

Jensen, L. A., Arnett, J. J., Feldman, S. S., & Cauffman, E. (2002). It's wrong, but everybody does it: Academic dishonesty among college and high school students. *Contemporary Educational Psychology, 27*, 209–228.

Kahneman, D., Knetsch, J. L., & Thaler, R. (1986). Fairness as a constraint on profit seeking: Entitlements in the market. *The American Economic Review, 76*, 728–741.

Kahneman, D., & Tversky, A. (1979). Prospect theory: An analysis of decision under risk. *Econometrica, 47*, 263–291.

Kahneman, D., & Tversky, A. (1984). Choices, values, and frames. *American Psychologist, 39*, 341–350.

Markowitz, H. (1952). The utility of wealth. *The Journal of Political Economy, 60*, 151–158.

Mazar, N., Amir, O., & Ariely, D. (2008). The dishonesty of honest people: A theory of self-concept maintenance. *Journal of Marketing Research, 45*, 633–644.

McCusker, C., & Carnevale, P. J. (1995). Framing in resource dilemmas: Loss aversion and the moderating effects of sanctions. *Organizational Behavior and Human Decision Processes, 61*, 190–201.

Merriman, K. K., & Deckop, J. R. (2007). Loss aversion and variable pay: a motivational perspective. *International Journal of Human Resource Management, 18*, 1026–1041.

Mitchell, G. J. (2007). *Report to the Commissioner of Baseball of an independent investigation into the illegal use of steroids and other performance enhancing substances by players in Major League Baseball*. Retrieved December 13, 2007 from http://files.mlb.com/ mitchrpt.pdf

Mummendey, A., Simon, B., Dietze, C., Grünert, M., Haeger, G., Kessler, S., Lettgen, S., & Schäferhoff, S. (1992). Categorization is not enough: Intergroup discrimination in negative outcome allocation. *Journal of Experimental Social Psychology, 28*, 125–144.

Neale, M. A., & Bazerman, M. H. (1985). The effects of framing and negotiator overconfidence on bargaining behaviors and outcomes. *The Academy of Management Journal, 28*, 34–49.

Pope, D. C. (2001). *Doing school: How we are creating a generation of stressed-out, materialistic, and miseducated students.* New Haven: Yale University Press.

Schab, F. (1991). Schooling without learning: Thirty years of cheating in high school. *Adolescence, 26*, 839–847.

Schweitzer, M. E., DeChurch, L. A., & Gibson, D. E. (2005). Conflict frames and the use of deception: Are competitive negotiators less ethical? *Journal of Applied Social Psychology, 35*, 2123–2149.

Schweitzer, M. E., Ordóñez, L., & Douma, B. (2004). Goal setting as a motivator of unethical behavior. *Academy of Management Journal, 47*, 422–432.

Smith, K. W., & Kinsey, K. A. (1987). Understanding taxpaying behavior: A conceptual framework with implications for research. *Law and Society Review, 21*, 639–663.

Williams, L., & Fainaru-Wada, M. (2004, 3 December). What Bonds told BALCO grand jury. *San Francisco Chronicle*, A1.

Yale Law School Career Development Office (2007). *The truth about billable hours.* Retrieved January 25, 2008 from www.law.yale.edu/documents/pdf/CDO_Public/cdo-billable_hour.pdf

CHAPTER 6

WHY LEADERS FEEL ENTITLED TO TAKE MORE

Feelings of Entitlement As a Moral Rationalization Strategy

David De Cremer
Erasmus University

Eric van Dijk
Leiden University

Chris P. Reinders Folmer
Tilburg University

As most of us will have noticed, recent years have shown a growing concern regarding the exorbitant salaries of top managers, their desire to obtain higher bonuses each fiscal year, and their tendency to make allocation decisions that primarily favor those in higher hierarchical positions. These kinds of behaviors have received increasing exposure in the media, so that nowadays a common belief seems to be that unethical behavior by those in

Psychological Perspectives on Ethical Behavior and Decision Making, pages 107–119
Copyright © 2009 by Information Age Publishing
107

charge is pervading contemporary organizations and groups. Indeed, such practices have given rise to the idea that leaders are by definition self-interested (i.e., a myth of self-interest is created regarding the decisions that leaders make, cf., Miller, 1999), and as a result claims such as "top managers should receive high payments because they will otherwise leave for 'where the money is'," seem to have become widely accepted.

Although the unethical behavior of leaders is often denied, and actually is a practice that most organizations prefer to keep silent about (see Elvira, 2001; Perlow & Williams, 2003), the emergence of these types of behaviors may lead us to think whether general thinking about the concept of leadership needs to be re-evaluated. Indeed, the idea of a self-serving leader does not fit with popular conceptualizations that portray leaders as people who are expected to (a) facilitate contributions to the collective welfare (e.g., De Cremer & Van Vugt, 2002; Tyler & Huo, 2002), (b) treat members in fair and respectful ways (De Cremer, 2003b), and (c) display a social responsible orientation toward the collective and its members (Yukl, 1998). Therefore, the question may be raised whether our leaders are by definition "bad apples"—who willingly and happily engage in unethical resource allocations—or whether social psychological processes are involved that can turn *any* individual into a self-serving leader figure, who may not even be aware that his or her behavior may be seen unethical. In the present chapter, we reveal how a social psychological approach may help us understand why even the practice of assigning roles like "leader" or "follower" can have powerful consequences for people's willingness to engage in objectively unethical behavior—and how cognitive processes can make that actions that are objectively unethical are not always seen as such.

ROLES AND RESOURCE ALLOCATIONS: A SOCIAL PSYCHOLOGICAL APPROACH

In the wake of recent examples of fraud, corruption, stealing and other types of unethical behavior, there has been increasing attention for the possibility that such behaviors may not only displayed by a few "bad apples," but that given particular circumstances, almost any individual may engage in them. Such a perspective is social psychological in that it argues that the display of ethical or unethical behavior depends on the kind of relationship one has with others (e.g., whether one is a follower or a leader) in a specific situation (e.g. in the context of economic resource allocations). We adopted this social psychological perspective as our starting point to study the impact of people's roles on the ethicality of their allocation decisions.

1. Self-Serving Allocations and Leadership: The Instant Entitlement Bias

In order to explain why people in leader positions seem to deviate from fairness norms when allocating resources, we looked at the social cognition literature. Specifically, we assumed that social cognitive processes may play a role in the tendency of leaders to take more for themselves and to give less to others, because these processes allow them to minimize the unethicality of their actions and thus still enable them to affirm themselves as a moral person. This process is closely linked to what has been called *moral rationalization* (Bandura, 1999). Moral rationalization can be defined as "cognitive process that individuals use to convince themselves that their behavior does not violate their moral standards" (Tsang, 2002, p. 26). According to Tsang (2002), one specific situational factor that can elicit a moral rationalization strategy is the role that people occupy. Applying this logic to the present question whether adopting the role of a leader or follower may impact allocation decisions, we assume that the role of leader (relative to that of follower) may evoke expectations and beliefs that rationalize unethical and unfair behavior, and even may legitimize this kind of behavior. If indeed this is the case, then it follows that being called the leader may motivate unethical allocation decisions, and that people in this role may see this unethical behavior not as unethical (i.e., they may automatically feel entitled to it).

In the social psychology literature some support for this idea can be found in the literature on cognitive schemas (Fiske, 1993) and equity theory (Adams, 1965). More precisely, when people are referred to as leader, role schemas are evoked that are consistent with that label (cf., Phillips & Lord, 1982), and one such specific schema is the expectation that leaders deserve more privileges than subordinates do (Fiske, 1993; Messé, Kerr, & Sattler, 1992). Moreover, being assigned the leader position may also evoke expectations that one will have to put more effort and work into the situation than followers, thus making one feel entitled to higher outcomes (Adams, 1965; Walster, Walster, & Berscheid, 1978).

These insights thus suggest that merely referring to an individual as "the leader" may be enough for him or her to benefit him- or herself at the expense of others. We suggest that if people are assigned the role of leader without any additional information about the leader role or task at hand, they will rely on category-consistent information to base their evaluations and decisions on (see Phillips & Lord, 1982). In the case of an allocation of resources between themselves and others, this information may be the notion that a leader is entitled to pursue privileges and his or her self-interest. In other words, when labeled as the "leader," people may immediately adopt the self-interested perspective of entitlement (cf., Epley & Caruso,

2004, for the idea that self-interest is immediate). As a consequence, this *instant entitlement bias* may cause leaders to perceive their selfish actions as justified rather than as violating norms of fairness, thus making it a moral rationalization strategy.

In a series of studies, we aimed to examine how being labelled a leader or follower may influence people's resource allocations, and whether feelings of entitlement may play a role. In these studies, participants are usually part of a group of six people, who share a collective resource from which the individual members can harvest (i.e., a social dilemma; Komorita & Parks, 1994). Each participant learns that (a) individual members earn more if they do not restrict their harvests, but also that (b) the collective interest is furthered if all group members restrict their harvests (i.e., individual group members learn that they earn more the more they harvest, but also that if the total harvests of the group exceed the available resource, all members end up with nothing; see Messick, Wilke, Brewer, Kramer, Zemke, & Lui, 1983). After this is made clear to the participants, they are told that allocations will be sequential, that is, one group member harvests first, followed by the second, and so forth.

In our studies, participants always learned that they would be the first to take from the resource. We reasoned that being the first to take would create a situation in which participants could not anchor their harvests on the decisions of others, and thus would rely primarily on their own conceptions of what constitutes a good and fair decision (a value which we expected to be colored by how their position in the group was labeled). Interestingly, some prior research has shown that if people are the first in their group to take from the resource, they are likely to anchor their decisions on the *equal division rule* (i.e., the rule that all decision-makers should take an equal amount from the common resource; see Allison & Messick, 1990; Rutte, Wilke, & Messick, 1987), as this rule is easy to follow and satisfies a general norm of fairness (i.e., equality; Deutsch, 1975; Harris & Joyce, 1980). Thus, this set-up makes it easy to test whether people deviate or adhere to what is right and fair when they are labeled as leader or follower.

Across several studies (De Cremer, 2003a; De Cremer & Van Dijk, 2005; Stouten, De Cremer, & Van Dijk, 2005; Van Dijk & De Cremer, 2006), the results showed that those labelled as leaders clearly and significantly deviate from the fairness rule, and consistently take more than those labelled as followers—who, interestingly, adhere to fairness rules (note that their label is the only information given to participants!). Moreover, this effect was consistently explained by the fact that participants felt more entitled to take more than a fair share from the resource in the role of leader than in the role of follower. Thus, role schemas associated with leadership create a feeling of being entitled to higher outcomes, and consequently affect harvesting behavior. These findings thus provide compelling evidence that simply being labelled as leader may legitimize unethical allocation behavior.

From an ethical perspective, these results are disturbing, and may cause worry about leader and management practices throughout all kind of groups and organizations. However, we also conducted several studies to examine whether there may be boundary conditions to this instant entitlement bias, and whether under different circumstances people in the leader role may act less selfishly, and more like those in the follower role. The conditions that we will discuss here are: (a) the extent to which people are accountable and have to justify their choices to others, (b) the social values of those assigned to the leader-follower role, and (c) the procedure by which people are assigned to the leader role.

2. Boundary Conditions of the Instant Entitlement Bias

a. Accountability and the Instant Entitlement Bias

In complex social systems like groups and organizations (see Pfeffer, 1997), people rarely have the opportunity to act without regard for the social consequences of their decisions. Rather, in such contexts, people are often expected to justify their actions (Staw, 1979): They often are accountable to others for their actions and decisions (Lerner & Tetlock, 1999). In many of their decisions, people therefore must take the potential social consequences of their actions into account—what will the others think, and how will they react? In organizational life, leaders are often considered to carry the greatest responsibility, for example for the division of resources. We therefore reasoned that accountability might moderate the effect of the immediate entitlement bias on their resource allocations.

Research on accountability has provided strong evidence that being accountable influences decision-makers' behavior and goals (Lerner & Tetlock, 1999). When individuals feel accountable to the person they are interacting with in an allocation situation, they may be more concerned about how that person views their actions (e.g., as being selfish or unethical). People seek approval and respect from others for many reasons (e.g. self-esteem maintenance, standing within the organization, Baumeister, 1982, 1993; Tyler & Lind, 1992), and therefore accountability may activate self-presentational concerns (Baumeister & Hutton, 1987). In turn, these concerns may constrain people's actions, in such a way that accountable decision-makers may be more likely to display normative and ethical behavior (De Cremer, Snyder, & Dewitte, 2001; De Kwaadsteniet, Van Dijk, Wit, De Cremer, & Van Rooij, 2007).

Because leaders hold jobs with much responsibility, these individuals may be particularly worried about self-presentation. Thus, if accountability is high, self-presentational and reputational concerns will come into play, making leaders aware of their responsibility, and consequently making them more likely to adhere to normative expectations. As a result, leaders may then display more ethical behavior, because using fair procedures will provide them with an image of being a fair and responsible person. In contrast, accountability may be less likely to affect the decisions of followers, as they do not suffer from the immediate entitlement bias and stick to normative expectations. De Cremer (2003a) tested these predictions, again using a six-person group whose members needed to manage a collective resource. His results showed that participants labelled as leaders harvested more than those labelled as followers, and that their harvests deviated significantly from the equal division rule. However, this difference in allocation behavior disappeared when participants were made accountable to the other members of their group. Thus, if conditions are created where they explicitly have to consider whether they can justify their decisions to others, people in the leader role seem less likely to make unethical allocations.

What do these results mean in light of the instant entitlement bias? One possible explanation may be that accountability affects people's processing abilities (cf., Lerner & Tetlock, 1999). Whereas assigned leaders are at first not aware of the fact that they show unethical behavior (i.e., they feel entitled and consider it justified to take a larger share from common resources) accountability makes them reflect upon and more conscious of social responsibility issues. As a result, the automatic evaluation of feeling entitled to a larger share may be interpreted differently from the elicited social responsibility perspective.

b. *Social Values and the Instant Entitlement Bias*

Of course, not only situational variables may be boundary conditions of the immediate entitlement bias; it is also possible that people's proneness to this bias may depend on their personality. A focus on personality variables has always been very popular in the ethics and morality literature, and research on ethical decision making has focused significantly on it (e.g. Ashkanasy, Windsor, & Treviño, 2006; Eisenberg, 2000; Forte, 2005). A social psychological approach also recognizes the value of personality, but understands its effects particularly in relation to the context in which it operates. As such, this approach represents a dynamic interactionist perspective (see e.g. Snyder & Cantor, 1998), where attributes of persons (e.g., their beliefs and values) and features of their situations (e.g., their role of leader or follower) are integrated by individuals as they construct and pursue agendas for action (and hence interact to produce ethical or unethical behavior, for example; see also Kelley, 2000). The use of such an interactionistic perspective has also been advocated by Treviño (1986) in the context of ethical decision making.

Reasoning from this perspective, under which circumstances will personality differences have the greatest impact on ethical decision making?

In other words, will personality influence resource allocations more when the role of leader is salient, or when that of follower is? To answer this question, we turned to the work of Keltner, Gruenfeld, and Anderson (2003) on the effects of power positions. These authors argued that assignment to *higher* positions would induce people to "behave in more state- and trait-consistent fashion" (p. 275)—an argument that is in line with our findings that people take more from shared resources as leaders than as followers. However, Keltner et al. (2003) further argued that, "one would also expect the personality traits of high-power individuals to be more predictive of their social behavior" (p. 276). Thus, this suggests that personality differences may have more impact on allocation behavior when people interact as leaders than when they interact as followers. But which personality difference may have this effect, and may influence people's proneness to the immediate entitlement bias? We reason that this may depend on their social value orientations.

Social value orientations are individual differences in how people evaluate outcomes for themselves and others (Kuhlman & Marshello, 1975; Messick & McClintock, 1968). Depending on the weight they assign to their own outcomes and those of others, people are more or less likely to take the interests of others into account when they make decisions. From the relative weight they assign to these outcomes, many orientations can be distinguished. Most people can be classified as having a prosocial, individualistic, or competitive orientation, however (Van Lange, 1999). Prosocials prefer to maximize joint outcomes and equality in outcomes. Individualists seek to maximize their own outcomes, regardless of the consequences for others' outcomes. Competitors are motivated to maximize the difference between their outcomes and those of others. These latter two categories— individualists and competitors—are usually taken together and defined as proselfs (Van Lange & Kuhlman, 1994), because they both assign a higher weight to outcomes for themselves than to the outcomes of others. In sum, social value orientations therefore directly address what we consider to be at the heart of leader-follower effects on allocations: whether people are motivated to put their own interests first or not. As this stable personality trait is widely acknowledged to affect decisions in situations of interdependence, it is likely that it will also have a pivotal influence on people's allocations to others in the present context (see for a recent overview, Van Lange, De Cremer, Van Dijk, & Van Vugt, 2007).

Van Dijk and De Cremer (2006) set out to integrate the work of Keltner et al. (2003) and insights into social value orientation, by testing the interactive hypothesis that people's social value orientations will have a stronger impact their allocations when they are assigned to higher positions (e.g., the role of leader) than when they are assigned to lower positions (e.g., the role of followers). Again using the same resource paradigm and sequential decision making procedure as discussed earlier, they indeed found support for this notion: social values were found predict allocation behavior only when participants were assigned the role of leader, and not when they were assigned the role of follower. More specifically, in the role of leader, pro-selfs were found to take more from the resource than prosocials. Interestingly, prosocial leaders harvested no more than followers (who harvested an equal amount regardless of their social value orientation). In addition, further analyses showed that relative to prosocial leaders and to followers, the high harvesting behavior of proself leaders was explained by feelings of entitlement. Therefore, these findings clearly show that personality and context can interact to produce (un)ethical allocation decisions, and that the emergence of unethical decisions is motivated by the tendency to put one's own interests first.

3. Leader selection and the Instant Entitlement Bias

As noted earlier, the idea of an absolute self-serving leader does not fit with popular conceptualizations, which portray leaders as people who are concerned with the welfare of their followers, and do their utmost for their group. Therefore, an important question is when leaders may disregard their self-interest, and instead may focus on their social responsibility (motivated by the moral consideration of how one ought to act, Fiske, Kitayama, Markus, & Nisbett, 1998; cf., Cialdini, Kallgren, & Reno, 1991). One relevant variable that may affect this shift in focus is the selection procedure used to assign someone to the role of leader. In some cases, leaders may be appointed by an (external) authority, and the group may have little say in it. In other cases, groups themselves may elect who they wish to be in charge. Leaders can thus be appointed or elected. How may these procedures affect their allocation decisions?

With regard to an elected leader, the group is believed to support one specific person, and thus in a way transfers hopes and expectations upon that individual. Indeed, Hollander and Julian (1970) argue that, "election builds higher demands on the leadership role" (p. 66). Moreover, research by Ben-Yoav, Hollander and Carnevale (1983) suggests that elected leaders are perceived as more responsive to the needs of followers and the interests of the group. As a result, we argue that the idea of an elected leader will create a socially shared expectation that the leader will do things right, and will act in a socially responsible way. After all, the notion of election holds that the group has voted for him and thus expects certain displays of reciprocity (Kenney, Schwartz-Kenney, & Blascovich, 1996). With regard to an appointed leader, however, matters look rather differently. Because appointed leaders do not "owe" their election to the group, they may not feel obliged to live up to the group's expectations to be a fair and socially responsible decision maker. In fact, research suggests that people expect appointed leaders to devote less attention to the needs and interests of the group members (Kenney et al., 1996), perceive such leaders as less legitimate, and expect less from them in terms of performance (see De Cremer & Van Vugt, 2002; Hollander, 1992; Hollander & Julian, 1970).

These insights thus suggest that people labeled as "elected leaders" will be more likely to make fair and ethical allocation decisions than people labeled as "appointed leaders," because the former label is cognitively associated with a focus on social responsibility. To test these predictions, De Cremer and van Dijk (2008) conducted three experimental studies. In a first study, they presented participants with a scenario in which a leader, who was either elected or appointed, acted in an ethical way (i.e., he/she took an equal share from the common resource) or in an unethical way (i.e., he/she violated the equality-rule and thus took more than a fair share). Participants' ratings revealed that they were more accepting of unethical behavior from an appointed leader than from an elected leader. This finding thus reveals that lay people indeed believe that elected leaders should be more responsible than appointed leaders. In a second study, these authors tested this notion by examining whether people labeled as elected leaders were less inclined to make selfish allocations than people labeled as appointed leaders. The results of this study indeed revealed that participants assigned to the role of appointed leader took more from the collective resource than participants assigned to the role of elected leader did. Interestingly, elected leaders took no more from the collective resource than participants assigned to the role of follower. In a final and third study, the authors further investigated this relationship by examining whether activation of the concept of social responsibility (via a priming method) might reduce the tendency of appointed leaders to make unethical allocation decisions. Indeed, in the social responsibility prime condition (where participants were asked to write about their ideas concerning social responsibility), participants who were appointed as leaders took no more from the collective resource than participants who were elected. In the neutral condition (where participants were asked to describe the characteristics of a chair), however, participants who were appointed as leader made more unethical allocations than participants who were elected. Thus, these findings reveal that procedures which bind leaders to their group may increase their feelings of responsibility, and thus may make them less likely to engage in unethical practices—and more likely to put their group's interests above their own.

CONCLUSION

The findings from our research program clearly identify a mechanism whereby leadership may easily invite self-serving and unethical behaviors: it seems to be the case that the role of leader (or even the label in itself) evokes particular expectations of entitlement, which cause leaders to deviate from normative and ethical behaviors—such as following an equal division rule in resource-sharing tasks. In contrast, the role of follower does not evoke such egocentric expectations, and in a way may facilitate ethical and normative behavior (i.e., adherence to an equality-rule). Furthermore, these findings suggest that leaders may not always recognize or be aware of the unethical implications of their selfish actions for the collective, as they simply do not perceive or evaluate their behavior as unfair (i.e., self-interest is automatic and immediate without reasoning, Epley & Caruso, 2004).

In this respect, we think that the notion of instant entitlement bias and its behavioral consequences may be a valuable lesson to be taught in training sessions for those new to management roles. As ethical and moral theoretical models have emphasized before us, unethical behavior is less likely to emerge if people are aware of the moral implications of their decisions (Rest, 1986). For this reason, it is vital that leaders and managers are informed about the social cognitive processes that in implicit ways may affect their decisions. On a more positive note, however, the present findings also reveal several ways in which organizations can limit unethical behavior among their leaders. By asking leaders about the reasons for their decisions (i.e., increasing accountability), leaders may become more conscious and aware of the moral implications of their actions. By fostering prosocial values leaders may be more inclined to consider the interests of their group. And finally, by appointing leaders which are supported by their groups, leaders may feel more responsible for the wellbeing of their group, and may put its interests above their own.[1] Such interventions therefore may also limit the likelihood that leaders unconsciously slip into unethical behavior.

NOTE

1. Interestingly, groups may be more likely to elect leaders who are concerned with their interests, making those with excessively selfish orientations (i.e., proselfs) less likely to attain positions of power—and thereby reducing the likelihood of unethical practices.

REFERENCES

Adams, J. S. (1965). Inequity in social exchange. In L. Berkowitz (Ed.), *Advances in experimental social psychology* (Vol. 2, pp. 267–299). New York: Academic Press.

Allison, S. T., & Messick, D. M. (1990). Social decision heuristics in the use of shared resources. *Journal of Behavioral Decision Making, 3,* 195–204.

Ashkanasy, N. M., Windsor, C. A., & Treviño, L. K. (2006), Bad apples in bad barrels revisited: cognitive moral development, just world beliefs, rewards, and ethical decision-making. *Business Ethics Quarterly, 16,* 449–73.

Bandura, A. (1999). Moral disengagement in the perpetration of inhumanities. *Personality and Social Psychology Review, 3,* 193–209.

Baumeister, R. F. (1982). A self-presentational view of social phenomena. *Psychological Bulletin, 91,* 3–26.

Baumeister, R. F. (1993). *Self-esteem: The puzzle of low self-regard.* Hillsdale, NJ: Lawrence Erlbaum.

Baumeister, R. F., & Hutton, (1987). Self-presentation theory: Self-construction and audience pleading. In B. Mullen and G. R. Goethals (Eds.), *Theories of group behavior* (pp. 71–87). New York: Springer Verlag.

Ben-Yoav, O., Hollander, E. P., & Carnevale, P. J. D. (1983). Leader legitimacy, leader-follower interaction, and followers' ratings of the leader. *Journal of Social Psychology, 121,* 111–115.

Cialdini, R. B., Kallgren, C. A., & Reno, R. R. (1991). A focus theory of normative conduct: A theoretical refinement and reevaluation of the role of norms in human behavior. In M Zanna (Ed.), *Advances in experimental social psychology* (Vol. 24, pp. 201–234). New York: Academic Press.

De Cremer, D. (2003a). How self-conception may lead to inequality: Effect of hierarchical roles on the equality-rule in organizational resource-sharing tasks. *Group and Organization Management, 28,* 282–302.

De Cremer, D. (2003b). Why inconsistent leadership is regarded as procedurally unfair: The importance of social self-esteem concerns. *European Journal of Social Psychology, 33,* 535–550.

De Cremer, D., Snyder, M., & Dewitte, S. (2001). "The less I trust, the less I contribute (or not)?" Effects of trust, accountability, and self-monitoring in social dilemmas. *European Journal of Social Psychology, 31,* 93–107.

De Cremer, D., & Van Dijk, E. (2005). When and why leaders put themselves first: Leader behavior in resource allocations as a function of feeling entitled. *European Journal of Social Psychology, 35,* 553–563.

De Cremer, D., & van Dijk, E. (2008). Leader-follower effects in resource dilemmas: The roles of selection procedure and social responsibility. *Group Processes and Intergroup Relations, 11,* 355–369.

De Cremer, D., & Van Vugt, M. (2002). Intergroup and intragroup aspects of leadership in social dilemmas: A relational model of cooperation. *Journal of Experimental Social Psychology, 38,* 126–136.

De Kwaadsteniet, E., Van Dijk, E., Wit, A., De Cremer, D., & Van Rooij, P. (2007). Justifying decisions in social dilemmas: Effects of accountability and resource size uncertainty. *Personality and Social Psychology Bulletin, 33*(12), 1648–1660.

Deutsch, M. (1975). Equity, equality, and need: what determines which value will be used as the basis for distributive justice? *Journal of Social Issues, 31*, 137–150.

Eisenberg, N. (2000). Emotion, regulation, and moral development. *Annual Review of Psychology, 51*, 665–697.

Elvira, M. M. (2001). Pay me now or pay me later—Analyzing the relationship between bonus and promotion incentives. *Work and Occupations, 28*, 346–370.

Epley, N., & Caruso, E. M. (2004). Egocentric ethics. *Social Justice Research, 17*, 171–187.

Fiske, A. P., Kitayama, S., Markus, H. R., & Nisbett, R. E. (1998). The cultural matrix of social psychology. In DT Gilbert, ST Fiske et al. (Eds), *The handbook of social psychology* (Vol. 2, pp. 915–981). Boston, MA: McGraw-Hill.

Fiske, S. T. (1993). Social cognition and social perception. In M. R. Rosenzweig & L. W. Porter (Eds), *Annual review of psychology*. Palo Alto, CA: Annual Reviews.

Forte, A. (2005). Locus of control and the moral reasoning of managers. *Journal of Business Ethics, 58*, 65–77.

Harris, R. J., & Joyce, M. A. (1980). What's fair? It depends on how you phrase the question. *Journal of Personality and Social Psychology, 38*, 165–179.

Hollander, E. P. (1992). Leadership, followership, self, and others. *Leadership Quarterly, 3*, 43–54.

Hollander, E. P., & Julian, J. W. (1970). Studies in leader legitimacy, influence, and innovation. *Advances in Experimental Social Psychology, 5*, 33–69.

Kelley, H. H. (2000). The proper study of social psychology . *Social Psychology Quarterly, 63*, 3–15.

Keltner, D., Gruenfeld. D. H., & Anderson, C. (2003). Power, approach, and inhibition. *Psychological Review, 110*, 265–284.

Kenney, R. A., Schwartz-Kenney, B. M., & Blascovich, J. (1996), Implicit leadership theories: defining leaders described as worthy of influence. *Personality and Social Psychology Bulletin, 22*, 1128–1143.

Komorita, S. S., & Parks, C. D. (1994). *Social dilemmas*. Dubuque, IA: Brown & Benchmark.

Kuhlman, D. M., & Marshello, A. F. J. (1975). Individual differences in game motivation as moderators of preprogrammed strategy effects in the Prisoner's Dilemma. *Journal of Personality and Social Psychology, 5*, 922–931.

Lerner, J. S., & Tetlock, P. E. (1999). Accounting for the effects of accountability. *Psychological Bulletin, 125*, 225–275.

Messé, L. A., Kerr, N. L., & Sattler, D. N. (1992). "But some animals are more equal than others": The supervisor as a privileged status in group contexts. In S. Worchel, W. Wood, & J. A. Simpson (Eds.), *Group processes and productivity* (pp. 203–222). Newbury Park, CA: Sage.

Messick, D. M., & McClintock, C. G. (1968). Motivational basis of choice in experimental games. *Journal of Experimental Social Psychology, 4*, 1–25.

Messick, D. M., Wilke, H. A. M., Brewer, M. B., Kramer, R. M., Zemke, P. E., & Lui, L. (1983). Individual adaptations and structural change as solutions to social dilemmas. *Journal of Personality and Social Psychology, 44*, 294–309.

Miller, D. T. (1999). The norm of self-interest. *American Psychologist, 54*, 1053–1060.

Perlow, L. & Williams, S. (2003). Is silence killing your company? Harvard Business Review, 81, 52–58.

Pfeffer, J. (1997). *New directions for organizational theory*. New York: Oxford University Press.

Phillips, J. S., & Lord, R. G. (1982). Schematic information processing and perception of leadership in problem solving groups. *Journal of Applied Psychology, 67,* 486–492.

Rest, J. R. (1986). *Moral development: advances in research and theory*. New York: Praeger.

Rutte, C. G., Wilke, H. A. M., & Messick, D. M. (1987). The effects of framing social dilemmas as give-some or take-some games. *British Journal of Social Psychology, 26,* 103–108.

Snyder, M., & Cantor, N. (1998). Understanding personality and social behavior: A functionalist strategy. In D. Gilbert, S. Fiske, and G. Lindzey (Eds.), *Handbook of social psychology, Vol. 1* (pp. 635–679). New York: McGraw-Hill.

Staw, B. M. (1979). Rationality and justification in organizational life. In B. M. Staw & L. L. Cummings (Eds.), *Research in organizational behavior, Vol. 2* (pp. 45–80). Greenwich, CT: JAI Press.

Stouten, J., De Cremer, D., & Van Dijk, E. (2005). I'm doing the best I can (for myself): Leadership and variance of harvesting in social dilemmas. *Group Dynamics: Theory, Research, and Practice, 9,* 205–211.

Tsang, J.-A. (2002). Moral rationalization and the integration of situational factors and psychological processes in immoral behavior. *Review of General Psychology, 6,* 25–50.

Treviño, L. K. (1986). Ethical decision making in organizations: A person-situation interactionist model. *Academy of Management Review, 11,* 601–617.

Tyler, T. R., & Huo, Y. J. (2002). *Trust in the law*. New York: Russell Sage Foundation.

Tyler, T. R., & Lind, E. A. (1992) A relational model of authority in groups. *Advances in Experimental Social Psychology, 25,* 115–191.

Van Dijk, E., & De Cremer, D. (2006). Self-benefiting behavior in the allocation of scarce resources: Leader–follower differences and the moderating effect of social value orientations *Personality and Social Psychology Bulletin, 32,* 1352–1361.

Van Lange, P. A. M. (1999). The pursuit of joint outcomes and equality in outcomes: An integrative model of social value orientation. *Journal of Personality and Social Psychology, 77,* 337–349.

Van Lange, P. A. M., De Cremer, D., Van Dijk, E., & Van Vugt, M. (2007). From aggression to altruism: Basic principles of social interaction. In E.T. Higgins & A. W. Kruglanski (Eds.), *Social psychology: Handbook of basic principles* (pp. 540–561). New York: Guilford.

Van Lange, P. A. M., & Kuhlman, D. M. (1994). Social value orientations and impressions of partner honesty and intelligence: A test of the Might versus Morality Effect. *Journal of Personality and Social Psychology, 67,* 126–141.

Walster, E., Walster, G. W., & Berscheid, E. (1978). *Equity: theory and reserch*. Boston: Allyn & Bacon.

Yukl, G. (1998). *Leadership in organizations* (4th ed.). Englewood Cliffs, NJ: Prentice Hall.

CHAPTER 7

ACTUAL AND POTENTIAL EXCLUSION AS DETERMINANTS OF INDIVIDUALS' UNETHICAL BEHAVIOR IN GROUPS

Madan M. Pillutla
Stefan Thau
London Business School

Employees often justify their unethical actions by referring to how their organizations benefited from these actions. These justifications are not necessarily post-hoc rationalizations of bad behavior as the actions may have been undertaken to help the organization. Take for example the description of the General Electric executives who were caught when conspiring to fix prices as "good organizational men who surrendered their own individualities to the corporate gods they served" (Randall, 1987, p. 466). Or the case of the prosecution of Gulf Oil executives for bribery where the Security and Exchange Commission stated, "there is no reason to suspect or believe that the motive of the employee or officer was anything other than a desire

Psychological Perspectives on Ethical Behavior and Decision Making, pages 121–133
Copyright © 2009 by Information Age Publishing
121

to . . . act solely in the best interest of Gulf and its shareholders" (Ermann & Lundmann, 1982, p. 119).

On the other hand, there are many examples of unethical behavior by individuals which are clearly intended to harm the organizations of which they are members. A famous case is Nick Leeson who broke all rules of trading in securities and incurred heavy losses that eventually led to the bankruptcy of Barings, one of Great Britain's oldest merchant banks (Stein, 2000). Leeson, who considered himself an outsider in an organization dominated by the British upper class, did attempt to defend his actions as helping the bank as one would expect, but most observers believe that his actions were not motivated by a desire to help the organization (Stein, 2000).

Clearly, people whose unethical actions are motivated by a desire to help their group or organization have a different relationship with their group than individuals whose unethical actions are undertaken without any regard for the benefits that accrue to the group. Surprisingly, little attention has been paid to how individuals' relationship with their organization or group affects their propensity to engage in unethical behavior. In this paper, we examine how an individual's standing within a group affects the likelihood that he or she will engage in unethical behavior. Specifically, we examine how the risk or exclusion from a group or actual exclusion from the group affects individual propensity to engage in unethical behavior.

SOCIAL EXCLUSION AND UNETHICAL BEHAVIOR

Group membership probably maximized people's chances of survival and reproduction in the ancestral environment (Stevens & Fiske, 1995). Groups provided food and mates, and helped care for offspring. Groups also helped in the accomplishment of survival tasks such as hunting and guarding against enemies. Thus evolution would have favored those who showed a preference to belong to groups and a propensity to form attachments. The 'need to belong' must therefore be an innate characteristic of all human beings and has been recognized as such in the psychological literature where authors have given it a status as one of the most fundamental of human needs (e.g. Freud, 1930; Maslow, 1968; Bowlby, 1969, 1973). In an extensive review, Baumeister and Leary (1995) present a large body of empirical evidence supporting the fundamental nature of the need to belong. Their literature review led them to assert that "a need to belong, that is, a need to form and maintain at least a minimum quantity of interpersonal relationships, is innately prepared (and hence nearly universal) among human beings" (1995, p. 502).

Baumeister and Leary (1995) suggest that the need for belongingness is not derived from any particular relationship (although family bonds are particularly important, e.g., De Cremer, Brebels, & Sedikides, 2008), and can, in principle, be directed, towards any human being. As a result, the loss of a relationship with any one person can be replaced by a relationship with another though formation of a new relationship takes time. The two main features of the need to belong is that people desire frequent contact or interaction with the other person and desire for these interactions to be free of conflict and negative affect. Thus, frequent contact with disliked others or sporadic pleasant interaction with strangers does not satisfy this need.

Given the importance of belonging to healthy individual functioning, it follows that people who are socially deprived or excluded from groups exhibit a variety of ill effects. Many empirical studies in social psychology and organizational behavior have provided empirical evidence on detrimental effect of social exclusion on those who have been socially excluded from groups. For example, Leary (1990) found that people felt depressed or grief stricken when their connections with certain other people were severed. Barden, Garber, Leiman, Ford & Masters (1985) found that children become anxious when excluded from groups. And Baumeister and Leary (1995) concluded that people who are excluded "suffer higher levels of mental and physical illnesses and relatively highly prone to a broad range of behavioral problems, ranging from traffic accidents to suicide" (p. 511).

If the need to belong is a fundamental human drive, then as with any other drive, the thwarting of this drive, should lead to a desire to seek alternative methods of satisfying this drive. One would therefore expect social exclusion to stimulate a desire to affiliate or reconnect with others. However, research shows mixed findings for this hypothesis, with some research showing that exclusion can sometimes promote interpersonal withdrawal and even contempt (Twenge & Campbell, 2003), harmful (Thau, Aquino & Poortvliet, 2007) and retaliatory behaviors (Stouten, De Cremer & Van Dijk, 2008). Research also shows that excluded people show a lowered capacity for self-regulation (Baumeister, DeWall, Ciarocco & Twenge, 2005) and empathy (Twenge, Baumeister, DeWall, Ciarocco & Bartels, 2007).

These finding, which suggest that social exclusion leads to contempt for the group, harmful, retaliatory behaviors, decreased capacity for self-regulation and an increased tolerance to risk suggests fairly straightforward implications for unethical behavior by individuals in organizations. Individuals who are socially excluded from their work-groups or from their organizations are more likely to behave in an unethical manner (i.e., a counter-normative manner) as they are ego-depleted, do not care about their co-workers, and do not pay attention to the normative demands of the social context (Thau et al., 2007).

While Baumeister and his colleagues have focused on the ill effects of being socially excluded, recent work suggests that people may also react badly when they are at risk of being socially excluded. For example, Allen and

Badcock (2003), also inspired by the evolutionary perspective, talk about the cognitive and behavioral consequences of being at risk of being socially excluded. They propose that 'social investment potential' or the balance of benefits and burdens that an individual brings to the group determines that particular individual's social risk within his or her group. People whose burdens on the group outweigh the benefits they bring to the group are most at risk of being socially excluded. People are likely to be aware of their risk of exclusion as evolution is likely to have equipped people with specialized cognitive and behavioral modules for being attentive to and minimizing the risk of social exclusion. (e.g., Allen & Badcock, 2003; Baumeister & Leary, 1995; Stevens & Fiske, 1995) given the adaptive significance of the task.

In reality, the distinction between actual and potential exclusion will vary on a continuum and differ depending on the individual, with some individuals seeing exclusion where others only seeing a risk of one. However, we talk about them in the following pages as though they are two distinct categories. This simplification is for analytical convenience and should not affect the substantive hypotheses that we generate. Distinguishing between actual and potential exclusion raises the possibility that people who are at risk of being socially excluded behave differently compared to people who have already been excluded. People at risk may attempt to reduce their risk of exclusion by increasing the social value that they bring to the group. One way they can increase value is by making themselves more popular through taking up tasks that others within the group are unable or unwilling to do. Central members of the group may be unwilling to act unethically even if they see it benefiting the group. While it is clear that groups and organizations benefit from undetected unethical behavior committed to benefit them, the negative consequences which include a tarnished reputation, possibility of criminal trials, etc., are so large that central members will not see any benefits for themselves in undertaking these risks. Marginalized members, or members who are at risk of being excluded, on the other hand, have less to lose and may therefore take the risk of acting unethically as long as they believe that it could help the group. Thus, people who are at risk of being socially excluded may act in an unethical manner to reduce their risk of social exclusion.

The preceding discussion suggests that both actual exclusion and the risk of exclusion lead to unethical behavior. However, the type of unethical behavior differs in the two cases. With actual exclusion, people's unethical behavior hurts the group. With potential exclusion, on the other hand, people's unethical behavior may be motivated by a desire to help the group.

In this paper, we explore the role that actual and potential exclusion play in unethical behavior by individuals. We begin with a definition of unethical behavior and then present a brief description of a typology of unethical behavior developed by Narayanan, Ronson & Pillutla (2006). We then develop arguments about how potential and actual exclusion influences the likelihood of commitment of different types of unethical behavior by individuals in a group. It must be noted that our level of analysis is the individual in a group, rather than the group, as we are primarily interested in how different kinds of unethical behavior by individuals are affected by the groups to which they belong. The group is therefore the context in which we examine unethical behavior by individuals. Although we conceptualize the group as primarily the work group to which an individual belongs, this analysis could be extended to the organizational level, where we would expect the individual's exclusion from the organization to have a similar influence on his or her tendency to commit unethical acts on behalf of or against the organization.

We define unethical behavior as any intentional action performed by an individual that violates societal values, mores, and standards of conduct. This definition implies that intentions are important in identifying unethical behavior, i.e., unethical acts requires that the individual intended to commit the act. Otherwise, we may characterize mistakes that result in bad outcomes as unethical behaviors. While the action needs to be intentional, it is not necessary that the actor view the act as unethical. Individuals can and do distort their beliefs in a self-serving manner and this distortion facilitates unethical actions. These potential distortions also suggest that individuals' beliefs about the ethicality of actions cannot serve as the basis for deciding whether an act is ethical or unethical; clear external standards are also required (cf., Pillutla & Murnighan, 2003 for similar arguments about individuals' perceptions of fairness and standards of fairness).

UNETHICAL BEHAVIORS BY INDIVIDUALS IN GROUPS

Our view of unethical behavior, as can be seen in the definition that we adopted, is that it is goal directed. As with any goal directed behavior, unethical action has an intended beneficiary. Narayanan et al., (2006) presented a typology of unethical behaviors based on whether the intended beneficiary of the unethical act is the individual herself or the group of which she is a member. Thus behaviors could (a) help the individual and the group of which she is a member (*mutual behaviors*); or (b) help the individual but harm the group (*egotistic behaviors*); (c) harm the individual but help the group (*martyrly*); and (4) harm the individual and the group (*spiteful*). (Note that the Narayanan et al., 2006 typology also included categories of unethical behavior that was neutral for the individual or for the group. We concentrate on the four categories that are relevant for understanding the effects of social exclusion).

Our hypothesis is that excluded group members are more likely to act in a manner that hurts the group. Thus their unethical behavior will be directed towards hurting the group or at a minimum not helping the group. Individuals who are at risk of being excluded, but are not yet excluded, on the other hand, will take risks and act unethically if they believe that these actions may help the group. We expand on these hypotheses in the following sections beginning with actual exclusion and its impact on unethical behaviors. But before we do that, we present a well-respected stage model of ethical decision making. We then examine how potential and actual exclusion affects each of the stages of decision making process that leads to unethical behavior.

A MODEL OF ETHICAL DECISION-MAKING

According to Rest (1986), ethical decision-making is a 4-component process. The first step is moral awareness or the degree to which the individual understands that the situation involves a moral dilemma. The second step is where the individual makes a moral judgment. The third step is where the individual makes a decision about how he or she intends to act and the final step is the act itself.

This model recognizes that real ethical dilemmas are ambiguous and most individuals look past them, unaware that they exist. For example, when a legitimate authority makes a request, individuals tend *not* to process the situation as one involving a choice where they should ask if they "want" to perform the requested act (Kelman & Hamilton, 1989). In other words, the automatic compliant response to orders from authority figures would prevent an individual from viewing an unethical action demanded by a legitimate authority as an ethical dilemma, as they would not even perceive that they have a decision to make. Moral awareness also depends on the cognitive expenditure the actor is willing to put forth, which is determined by situational factors like personal relevance and accountability, and personal factors like the need for cognitive closure (Street, Douglas, Geiger & Martinko, 2001).

Moral judgments are affected by the stage of cognitive moral development of the individual and the moral intensity of the act. People at higher stages of Kohlberg's (1966) hierarchy of cognitive moral development are more likely to judge corrupt actions as unethical (Rest, 1986), as they rely less on the expectations of others, and more on universal principles. Unethical acts with higher levels of moral intensity are also more likely to be judged as unethical (Jones, 1991). Morally intense acts contain some element of moral imperative, which is determined by the magnitude of the consequences of the action, the existence of social consensus, the temporal closeness of the act, the social, cultural or psychological proximity of those affected by the act, and the concentration of the consequences of the act (Jones, 1991).

The intention that follows moral judgment may differ from the judgment itself, because people have motivations other than ethical considerations. For example, the individual might recognize that the action is unethical, but decide to do it anyway because some other factor—e.g. need—justifies or outweighs the ethical concern. Finally moral action may differ from the intention, because not all intended actions are carried through.

This model indicates that the likelihood of someone acting unethically increases with the likelihood that (a) they view the situation as one that does not involve an ethical dilemma, (b) they do not judge the act as unethical, or (c) they can find reasons to justify acting unethically.

We now turn to an examination of how actual exclusion affects this process.

ACTUAL EXCLUSION AND UNETHICAL BEHAVIOR

As mentioned above, social exclusion leads to a number of negative effects such as being more likely to suffer physical and mental illnesses, being more prone to suicide and becoming more vulnerable to resorting to criminal activity (Baumeister & Leary, 1995). Given these negative consequences one would expect excluded individuals to attempt to reconnect with their groups. But rather than do that (i.e., attempt to reconnect to the group from which they have been excluded), excluded individuals withdraw and even show contempt towards the excluders (Twenge & Campbell, 2003), rate them negatively and as hostile (Maner, DeWall, Baumeister, & Schaller, 2007), and provide them with very low rewards when they are in a position to allocate rewards (Maner et al., 2007). These results suggest that excluded individuals are hostile towards their excluders. Any attempt at reconnection may be towards new others, but they are not normally directed at the excluders (Maner et al., 2007).

Research also suggests that socially excluded people are more likely to engage in self-defeating behaviors such as showing a greater preference for risky long shot lotteries, procrastinating more, and making unhealthy eating choices (Twenge, Catanese, & Baumeister, 2002). Social exclusion also leads to increased gambling behavior (Ocean & Smith, 1993). Baumeister, DeWall, Ciarocco, and Twenge (2005) argue that the psychological basis for these ill-effects is a decreased capacity to self-regulate following exclusion. In their empirical study, Baumeister et al., (2005) showed that social exclusion impaired self-regulation (measured by consumption of healthy and non-tasty drinks, resistance to eating non-healthy snacks or by persistence in unsolved puzzle task). Interestingly, self-regulation did not improve for socially excluded individuals, even when they were offered money as an incentive to self-regulate. This suggests that the self regulation deficits that follow exclusion results from an inability rather than an unwillingness to self regulate.

And finally, there is ample evidence that shows that socially excluded individuals show little concern for the normative demands of their context. For example, Twenge, Baumeister, Tice and Strucke (2001) argued that without the socializing influence of a group pro-social behavior fades and the more instinctual and impulsive tendency of aggressiveness emerges. In an empirical test of their argument, they manipulated social exclusion by either providing experimental participants with bogus feedback after filling a personality questionnaire saying they are likely to end up alone in the future, or by telling participants they were rejected from other people in their experimental group. Results showed that social exclusion led to an increase in aggression toward a person who insulted them. More interestingly, excluded individuals were more aggressive even toward an innocent other. Using a similar exclusion manipulation, Twenge et al., (2007) showed that excluded people were less helpful to victims of a mishap, cooperated less with others is a mixed-motive game and trusted others less. Note that these others were not the excluders. Yet exclusion led to a general reduction in pro-social behavior.

In sum, these findings suggest that social exclusion leads individuals to treat the excluders with hostility. It leads individuals to have an increased tolerance for risk and a propensity to ignore the normative demands of the context. And finally, it impairs their ability to self-regulate. In applying these findings to the decision making model presented above, one could argue that the increased tendency to ignore the normative demands of the contexts will prevent the recognition of ethical issues in any given situation, their inability to self-regulate and increased propensity to take risk will allow them to act even though they recognize an action as unethical and their hostility towards the group provides them with a justification for acting in an unethical manner. Thus social exclusion facilitates unethical behavior. But the hostility towards the group ensures that this unethical behavior will not be undertaken to benefit the group, it may, in fact be taken with the active aim of causing harm to the group. The deficit in self-regulation also suggests that the action may be taken even if it harms the individuals themselves. Thus:

Proposition 1: *Actual exclusion will result in the increased likelihood that individuals will take unethical actions that hurt the group.*

POTENTIAL EXCLUSION AND UNETHICAL BEHAVIOR

Allen and Badcock (2003) argue that individuals' risk of being socially excluded from their groups is determined by their social investment potential, which they defined as a person's social value relative to the person's social burden. Social value refers to the positive contributions that people make to a group's well-being. Social burden, in turn, refers to the negative contributions made to a group's well-being.

Social value and social burden jointly determine an individual's social investment potential and, by extension, an individual's risk of social exclusion. The reason why social value and social burden are key to understanding a person's social investment potential is that groups lose the individual's contributions to common tasks when they exclude members (Hirshleifer & Rasmusen, 1989): The group will be reluctant to exclude a member who has high social value, even if the member is burdensome in other ways. The person then still contributes to the group's well-being and is worthy of social investments. However, the group does not lose much by excluding a highly burdensome member who has low social value. In this case, the person's net contribution to the group's well-being is low, so the person is no longer worthy of social investments and is at risk of social exclusion. These arguments imply a compensatory mechanism, whereby negative contributions to the group's well-being lower social investment potential (and increase social risk) particularly when positive contributions to the group's well-being are low.

Individuals' should have a fairly good idea of their social investment potential as there appear to be at lest two fitness enhancing benefits that emerge from an accurate understanding of one's social investment potential in a particular group. First, it (an accurate understanding) allows individuals to successfully negotiate uncertain social opportunities and more importantly to detect when investment in such opportunities were likely to fail (Allen & Badcock, 2003). In other words, an accurate understanding will enable success in exchange interactions within the group. Second, an accurate understanding will enhance one's ability to manage resources in a given social environment. For instance, if an individual's social value exceeds his or her social burden in a particular group, he or she can demand more from that particular group. Similarly, if burden exceeds value, it is a signal that he or she has to reduce the burden or enhance the benefits.

A similar process applies to work groups. Group members whose negative contributions to the work group outweigh their positive contributions have little social investment potential and are at risk of being excluded from their fellow coworkers. When social investment potential is high, however, employees face no risks of social exclusion. And individuals should have a fairly accurate view of their risk of social exclusion.

So, how would individuals reduce the risk of social exclusion? Considerable research suggests that individuals gain status within their group by offering to help others within the group (cf. reviews by Flynn, 2006; Penner, Dovidio, Piliavin & Schroeder, 2005). Thus, individuals who are at risk of being socially excluded can reduce their risk by offering to help. However, their very status as being at risk suggests that they are not able to help the group in obvious ways (i.e., in contributing more towards the central functions of the group). Thus, they are more likely to offer to do the work that others in the group are unwilling to do.[1] The work would have to benefit the group of course as only helping behaviors that benefit the group are likely to lead to increased status.

Unethical behaviors are one example of actions that more central group members may be unwilling to take despite the benefits that it offers the group. This provides the opportunity for individuals who are at risk of being excluded to perform behaviors that help the group and consequently enhance their status. Thus:

Proposition 2: *Individuals who are at risk of being socially excluded are more likely to behave in an unethical manner to help their group or organization.*

It should be noted here that the limited research that differentiates actual from potential exclusion suggests that individuals who are at risk of being socially excluded appear not to have the self-regulation deficits that the actually excluded people display. This research indicates that socially excluded individuals take less social risks compared to individuals at risk (and to a control group, Derfler-Rozin, Pillutla & Thau, 2008). They also appear to pay more attention to the normative demands of their context than the excluded people. This suggests that the mechanism through which people at risk of being socially excluded is not because of a reduced sensitivity to unethical behaviour, but through a process of justification.

DISCUSSION AND CONCLUSION

In this paper we argue that an individual's relationship with his or her group will determine the likelihood that they will engage in unethical behavior. This account complements the individual and situational accounts of unethical behavior which are currently in vogue in the ethics literature. In conceptualizing unethical behavior as either helping or hurting the group we take our lead from work in social-psychology that looks at determinants of pro-social behavior within groups (cf., Penner et al., 2005). This work suggests that helping behaviors enhance status and standing within groups allowing us to hypothesize that unethical behavior which helps the group is an avenue open to people who are risk of being excluded from groups to increase their standing in the group.

There are clear parallels with the model that we develop here and the work on cooperation in organizations that has been inspired by social identity theory (e.g., Tyler, 2001). That work too, takes individual relationship with the group as the point of departure in analyzing why individuals choose to cooperate with group members or at a minimum refrain from hurting groups of which they are members. While that research focuses on social-identification processes and their impact on individual behavior within groups, we focus on an individual's actual or potential exclusion as the motivational basis for unethical behavior. Given the parallels, it may be worthwhile to investigate commonalities and differences in these two approaches.

As noted briefly before, there would be individual differences in perceptions about exclusion. Circumstances which lead one individual to believe that he or she is excluded from a group may lead another, more optimistic, individual to believe that they can take action to prevent exclusion. These perceptions are in turn going to determine the likelihood of performance of different kinds of unethical behavior. But once, an individual believes that he or she has been excluded from the group, we hypothesize that rather than attempting to "correct" their social status by performing a service for the group, people will take actions that hurt their group. Groups and organizations are thus vulnerable when they exclude members and must be vigilant to prevent their actions from causing permanent damage.

People who perceive that they are only at risk of exclusion may see the situation as less deterministic and feel they have the opportunity to reduce that risk. They may therefore act in a manner that helps the group. But, given their relatively low status in their group, their only option may be to perform behaviors that others don't want to do. They may therefore end up acting unethically if they believe that these unethical behaviors help their groups. Unethical behaviors by group members that get detected can create severe reputational damage, especially if they are seen as benefiting the group. Thus groups should never encourage individuals to act unethically on their behalf. People who are at risk of social exclusion, should therefore be carefully managed so that they don't feel that they need to act unethically to reconnect with the group.

NOTE

1. We are not aware of any empirical studies that test this argument. However anecdotal evidence suggests that people who are on the low end of a status hierarchy end up doing work that others within the group don't do.

REFERENCE

Allen, N. B., & Badcock, P. B. T. (2003). The social risk hypothesis of depressed mood: Evolutionary, psychosocial, and neurobiological perspectives. *Psychological Bulletin, 129,* 887–913.

Barden, R. C., Garber, J., Leiman, B., Ford, M. E. &.Masters, J. C. (1985). Factors governing the effective remediation of negative affect and its cognitive and behavioral consequences. *Journal of Personality and Social Psychology, 49,* 1040–1053

Baumeister, R. F., DeWall, N., Ciarocco, N. J., & Twenge, J. M. (2005). Social exclusion impairs self-regulation. *Journal of Personality and Social Psychology, 88,* 589–604.

Baumeister, R. F., & Leary, M. R. (1995). The need to belong: Desire for interpersonal attachment as a fundamental human motivation. *Psychological Bulletin, 117*(3), 497–529.

Bowlby, J. (1969). *Attachment and loss: Vol. 1. Attachment.* New York: Basic Books.

Bowlby, J. (1973). *Attachment and loss: Vol. 2. Separation anxiety and anger.* New York: Basic Books.

De Cremer, D., Brebels, L. & Sedikides, C. (2008). Being uncertain about what? Procedural fairness effects as a function of general uncertainty and belongingness uncertainty. *Journal of Experimental Social Psychology, 44,* 1520–1525.

Derfler-Rozin, R., Pillutla, M., & Thau, S. (2008). Social connection revisited: The effects of social exclusion risk on reciprocity, trust, and general risk taking. Working paper.

Ermann, M. D., & Lundmann, R. J. (1982). *Corporate deviance.* New York; Holt, Reinhart & Stein.

Flynn, F. (2006). Subjective evaluations of cooperation in organizations. *Research in Organizational Behavior, 27,* 133–174.

Freud, S. (1930). *Civilization and its discontents* (J. Riviere, Trans.). London: Hogarth Press.

Jones, T. M. (1991). Ethical decision making by individuals in organizations: An issue-contingent model. *Academy of Management Review, 16,* 366–395.

Kelman, H. C., and Hamilton, V. L.(1989). *Crimes of obedience.* Binghampton, NY: Yale University.

Kohlberg, L. A. (1966) Cognitive-developmental analysis of children's sex-role concepts and attitudes. In E.E. Maccoby (Ed.), *The development of sex differences* (pp. 82–173). CA :Stanford University Press

Maner, J. E., DeWall, C. N., Baumeister, R. F., & Schaller, M. (2007). Does social exclusion motivate withdrawal or reconnection? Resolving the "porcupine problem." *Journal of Personality and Social Psychology, 92,* 42–55.

Maslow, A. H. (1968). *Toward a psychology of being.* New York: Van Nostrand.

Narayanan, J., Ronson, S. & Pillutla, M. M. (2006). Groups as enablers of unethical behavior: The role of cohesion on group member actions. In A. Tenbrunsel (Ed.), *Ethics in groups: Research on managing groups and teams* (Vol.8, pp. 127–247). Oxford: Elsevier.

Ocean, G., & Smith, G. J. (1993). Social reward, conflict, and commitment: A theoretical model of gambling behavior. *Journal of Gambling Studies, 9,* 321.

Penner, L. A., Dovidio, J. F., Piliavin, J. A., & Schroeder, D. A. (2005). Prosocial behavior: A multilevel approach. *Annual Review of Psychology, 56,* 365–392.

Pillutla, M. M., & Murnighan, J. K. (2003). Fairness in bargaining. *Social Justice Research, 16,* 241–262.

Randall, D. M. (1987). Commitment and the organization: The organization man revisited. *Academy of Management Review, 12,* 460–471.

Rest, J. R. (1986). *Moral development: Advances in research and theory.* New York: Praeger.

Stein, M. (2000). The Risk Taker As Shadow: A Psychoanalytic View Of The Collapse Of Barings Bank *Journal of Management Studies* 37, 1215–1230.

Stevens, L. E., & Fiske, S. T. (1995). Motivation and cognition in social life: A social survival perspective. *Social Cognition, 13,* 189–214.

Stouten, J., De Cremer, D., Van Dijk, E. (in press). When being disadvantaged grows into vengeance: The effects of asymmetry of interest and social rejection in social dilemmas. *European Journal of Social Psychology.*

Street, M. D., Douglas, S. C., Geiger, S. W., & Martinko, M. J. (2001). The impact of cognitive expenditure on the ethical decision-making process: The cognitive elaboration model. *Organizational Behavior and Human Decision Processes, 86,* 256–277.

Thau, S., Aquino, K. & Poortvliet, P. M. (2007). Self-defeating behaviors in organizations: The relationship between thwarted belonging and interpersonal work behaviors. *Journal of Applied Psychology, 92,* 840–847.

Twenge, J. M., Baumeister, R. F., DeWall, C. N., Ciarocco, N. J., & Bartels, J. M. (2007). Social exclusion decreases prosocial behavior. *Journal of Personality and Social Psychology, 92,* 56–66.

Twenge, J. M., Baumeister, R. F., Tice, D. M., & Stucke, T. S. (2001). If you can't join them beat them: Effects of social exclusion on aggressive behavior. *Journal of Personality and Social Psychology, 81,* 1058–1069.

Twenge, J. M., & Campbell, W. K. (2003). "Isn't it fun to get the respect that we're going to deserve?" Narcissism, social rejection, and aggression. *Personality and Social Psychology Bulletin, 29,* 261–272.

Twenge, J. M., Catanese, K. R., & Baumeister, R. F. (2002). Social exclusion causes self-defeating behavior. *Journal of Personality and Social Psychology, 83,* 606–615.

Tyler, T. R. (2001). Cooperation in organizations. In M. A. Hogg & D. J. Terry (Eds.), *Social identity processes in organizational contexts.* (pp. 149–166). Philadelphia: Psychology Press.

CHAPTER 8

WHEN THE NEED TO TRUST RESULTS IN UNETHICAL BEHAVIOR

The Sensitivity to Mean Intentions (SeMI) Model

Mario Gollwitzer
Tobias Rothmund
University of Koblenz-Landau

Tax evasion is a ubiquitous problem in many countries. The German Tax Union estimates that fiscal authorities forgo approximately 30 billion Euros every year. Folk theory holds that tax evasion is an offense most likely committed by managers or politicians, and popular cases like the "Liechtenstein affair," in which—among others—the former CEO of Deutsche Post, Klaus Zumwinkel, was suspected of having evaded 1 million Euros of taxes, fortify this theory. However, tax evasion is an offense that is committed in all social milieus, independent of class, age, or income. According to recent estimations, 15 billion Euros of unpaid taxes in Germany are accumulated

Psychological Perspectives on Ethical Behavior and Decision Making, pages 135–152
Copyright © 2009 by Information Age Publishing

by people with a monthly income of 4,000 Euros or lower (Brönstrup & Peters, 2008).

Why do people evade taxes? Economists argue that saving money by evading taxes is perfectly in line with a fundamental self-interest motive. According to the economic rational-choice model, the only reason why people do not evade taxes is that they are deterred by legal punishment (e.g., Allingham & Sandmo, 1972; Becker, 1968). However, rational-choice based models have been criticized for not being able to predict tax compliance correctly: They obviously tend to overestimate the frequency of tax evasion (e.g., Frey & Feld, 2002).

Recent theorizing has therefore begun taking psychological factors such as norms, motives, identity, social cognitions, and emotions, into account (e.g., Braithwaite & Wenzel, 2008; Feld & Frey, 2007; Torgler, 2003). One of the most influential psychological variables related to tax compliance (vs. tax evasion) is trust. Trust is usually defined as an "...expectancy held by an individual or a group that the word, promise, verbal or written statement of another individual or group can be relied upon" (Rotter, 1967, p. 651), "...an expectation of the persistence and fulfillment of the natural and the moral orders" (Barber, 1983, p. 9), or "...a psychological state comprising the intention to accept vulnerability based upon positive expectation of the intentions or behavior of another" (Rousseau, Sitkin, Burt, & Camerer, 1998, p. 395). The common element in these definitions is that trust manifests itself in an expectation regarding other people's intentions or behavior. Regarding tax evasion, trust therefore manifests itself in the expectation that other people intend to comply with tax rules.

A large body of empirical findings shows that such expectations regarding other people's intentions are positively correlated with one's own behavior. For example, taxpayers' norm-compliance correlates with their expectation that other people are as well norm-compliant (e.g., Bosco & Mittone, 1997; De Juan, Lasheras, & Mayo, 1994; Webley, Robben & Morris, 1988). Correlations of this kind have also been found in other areas, such as insurance fraud (e.g., Fetchenhauer, 1998), making donations in order to secure the maintenance of a public good (e.g., a cross-country skiing slope, cf., Heldt, 2005), or solidarity with the disadvantaged (e.g., students' willingness to help out other students who are economically worse-off; cf., Frey & Meier, 2004). All these examples represent social dilemmas. Social dilemma situations have the following characteristics: First, deciding to behave morally, cooperatively, or considerately would be the right thing to do in the sense that it would benefit the community's common interest. Paying taxes or purchasing a ticket for the subway helps maintaining a system that everybody profits from. However, deciding to behave immorally, egoistically, or ruthlessly is enticing; it would benefit one's own interest. A second key element of social dilemmas is that they introduce a certain kind of interdependence between the actors involved in it: Cooperation only pays off if others cooperate as well, but cooperation is costly if others do not cooperate. Being the only one who pays taxes, who purchases tickets for the subway, or who complies with legal or social norms means being the "sucker." Third, social dilemma situations imply a certain amount of social uncertainty (Yamagishi, 2001). In general, people do not know how other people will decide or behave in a social dilemma situation. One cannot be sure that potential partners will cooperate. Therefore, it is not surprising that individuals' expectations regarding others' intentions are crucial for how they decide in a social dilemma (e.g., Brann & Foddy, 1987; De Cremer, Snyder, & Dewitte, 2001; Dawes, 1980; Kelley & Stahelski, 1970; Messick et al., 1983).

The term "fear of being exploited" (or "sugrophobia"; cf., Vohs, Baumeister, & Chin, 2007) is widely used in the social dilemma literature. It has been referred to as a motivation behind players' decisions in social dilemmas (e.g., Coombs, 1973; Dawes, 1980; Rapoport & Eshed-Levy, 1989; Yamagishi & Sato, 1986). Being exploited or being the "sucker" implies being a victim of injustice: The "sucker" always has a lower payoff than the "free-rider." Those who purchase a ticket for the subway or those who work hard on a group task subsidize those who do not.

Beyond the inequity and the social inequality that is implied in being the sucker, there is another kind of victimization: Being the sucker means being stupid. In a social community in which the norm of self-interest is considered powerful and ubiquitous (Miller, 1999; Miller & Ratner, 1996), suckers have a low social status. People who let themselves be exploited by others supposedly lack social intelligence, power, and competence. Gullibility and naivety are socially undesirable traits. Becoming aware of the fact that one has been exploited by others leads to shame and self-blame (Vohs et al., 2007).

Taken together, it is not surprising that in light of these aspects of victimization, people try hard to avoid being the sucker. More precisely, this means that (a) people are sensitive towards the possibility that they might be exploited by others, and that (b) people withdraw their cooperation if there is reason to believe that they will be exploited by others. There is ample empirical evidence for both notions. An important finding is that people appear to be more sensitive towards cues that indicate dishonesty than towards cues that indicate honesty (Fein, Hilton, & Miller, 1990). One single instance of dishonesty is more likely to be attributed to bad character, whereas multiple instances of honesty are not necessarily likely to be attributed to good character (Miller, Visser, & Staub, 2005). Other findings suggest that evolution has equipped humans with a particular sensitivity toward cues that suggest that other people might harbor mean intentions (Cosmides & Tooby, 1992; Stone, Cosmides, Tooby, Kroll, & Knight, 2002). If there is reason to believe that one might end up being the "sucker," people swiftly withdraw their cooperation. This has been demonstrated in social dilemma games (e.g., Deutsch, 1958; Pillutla, Malhotra, & Murnighan, 2003; Yamagishi & Sato, 1986) or in group tasks that allow social loafing (Latané, Williams, & Harkins, 1979).

Taken together, our brief review suggests (a) that being exploited is the risk that comes with cooperative behavior in social dilemma situations, (b) that being exploited is generally highly aversive and motivates people to avoid it, (c) that fear of being exploited depends on the expectation regarding others' intentions, and (d) that fear of being exploited can be considered an affective "warning sign" that prevents one from being exploited.

The theoretical model that we will describe in the present chapter expands these notions by a personality perspective. We believe that the motivation to avoid being exploited differs on an interindividual level. The combination of a strong trust motive and a generalized expectation that others are not trustworthy results in a personality feature that we will refer to as "Sensitivity to Mean Intentions" (SeMI). SeMI is defined as the generalized aversive expectation that one will be exploited by others. We will describe and define this construct in the following, and we will present a model that describes and explains why and when a high SeMI results in unethical behavior.

SENSITIVITY TO MEAN INTENTIONS AS A PERSONALITY CONSTRUCT

We believe that people differ with regard to their aversive expectation that other people harbor mean intentions, and that these expectations are to a certain degree cross-situationally consistent and stable. It is important to note that this trait conception is related to, but not redundant with, the concept of dispositional trust. "Trait-trust" has been defined as the generalized expectation that other people are reliable (Rotter, 1967) or as a general belief in human benevolence (Yamagishi & Yamagishi, 1994). The crucial difference between SeMI and "trait-trust" is that the latter lacks a motivational aspect. The expectation that other people are more or less trustworthy can be principally independent from the value or the importance that a person places on trustworthiness. In other words, a person may think that others are untrustworthy in general, but the same person can, at the same time, be emotionally indifferent toward this expectation. A second person may also think that others are untrustworthy, and this thought makes this person feel worried, helpless, outraged, or angry.

The notion that people differ not only with regard to their *expectations* of benevolence ("trait-trust") but also with regard to their *need* to trust is consistent with a number of theoretical notions. Fiske (2002, 2004) considers the need to trust others as one of the five core social motives. According to her theory, viewing other people as benevolent enables people to participate in group activities without undue suspicion or vigilance. In particular, trust is necessary for building up and maintaining a positive sense of the self, of others, and the world, it helps us to make use of the profits of social learning and interpersonal communication (e.g., to behave efficiently even in novel situations). It is not surprising that trust is considered to be at the roots of the economic system, the core of social capital, the driving machine of democratic societies (Coleman, 1990; Putnam, 2000). Without trust, there would be no functioning social order, no group cohesion, and no interpersonal attachment. Trust is a key component in many social interactions, from bargaining to loving. Or, as Graham Greene (1993/1943) puts it, "it is impossible to go through life without trust: That is to be imprisoned in the worst cell of all, oneself" (p. 43).

An additional aspect of this assumption which is not inherent in Fiske's theory is that people differ with regard to the strength of their trust motive. Since all motives vary individually with regard to their strength, there is reason to assume that the trust motive does likewise. For example, the need to belong, although regarded universal in humans (e.g., Baumeister & Leary, 1995; Fiske, 2002), varies in strength between individuals (De Cremer & Alberts, 2004; De Cremer & Blader, 2006). Likewise, the need for control (cf., Fiske, 2002) varies in strength between individuals (e.g., Burger & Cooper, 1979).

A central proposition of our model is that people who have a strong trust motive and who, at the same time, harbor generalized expectations of others' malevolence are particularly sensitive toward cues of untrustworthiness. This is why we call our trait concept "Sensitivity to Mean Intentions" (SeMI). People high on this sensitivity have a high need to trust, but are at the same time not trusting. This combination results in a heightened dispositional sensitivity towards cues that suggest that other people harbor mean intentions.

It is interesting to note that similar conceptual arguments have already been made for other social motives. For example, people differ with regard to how much they value affiliation and social acceptance, and how negatively they react towards social rejection. Furthermore, people differ with regard to their generalized expectation that others will or might reject them. The combination of the personal relevance of not being rejected and the expectation of being rejected results in a heightened dispositional sensitivity towards cues that suggest rejection (Downey & Feldman, 1996). Recent experimental and neuroimaging studies suggest that rejection sensitivity (RS) appears to be "hard-wired" and connected to a general sensitivity for pain (e.g., Eisenberger, Jarcho, Lieberman, & Naliboff, 2006). In a laboratory experiment, Downey and Feldman (1996; Study 2) confronted participants with an ambiguous message of an ostensible fellow participant (the experimenter told participants that the other person did not want to continue a joint task that both had been working on for the last ten minutes). People high in RS reported much more emotional distress after receiving the message than people low in RS. In another study (Downey and Feldman, 1996; Study 3) these authors showed that rejection sensitivity is correlated with perceiving ambiguous, but potentially rejecting remarks by their intimate partners as hurtful and intentional. Thus, rejection sensitivity can be conceived of as a readiness to interpret ambiguous social stimuli in a way that fits one's anxious expectation.

The analogy between a dispositional Sensitivity to Mean Intentions (SeMI) and RS is useful since both constructs have at least four features in common. First, both sensitivity constructs are defined as a combination of a motivational aspect (RS: The need to belong; SeMI: The need to trust) and a cognitive aspect (RS: The expectation of being rejected; SeMI: The expectation of being exploited). Second, both constructs are asymmetrical sensitivities as we will show in the following paragraph. Third, both result in undesirable or inappropriate social behavior. Fourth, the influence of both sensitivity constructs on such undesirable behavior depends on the structure of a given situation. Thus, the way RS and SeMI translate into behavior cannot be explained by a simple "main effect" but rather by a particular ("synergistic") person × situation interaction (Schmitt, Eid, & Maes, 2003).

ASYMMETRICAL VERSUS SYMMETRICAL SENSITIVITIES

A central prediction of the SeMI model is that people high in SeMI (that is, high in need to trust and low in trust) are more sensitive towards cues that suggest that other people harbor mean intentions. On first glance, this seems to contradict the notion that people high in dispositional trust are more receptive towards information about trustworthiness (e.g., Kosugi & Yamagishi, 1998; Yamagishi, 2001). Empirical evidence, however, suggests that high- and low-trusters do not merely differ with regard to how sensitive they are in general, but rather *to which cues* they are sensitive to. More precisely, high-trusters appear to be sensitive both towards cues that suggest that others are trustworthy *and* to cues that suggest that others are mean. Low-trusters, on the other hand, are *selectively* sensitive towards cues that suggest that others harbor mean intentions. A noteworthy experiment in this regard was conducted by Parks, Henager, and Scamahorn (1996). Using an iterated prisoner's dilemma game, these authors investigated high- and low-trusters' reactions toward an alleged message from the other player. The message suggested that the other player would play either cooperatively or competitively. In a third (control) condition, the message was neutral with regard to the other player's intentions. The authors found that high-trusters made more cooperative decisions in the "cooperative message" condition than in the neutral condition, and they also made more non-cooperative decisions in the "competitive message" condition than in the neutral condition. Low-trusters, on the other hand, showed a different pattern: These people made more non-cooperative decisions in the "competitive message" condition than in the neutral condition, but they were not more cooperative in the "cooperative message" condition than in the neutral condition. Thus, whereas high-trusters are symmetrically sensitive, low-trusters appear to be asymmetrically sensitive. According to the SeMI model, this asymmetrical sensitivity should even be more pronounced among people with a high need for trust. Rejection sensitivity is, by the way, also an asymmetrical sensitivity. Rejection-sensitive individuals give more weight to cues that indicate rejection, but not to cues that indicate acceptance.

UNDESIRABLE CONSEQUENCES

Rejection sensitivity has negative personal and social consequences. For example, the intimate relationships of people high in RS are more likely to end sooner than those of people low in RS (Downey, Freitas, Michaelis, & Khouri, 1998). Especially among those low in self-regulation capacities, RS is connected to low self-worth, substance abuse, and symptoms of a borderline personality (Ayduk et al., 2000; Ayduk et al., 2008). In a similar vein, Mendoza-Denton, Purdie, Downey, Davis, and Pietrzak (2002) demonstrated that African American students who were highly sensitive to being rejected on the base of their ethnicity (RS-race) had a stronger decrease in well-being and belonging across their first semesters at an American university. Additionally, RS-race was connected to a significant decline in university grades across time.

Sensitivity to Mean Intentions can also have negative personal and social consequences. We assume that SeMI triggers a state of suspiciousness, a cognitive-affective syndrome which we will refer to as "suspicious mindset." The suspicious mindset implies (a) an attributional bias, (b) a motivation to avoid being exploited, and (c) a heightened accessibility to cognitions that legitimize or rationalize one's own unethical behavior.

Attributional bias means that even slight or meaningless incidents or actions that are indicative of the untrustworthiness of another person are interpreted as evidence for this person's "mean intentions." For example, if a person A who is high in SeMI is hustled from behind by a person B while exiting the subway, then A is more likely to attribute this ambiguous incident to B's recklessness. If persons A and C were engaged in a prisoners' dilemma, and C chose to defect, then A is more likely to attribute his behavior to C's greed (although it might as well be attributable to C's fear of being exploited, to C's failure to understand the game, or to situational constraints; cf., Stouten, De Cremer, & Van Dijk, 2005, 2006). If A is pressed by a sports car behind him on a highway, A is more likely to attribute the other driver's behavior to his egoism and arrogance (instead of attributing it to the fact that, for example, the other driver needs to bring his pregnant wife to a hospital). These examples demonstrate that suspiciousness has much in common with the so-called "sinister attribution error." According to Kramer (1994), a sinister attribution error refers to the tendency to overattribute malevolent motives to others. There are also similarities to the hostile attribution bias (Dill, Anderson, Anderson, & Deuser, 1997; Dodge, 1993; Epps & Kendall, 1995), according to which aggressive people tend to attribute other people's objectively ambiguous behaviors to their hostile intentions.

Motivation to avoid being exploited, the second aspect of suspiciousness, has already been discussed at the beginning of this chapter. The mere contemplation of the possibility of being exploited is an aversive emotional state that involves a sense of threat, hyperarousal, hostility, and anticipations of regret, shame, and self-blame (Vohs et al., 2007). Thus, suspiciousness is connected to an avoidance-related motivational state (Carver, 1996; Elliot & Friedman, 2007). Trying to avoid being exploited is inherently prevention-oriented: In a state of suspiciousness, people are motivated to avoid or prevent a negative outcome (in this case, being exploited). The notion that an avoidance-related motivational state is connected to an asymmetrical sensitivity toward negative information, to more vigilance, hyperarousal, affective negativity, and undesirable behavioral and emotional consequences is in line with findings from regulatory focus theory (Higgins, 1997; Higgins & Spiegel, 2004), from the BIS/BAS[1] model (Amodio, Master, Yee, & Taylor, 2008; Gray, 1987), and from Gable's approach-avoidance model of social motivation (Elliot, Gable, & Mapes, 2006; Gable, 2006). A suspicious mindset should therefore have all social-cognitive features that are typical for a "prevention focus," such as subtractive counterfactual thinking (e.g., focusing on what might have happened if one had *not* made a particular choice in the past), generating less alternative explanations for things that happen to them, making more stable, universal, and personal attributions, a more conservative response bias, and a quicker, but also more tenacious goal-pursuit (Higgins & Spiegel, 2004).

Finally, *accessibility to legitimizing or rationalizing cognitions* means that in a state of suspiciousness, the threshold for adhering to ethical norms and moral standards is lowered. The fear of being exploited calls for vindicating actions that defend one from actually being exploited. In many social dilemmas, the vindicating action would be to defect, to refrain from contributing, and to behave uncooperatively. A person high in SeMI who is asked for a Euro at the train station and who suspects ulterior motives on the side of the asker will be less likely to do him or her this favor. A person who has reason to believe that his or her partners in a working team are social loafers would be less likely to put his own effort in the team work. A person who has reason to believe that his or her co-players violate the equality rule in a public goods dilemma would be less likely to contribute a lot to the common good. In all these cases, the high SeMI person perfectly knows that giving the Euro, working hard for the team, and contributing to the common good would be the right thing to do, but deviating from the social and moral standards that prescribe altruistic, collaborative, and cooperative behaviors is justified.

SYNERGISTIC PERSON × SITUATION INTERACTION

Snyder and Ickes (1985) have put forth the widely adopted principle that traits have their greatest impact in "weak" situations (Mischel, 1973; Ickes, 1982), whereas a "weak" situation is defined as normatively unstructured and unstandardized, as long as such a situation is functionally equivalent to the trait in question (Kammrath, Mendoza-Denton, & Mischel, 2005). The impact of traits in "weak" situations is most obvious on immediate cognitive responses to situations, such as perceptions and interpretations of the situation. Highly trait anxious individuals, for instance, selectively attend to threatening information and put more weight on threat signals than on security signals. As a consequence, they are not only alarmed earlier than individuals low in trait anxiety but also react more strongly to situations that differ in threat (Endler, 1997). Highly rejection sensitive individuals selectively attend to cues regarding a possible rejection and put more weight on rejection signals than on acceptance signals (Downey & Feldman, 1996). People who harbor "dangerous world beliefs" selectively attend to cues regarding potential danger and put more weight on danger signals than on security signals (Schaller, Park, & Müller, 2003). Accordingly, people high in SeMI selectively attend to cues regarding other people's mean intentions and put more weight on untrustworthiness signals than on trustworthiness signals.

What we mean to say by those analogies with other sensitivity constructs is that the effect that SeMI has on a person's behavior is inherently an interactionistic one. SeMI implies a lowered threshold for perceiving and processing cues of untrustworthiness in one's social environment. But without such cues, SeMI has no effect on behavior. People high in SeMI are not necessarily less altruistic, less moral, or less cooperative than people low in SeMI; maybe even on the contrary. Only situational cues that are to some extent indicative of untrustworthiness or other people's ulterior motives evoke a suspicious mindset among people high in SeMI, and therefore lead to unethical behavior.

SITUATIONAL CUES OF MEAN INTENTIONS

The aforementioned argument raises the question which situational cues are in fact indicative of other people's mean intentions and which are not. In general, all cues that contain a certain degree of validity for untrustworthiness are applicable here. These cues can be features of a person, an interaction, or a situation. Among the features of a person are cues such as certain facial postures or facial expressions (e.g., narrow eyes; cf., Ekman, 1992; Zebrowitz, 1997). Among the features of an interaction are explicit cues such as messages of intent (e.g., Deutsch, 1958; Parks et al., 1996), or implicit cues such as speech speed, hesitations, or incongruent gestures (cf., Vrij, 2000; Vrij, Edward, & Bull, 2001). Situational cues apply to the context that surrounds a particular interaction. Situational cues can be explicit (e.g., signs saying "beware of pickpockets") or more or less implicit. Implicit cues are merely associated with "meanness." They represent demand characteristics that can be interpreted as indicators of other people's meanness, even if such associations are stereotypical. For example, think of a scene in a shabby neighborhood in which you have lost your way, loosely crowded with shoddily dressed people that are staring at you in a peculiar way. Other situational cues might be associated with "meanness," such as foul odor, dim light, horrifying screams, whispers, or snickers. Even semantic cues that are associated with "meanness" (such as "might" versus "morality") may work as primes that activate a suspicious mindset and lead to uncooperative behavior in a social dilemma (Hertel & Fiedler, 1994; Smeesters, Warlop, Van Avermaet, Corneille, & Yzerbyt, 2003).

Another category of situational cues are information about base-rates of meanness. The information that 15 billion Euros of unpaid taxes in Germany are accumulated by people with a monthly income of 4,000 Euros or lower (Brönstrup & Peters, 2008) might serve as a prime for suspiciousness. Information about the relative number of cheaters, free-riders or defectors in a social dilemma situation should also prime suspiciousness. Confronting people with news about violent crimes that had been committed out of ulterior motives, with newspaper articles about cases of rape and murder, or even with works of fiction that contain strong indicators of bestial behavior might be sufficient to prime suspiciousness, first and foremost among people high in SeMI.

BUFFERS AGAINST UNETHICAL BEHAVIOR

The conceptual arguments that underlie the SeMI Model have almost completely been introduced and discussed by now. SeMI is considered a personality construct that results from a more or less strong need to trust others in combination with a more or less strongly held expectation that other people are not trustworthy. SeMI is defined as a dispositional sensitivity towards situational cues that suggest that other people harbor mean intentions. People high in SeMI are more likely to perceive such cues and they give more weight to cues that suggest untrustworthiness than they give to cues that suggest trustworthiness. In a situation that contains such cues, SeMI results in the evocation of a suspicious mindset. This mindset consists of an attributional bias towards corroborating the *a priori* expectation that other people are not trustworthy, a motivation to avoid being exploited, and a heightened accessibility to cognitions that legitimize one's own unethical behavior. Thus, the model describes a case of moderated mediation (cf., Muller, Judd, & Yzerbyt, 2005): Suspicious mindset is the variable that mediates the relation between cues of untrustworthiness and unethical behavior, and SeMI is the variable that moderates the impact of situational cues on the activation of a suspicious mindset (see Figure 8.1).

The SeMI Model makes one additional prediction. Not always does a suspicious mindset result in unethical behavior. There may be buffers such as strong situational constraints (e.g., strong norms, harsh punishment for norm violation etc.), high moral standards, or self-regulation capacities that mitigate unethical behavior even when a strong suspicious mindset is activated (e.g., Bandura, 1991). We do not go into details regarding the exact nature of this cluster of buffering variables; yet, we suggest referring to it as "moral self-regulation" as some sort of umbrella term. Self-regulation

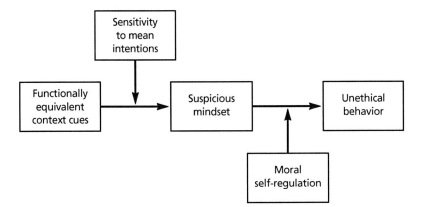

Figure 8.1   The sensitivity to mean intentions (SeMI) model.

capacities have, for example, also been found to mitigate the impact of rejection sensitivity on negative consequences (e.g., Ayduk et al., 2000; Ayduk et al., 2008). Figure 8.1 displays the full SeMI Model including all its components and hypothesized effects.

CONCLUSION

In the present chapter, we described and discussed a model that aims to explain under what conditions a need to trust may result in unethical behavior. Our model builds upon research on trust and on fear of being exploited and their effects on uncooperative or egoistic behavior. We suggest that people differ with regard to their sensitivity towards environmental cues that suggest that other people harbor mean intentions—a personality construct that we call Sensitivity to Mean Intentions (SeMI). First, we discussed the conceptual connection between trust, a need for trust, and SeMI. The most important difference between dispositional trust and SeMI is that trust refers to expectations regarding other people's benevolence, whereas SeMI refers to a particular combination of expectations (regarding other people's malevolence) and the aversiveness of these expectations (which represents a manifestation of the need to trust).

The SeMI model is interactionistic in nature. It assumes a particular "synergistic" interplay between personality (SeMI) and situational factors (cues that contain information regarding other people's trustworthiness). The interplay can be described in terms of the social-cognitive processes and mechanisms that it evokes. Moreover, the SeMI model explains why SeMI translates into unethical behavior. Among people high in SeMI, the perception of situational cues associated with other people's mean intentions activate a suspicious mindset, which consists, among other features, of legitimizing thoughts regarding one's own unethical behavior. This mindset is a mediator between apparent cues of untrustworthiness and unethical behavior, especially if moral self-regulation is low.

We believe that the SeMI Model can help integrate the many, sometimes contradictory findings that have been found in the literature on trust, fear of being exploited, and unethical behavior. It makes clear, testable assumptions about when and why unethical behavior results, it clarifies the role of trust, fear, and suspicion, and it fits well into recent approaches in personality psychology that aim at clearly describing and testing the social-cognitive processes by which personality factors translate into behavior (e.g., Cervone, 2004).

However, we do believe that much conceptual and empirical work needs to be done. First, individual differences in SeMI need to be measured. Trust scales (e.g., Rotter, 1967; Yamagishi & Yamagishi, 1994) might be a starting point for the construction of such a measure, but since these measures mainly focus on the expectation aspect of SeMI, they do not appear to be optimal. A scale measuring individual differences in SeMI should tap both the cognitive aspect (mistrust expectation) and the motivational aspect (need to trust). Such a scale could either consist of two subscales that are multiplicatively combined (cf., the Rejection Sensitivity Scale; Downey and Feldman, 1996), or it could consist of a single scale that combines both aspects within the same item (cf., the "Justice Sensitivity" scales; Schmitt, Gollwitzer, Maes, & Arbach, 2005). Second, the nature and quality of situational cues that evoke a suspicious mindset among people high in SeMI should be carefully investigated. Third, moderator variables that buffer the effect of suspiciousness on unethical behavior need to be much more clearly defined and operationalized. Fourth, the range of behaviors that the SeMI Model can be applied to needs to be empirically established. In general, we believe that the model can be applied to all kinds of immoral or unethical behaviors, ranging from non-cooperation in a social dilemma to more immediately socially relevant behaviors such as bystander apathy or tax evasion.

NOTE

1. BIS = Behavioral Inhibition System; BAS = Behavioral Activation System.

REFERENCES

Allingham, M. G., & Sandmo, A. (1972). Income tax evasion: A theoretical analysis. *Journal of Public Economics, 1*, 323–338.

Amodio, D. M., Master, S. L., Yee, C. M., & Taylor, S. E. (2008). Neurocognitive components of the behavioral inhibition and activation systems: Implications for theories of self-regulation. *Psychophysiology, 45*, 11–19.

Ayduk, Ö., Mendoza-Denton, R., Mischel, W., Downey, G., Peake, P.K., & Rodriguez, M. (2000). Regulating the interpersonal self: Strategic self-regulation for coping with rejection sensitivity. *Journal of Personality and Social Psychology, 79*, 776–792.

Ayduk, Ö., Zayas, V., Downey, G., Cole, A. B., Shoda, Y., & Mischel, W. (2008). Rejection sensitivity and executive control: Joint predictors of borderline personality features. *Journal of Research in Personality, 42*, 151–168.

Bandura, A. (1991). Social cognitive theory of moral thought and action. In W. M. Kurtines & J. L. Gewirtz (Eds.), *Handbook of moral behavior and development* (Vol. 1, pp. 45–103). Hillsdale NJ: Erlbaum.

Barber, B. (1983). *The logic and limits of trust.* New Brunswick, NJ: Rutgers University Press.

Baumeister, R. F., & Leary, M. R. (1995). The need to belong: Desire for interpersonal attachments as a fundamental human motivation. *Psychological Bulletin, 117*, 497–529.

Becker, G. S. (1968). Crime and punishment: An economic approach. *Journal of Political Economy, 76*, 169–217.

Bosco, L., & Mittone, L. (1997). Tax evasion and moral constraints: Some experimental evidence. *Kyklos, 50*, 297–324.

Braithwaite, V., & Wenzel, M. (2008). Integrating explanations of tax evasion and avoidance. In A. Lewis (Ed.), *The Cambridge handbook of psychology and economic behaviour* (pp. 304–331). Cambridge: Cambridge University Press.

Brann, P., & Foddy, M. (1987). Trust and the consumption of a deteriorating common resource. *Journal of Conflict Resolution, 31*, 615–630.

Brönstrup, C., & Peters, M. (2008, February 19). Die Rache des kleinen Mannes [Little man's revenge]. *Tagesspiegel, 60/2008*. Retrieved May 22, 2008, from http://www.tagesspiegel.de/wirtschaft/Steuerskandal;art271,2479383.

Burger, I. M., & Cooper, H. M. (1979). The desirability of control. *Motivation and Emotion, 3*, 381–393.

Carver, C. S. (1996). Emergent integration in contemporary personality psychology. *Journal of Research in Personality, 30*, 319–334.

Cervone, D. (2004). The architecture of personality. *Psychological Review, 111*, 183–204.

Coleman, J. S. (1990). *Foundations of social theory*. Cambridge, MA: Harvard University Press.

Coombs, C. (1973). A reparametrization of the prisoner's dilemma game. *Behavioral Science, 18*, 424–428.

Cosmides, L., & Tooby, J. (1992). Cognitive adaptations for social exchange. In J. Barkow, L. Cosmides, & J. Tooby (Eds.), *The adapted mind* (pp. 163–228). New York: Oxford University Press.

Dawes, R. (1980). Social dilemmas. *Annual Review of Psychology, 31*, 169–193.

De Cremer, D., & Alberts, H. (2004). When procedural fairness does not influence how good I feel: The effects of voice and leader selection as a function of belongingness needs. *European Journal of Social Psychology, 34*, 333–344.

De Cremer, D., & Blader, S. (2006). Why do people care about procedural fairness? The importance of belongingness in responding and attending to procedures. *European Journal of Social Psychology, 36*, 211–228.

De Cremer, D., Snyder, M., & Dewitte, S. (2001). "The less I trust, the less I contribute (or not)?" The effects of trust, accountability and self-monitoring in social dilemmas. *European Journal of Social Psychology, 31*, 93–107.

De Juan, A., Lasheras, M. A., & Mayo, R. (1994). Voluntary tax compliant behavior of Spanish income tax payers. *Public Finance, 49*, 90–105.

Deutsch, M. (1958). Trust and suspicion. *Journal of Conflict Resolution, 2*, 265–279.

Dill, K. E., Anderson, C. A., Anderson, K. B., & Deuser, W. E. (1997). Effects of aggressive personality on social expectations and social perceptions. *Journal of Research in Personality, 31*, 272–292.

Dodge, K. A. (1993). Social-cognitive mechanisms in the development of conduct disorder and depression. *Annual Review of Psychology, 44*, 559–584.

Downey, G., & Feldman, S. I. (1996). Implications of rejection sensitivity for intimate relationships. *Journal of Personality and Social Psychology, 70*, 1327–1343.

Downey, G., Freitas, A. L., Michaelis, B., & Khouri, J. (1998). The self-fulfilling prophecy in close relationships. *Journal of Personality and Social Psychology, 75*, 545–560.

Eisenberger, N. I., Jarcho, J. M., Lieberman, M. D., & Naliboff, B. D. (2006). An experimental study of shared sensitivity to physical pain and social rejection. *Pain, 126*, 132–138.

Ekman, P. (1992). *Telling lies: Clues to deceit in the marketplace, politics and marriage.* New York: Norton.

Elliot, A. J., & Friedman, R. (2007). Approach-avoidance: A central characteristic of personal goals. In B. R. Little, K. Salmela-Aro, & S. D. Phillips (Eds.), *Personal project pursuit* (pp. 97–118). Mahwah, NJ: Lawrence Erlbaum.

Elliot, A. J., Gable, S. L., & Mapes, R. R. (2006). Approach and avoidance motivation in the social domain. *Personality and Social Psychology Bulletin, 32*, 378–391.

Endler, N. S. (1997). Stress, anxiety, and coping: The multidimensional interaction model. *Canadian Psychology, 38*, 136–153.

Epps, J., & Kendall, P.C. (1995). Hostile attributional bias in adults. *Cognitive Therapy and Research, 19*, 159–178.

Fein, S., Hilton, J. L., & Miller, D. T. (1990). Suspicion of ulterior motivation and the correspondence bias. *Journal of Personality and Social Psychology, 58*, 753–764.

Feld, L. P., & Frey, B. S. (2007). Tax compliance as the result of a psychological tax contract: The role of incentives and responsive regulation. *Law and Policy, 29*, 102–120.

Fetchenhauer, D. (1998). *Versicherungsbetrug [Insurance fraud].* Baden-Baden, Germany: Nomos.

Fiske, S. T. (2002). Five core social motives, plus or minus five. In S. J. Spencer, S. Fein, M. P. Zanna, & J. Olson (Eds.), *Motivated social perception: The Ontario Symposium* (Vol. 9, pp. 233–246). Mahwah, NJ: Erlbaum.

Fiske, S. T. (2004). *Social beings: A core motives approach to social psychology.* New York: Wiley.

Frey, B. S., & Feld, L. P. (2002). *Deterrence and morale in taxation: An empirical analysis.* (CESifo Working Paper No. 760). München, Germany: CESifo Group.

Frey, B. S., & Meier, S. (2004). Social comparisons and pro-social behavior. Testing "conditional cooperation" in a field experiment. *American Economic Review 94*, 1717–1722.

Gable, S. L. (2006). Approach and avoidance social motives and goals. *Journal of Personality, 74*, 175–222.

Gray, J. A. (1987). *The psychology of fear and stress* (2nd ed.). New York: Cambridge University Press.

Greene, G. (1993). *The ministry of fear: An entertainment.* New York: Penguin Classics. (Original work published 1943)

Heldt T. (2005). *Sustainable nature tourism and the nature of tourists' cooperative behaviour: Recreation conflicts, conditional cooperation and the public good problem* (Economic Studies No. 86). Uppsala, Sweden: Department of Economics, Uppsala University.

Hertel, G., & Fiedler, K. (1994). Affective and cognitive influences in a social dilemma game. *European Journal of Social Psychology, 24,* 131–146.

Higgins, E. T. (1997). Beyond pleasure and pain. *American Psychologist, 52,* 1280–1300.

Higgins, E. T., & Spiegel, S. (2004). Promotion and prevention strategies for self-regulation: A motivated cognition perspective. In R. F. Baumeister, & K. D. Vohs (Eds.), *Handbook of self-regulation: Research, theory and applications* (pp. 171–187). New York: Guilford Press.

Ickes, W. (1982). A basic paradigm for the study of personality, roles, and social behavior. In W. Ickes, & E. S. Knowles (Eds.), *Personality, roles, and social behavior* (pp. 305–341). New York: Springer.

Kammrath, L. K., Mendoza-Denton, R., & Mischel, W. (2005). Incorporating if … then … personality signatures in person perception: Beyond the person-situation dichotomy. *Journal of Personality and Social Psychology, 88,* 605–618.

Kelley H. H., & Stahelski, A. J. (1970). Social interaction basis of cooperators' and competitors' beliefs about others. *Journal of Personality and Social Psychology, 16,* 66–91.

Kosugi, M., & Yamagishi, T. (1998). Generalized trust and judgments of trustworthiness. *The Japanese Journal of Psychology, 69,* 349–357.

Kramer, R. M. (1994). The sinister attribution error: Paranoid cognition and collective distrust in organizations. *Motivation and Emotion, 18,* 199–230.

Latané, B., Williams, K., & Harkins, S. (1979). Many hands make light work. The causes and consequences of social loafing. *Journal of Personality and Social Psychology, 37,* 822–882.

Mendoza-Denton, R., Purdie, V., Downey, G., Davis, A., & Pietrzak, J. (2002). Sensitivity to status-based rejection: Implications for African-American students' college experience. *Journal of Personality and Social Psychology, 83,* 896–918.

Messick, D. M., Wilke, H., Brewer, M. B., Kramer, R. M., Zemke, P. E., & Lui, L. (1983). Individual adaptations and structural change as solutions to social dilemmas. *Journal of Personality and Social Psychology, 44,* 294–309.

Miller, D. T. (1999). The norm of self-interest. *American Psychologist, 54,* 1053–1060.

Miller, D. T., & Ratner, R. K. (1996). The power of the myth of self-interest. In L. Montada, & M. J. Lerner (Eds.), *Current societal issues about justice* (pp. 25–48). New York: Plenum Press.

Miller, D. T., Visser, P. S., & Staub, B. D. (2005). How surveillance begets perceptions of dishonesty. The case of the counterfactual sinner. *Journal of Personality and Social Psychology, 89,* 117–128.

Mischel, W. (1973). Toward a cognitive social learning reconceptualization of personality. *Psychological Review, 80,* 252–283.

Muller, D., Judd, C. M., & Yzerbyt, V. Y. (2005). When moderation is mediated and mediation is moderated. *Journal of Personality and Social Psychology, 89,* 852–863.

Parks, C. D., Henager, R. F., & Scamahorn, S. D. (1996). Trust and reactions to messages of intent in social dilemmas. *Journal of Conflict Resolution, 40,* 133–150.

Pillutla, M. M., Malhotra, D., & Murnighan, J. K. (2003). Attributions of trust and the calculus of reciprocity. *Journal of Experimental Social Psychology, 39,* 448–455.

Putnam, R. D. (2000). *Bowling alone. The collapse and revival of American community.* New York: Simon & Schuster.

Rapoport, A., & Eshed-Levy, D. (1989). Provision of step-level public goods: Effects of greed and fear of being gypped. *Organizational Behavior and Human Decision Processes, 44,* 325–344.

Rotter, J. (1967). A new scale for the measurement of interpersonal trust. *Journal of Personality, 35,* 651–665.

Rousseau, D. M., Sitkin, S. B., Burt, R. S., & Camerer, C. (1998). Not so different after all: A cross-discipline view of trust. *Academy of Management Review, 23,* 393–404.

Schaller, M., Park, J. H., & Mueller, A. (2003). Fear of the dark: Interactive effects of beliefs about danger and ambient darkness on ethnic stereotypes. *Personality and Social Psychology Bulletin, 29,* 637–649.

Schmitt, M., Eid, M., & Maes, J. (2003). Synergistic person × situation interaction in distributive justice behavior. *Personality and Social Psychology Bulletin, 29,* 141–147.

Schmitt, M., Gollwitzer, M., Maes, J., & Arbach, D. (2005). Justice sensitivity: Assessment and location in the personality space. *European Journal of Psychological Assessment, 21,* 202–211.

Smeesters, D., Warlop, L., Van Avermaet, E., Corneille, O., & Yzerbyt, V. (2003). Do not prime hawks with doves: The interplay of construct activation and consistency of social value orientation on cooperative behavior. *Journal of Personality and Social Psychology, 84,* 972–987.

Snyder, M., & Ickes, W. (1985). Personality and social behavior. In G. Lindzey, & E. Aronson (Eds.), *Handbook of social psychology* (3rd ed., Vol. II, pp. 883–947). New York: Random House.

Stone, V. E., Cosmides, L., Tooby, J., Kroll, N., & Knight, R. T. (2002). Selective impairment of reasoning about social exchange in a patient with bilateral limbic system damage. *Proceedings of the National Academy of Sciences, USA, 99,* 11531–11536.

Stouten, J., De Cremer, D., & Van Dijk, E. (2005). All is well that ends well, at least for proselfs: Emotional reactions to equality violation as a function of social value orientation. *European Journal of Social Psychology, 35,* 767–783.

Stouten, J., De Cremer, D., & Van Dijk, E. (2006). Violating equality in social dilemmas: Emotional and retributive reactions as a function of trust, attribution, and honesty. *Personality and Social Psychology Bulletin, 32,* 894–906.

Torgler, B. (2003). *Tax morale. Theory and empirical analysis of tax compliance.* Unpublished doctoral dissertation, University of Basel, Switzerland.

Vohs, K. D., Baumeister, R. F., & Chin, J. (2007). Feeling duped: Emotional, motivational, and cognitive aspects of being exploited by others. *Review of General Psychology, 11,* 127–141.

Vrij, A. (2000). *Detecting lies and deceit: The psychology of lying and the implications for professional practice.* Chichester, UK: Wiley.

Vrij, A., Edward, K., & Bull, R. (2001). Stereotypical verbal and nonverbal responses while deceiving others. *Personality and Social Psychology Bulletin, 27,* 899–909.

Webley, P., Robben, H., & Morris, I. (1988). Social comparison, attitudes and tax evasion in a shop simulation. *Social Behaviour, 3,* 219–228.

Yamagishi, T. (2001). Trust as a form of social intelligence. In K. S. Cook (Ed.), *Trust in society* (pp. 121–147). New York: Russell Sage Foundation.

Yamagishi, T., & Sato, K. (1986). Motivational bases of the public goods problem. *Journal of Personality and Social Psychology, 50,* 67–73.

Yamagishi, T., & Yamagishi, M. (1994). Trust and commitment in the United States and Japan. *Motivation and Emotion, 18,* 129–166.

Zebrowitz, L. A. (1997). *Reading faces: Window to the soul?* Boulder, CO: Westview Press.

CHAPTER 9

THE NEURAL BASIS
OF MORALITY

Maarten A. S. Boksem
Tilburg University

David De Cremer
Erasmus University

The interest in ethical and, especially, unethical behaviour is rapidly increasing as witnessed by the many articles published in magazines and news papers on fraud, corruption and bad CEO behaviour. To understand how people come to violate ethical and moral norms, it is important to arrive at a better understanding of how and why people come to behave in an ethical manner in the first place. In this chapter, we will show that moral behaviour is deeply rooted in our biological system. Throughout our evolution as human beings, the social group that we belong to has played a role of central importance: belonging to a well functioning social group is essential for the survival of the individual. It is therefore not surprising that we have developed specialized biological and neural systems that allow us to function successfully within these social groups. These neural systems are proposed to form the basis of what we now call moral behaviour: taking into account the interests and integrity of individuals other than ourselves

Psychological Perspectives on Ethical Behavior and Decision Making, pages 153–166
Copyright © 2009 by Information Age Publishing
All rights of reproduction in any form reserved.

and the strong disapproval of behaviour that would harm others or would compromise our group.

In this chapter, we will explore how neuroscience methods have been applied to investigating moral behaviour. The overall aim of the present chapter is to present a short overview of recent neuroscientific research examining the processes and neural substrates involved in ethical decision-making and linking it to concepts of prosocial emotions and the biological basis of basic attachment between individuals. This may provide us with a better understanding of the origens and function of moral behaviour.

MORAL EVALUATIONS AND THE PREFRONTAL CORTEX

In recent years, functional magnetic resonance imaging (fMRI) has been employed to examine the neural substrate involved in the processing of emotional valence and moral content in social judgments. Using a strong magnetic field and high frequency radio waves, fMRI makes it possible to image both the anatomy, as well as the activation of specific brain structures. Basically, an fMRI scanner can detect local differences in blood oxygenation, which is a direct correlate of neural activity (active brain cells (neurons) require more oxygen than inactive neurons).

One of the first studies to convincingly show a neural network underlying moral evaluations was that of Moll, Oliveira-Souza, Bramati, & Grafman (2002). While in the scanner, subjects were requested to judge statements from three main conditions: emotionally unpleasant statements with moral connotations ("He shot the victim to death"), emotionally unpleasant statements without moral connotations ("He licked the dirty toilet"), and emotionally neutral statements ("He never uses a seat belt"). Subjects were asked to classify these statements as either right or wrong. Comparing brain activation elicited by unpleasant statements with or without moral connotation, the authors found increased activation in Brodmans Areas (BA) 10 and 11 (the anterior part of the medial orbitofrontal cortex (OFC)). This area of the brain has previously been implicated in estimating the outcome value of behavioural actions, suggesting that this brain area may also be critically involved in integrating moral knowledge with the emotions that determine the value of these actions (Moll et al., 2002).

Another early study took a slightly different approach, by scanning the brains of subjects solving moral dilemmas (Greene et al., 2001). One such dilemma is the trolley dilemma: A runaway trolley is speeding down the track towards five people who will be killed if it continues on its present course. The only way to save these people is for you to throw a switch that will diverge the trolley onto an alternate set of tracks where it will kill one person instead of five. Ought you turn the trolley in order to save five people at the expense of one? Most people would answer no. The footbridge dilemma poses a similar problem: as before, a trolley is bound to kill five people. You are standing next to a rather large stranger on a footbridge that spans the tracks, in between the oncoming trolley and the five people. In this scenario, the only way to save the five people is to push this stranger off the bridge, onto the tracks below. He will die if you do this, but his body will stop the trolley from reaching the others. Ought you save the five others by pushing this stranger to his death? While most people answer yes to the first dilemma, they say no to the second. The authors argue that the crucial difference between these dilemmas, lies in the fact that the footbridge dilemma tends to engage people's emotions in a way that the trolley dilemma does not. The thought of physically pushing someone to his death, they propose, is more emotionally and morally salient than the thought of operating a switch that will cause similar consequences. Supporting their hypothesis, Greene and colleagues (2001) found that the more personal dilemmas (like the footbridge dilemma) were associated with greater activation of brain areas similar to those reported by Moll and colleagues (BA 9 and 10; medial prefrontal cortex (mPFC); a brain area that is known to be involved in emotional processes), compared to the more impersonal dilemmas such as the trolley dilemma.

These, and other studies, converge on the fact that the medial areas of the prefrontal cortex (PFC) are primarily involved in moral evaluations. This is not to say that other areas are not involved. Indeed, also lateral areas of the PFC have been shown to be activated by moral tasks (Berthoz, Armony, Blair, & Dolan, 2002; Finger et al., 2006), as well as the amygdala (Moll et al., 2002; Greene et al., 2004; Berthoz et al., 2006), the cingulate cortex (Greene et al., 2001; Moll et al., 2002), superior temporal sulcus (Heekeren et al., 2003, 2005), and other brain areas, making moral evaluations a distributed, whole brain affair. However, the mPFC has been focused on the most in research on morality and we will therefore mainly limit our discussion to this area of the brain.

Recently, Koenigs and colleagues (2007) investigated the behaviour of patients with lesions to exactly this area of the brain, the ventro-medial PFC (vmPFC) on dilemmas such as those used by Greene and colleagues (2001). They found that, whereas normal subjects are likely to say that it is allright to throw a switch, killing one instead of five, but do not endorse pushing a bulky stranger onto the tracks to stop the train, vmPFC lesioned subjects judged both cases to be acceptable. Like Greene and colleagues (2001), these authors argued that it is the emotional salience of the actions involved in the more "personal" moral dilemmas (actually pushing another human being off a bridge) that is integrated into the decision-making process by the vmPFC that leads normal subjects to reject such actions. Patients with vmPFC lesions, by consequence fail to involve these emotional considerations in their decisions, making them more "utilitarian" (favouring the larger aggregate welfare over the welfare of fewer individuals). Although this is a tempting interpretation (emotional blunting is commonly observed in patients with frontal brain damage) it seems to be at odds with a second study by Koenigs and Tranel (2007).

In that study, patients with vmPFC damage played the "ultimatum game." In a typical instantiation of this game, two players are given one opportunity to split a sum of money. One player (the proposer) offers a portion of the money to the second player (the responder). The responder can either accept the offer (in which case both players split the money as proposed) or reject the offer (in which case both players get nothing). If the responder would act strictly utilitarian, he or she should accept any offer, no matter how low, because rejecting the offer would mean getting nothing at all. However, relatively small offers (20% of the total) have a 50% chance of being rejected (Bolton & Zwick, 1995). The "irrational" rejection of unfair Ultimatum Game offers has been correlated with feelings of anger (Pillutla & Murnighan, 1996), increased skin conductance responses (van't Wout et al., 2006), and activation of the insula (Sanfey et al., 2003), a brain area associated with negative emotional states (Phillips et al., 1997). Therefore, lacking such a strong emotional reaction to unfair offers, one would expect patients with vmPFC damage to no longer irrationally reject these unfair offers. Surprisingly, what Koenigs and Tranel (2007) found was that vmPFC patients rejected unfair offers even more often that control subjects did. These patients allowed the negative emotions provoked by receiving such an unfair offer to overrule their utilitarian reason more than normal subjects would do. This makes the emotional blunting in these patients seem like an unlikely explanation for the findings in the moral dilemma study by Koenigs et al. (2007).

A more plausible interpretation of these findings was provided by Moll and deOlivera-Souza (2007). They suggested that the vmPFC may be involved in the experience of prosocial moral sentiments, such as guilt, compassion and empathy, and the integration of these emotions with cognitive mechanisms. These prosocial sentiments are proposed to emerge when emotional states mediated by the limbic system, are integrated with mechanisms mediated by more anterior sectors of the PFC, such as prospective evaluation of action outcomes. This integration of emotions and cognition would allow us to assess the consequences of our own actions upon the well-being of others (Moll et al., 2005; Moll & deOlivera-Souza, 2007).

While vmPFC is suggested to be involved in the experience of prosocial moral sentiments, more lateral areas of the PFC, such as dorsolateral PFC and lateral OFC are more important for self-centered and other-aversive emotional experience (e.g. anger, frustration or moral disgust) (Moll et al., 2002; 2005; 2006). Selective damage to the vmPFC, along with more lateral areas being spared, may explain the otherwise puzzling discrepancy in the findings in the two studies by Koenigs and colleagues. The vmPFC-damaged patients playing the ultimatum game let emotions such as anger and frustration guide their actions towards the non-utilitarian decision to reject unfair offers. On the other hand, vmPFC patients were more utilitarian when solving moral dilemmas, because the damage to this part of their prefrontal cortex reduced their prosocial sentiments, steering them towards decisions that favour agregate total welfare over the wellbeing of individuals.

Prosocial, or moral emotions such as guilt, shame, compassion, promote the helping of others, cooperation and conforming to social norms, probably by invoking feelings of social attachment (Eisenberg, 2000). They function to regulate social behaviours, often in the long-term interests of a social group rather than the short-term interests of the individual person (Haidt, 2001). The importance of actually feeling these emotions is painfully clear from observations of people who apparently do not have these feelings. Psychopathy, or sociopathy, is a type of antisocial personality that physicians in the 19th century labelled "moral insanity" (Berrios, 1999). It is a developmental disorder (Lynam et al., 2007) that involves emotional dysfunction, characterized by reduced guilt, empathy and attachment to significant others. As Blair (2007) puts it:

These people can steal from their friends, dismember live animals, and even murder their parents to collect insurance benefits without showing any trace of remorse or, when caught, of shame. Psychopaths know the rules of social behaviour and they understand the harmful consequences of their actions for others. They simply do not care about those consequences.

Neuroimaging studies on psychopathy have found that individuals with psychopathy show reduced activation of both the amygdala and the rostral anterior cingulate cortex/vmPFC, compared to normal subjects (Kiehl et al., 2001; Birbaumer et al., 2005). Although damage to specific brain areas is not associated with psychopathy, damage to ventral, medial and polar aspects of the frontal cortex results in severe personality changes and behaviour very similar to that observed in psychopaths. This condition has been called acquired sociopathy (Anderson, et al., 1999) and is associated with injury to specific brain areas, particularly the orbitomedial and polar frontal cortex, the medial frontal lobe, and several basal forebrain structures (Adolphs, Tranel, & Damasio., 1998; Blair & Cipolotti, 2000). Like primary psychopaths, such acquired sociopaths often remain perfectly able to tell right from wrong and to articulate sound statements on morality and social appropriateness, that stand in sharp contrast to their actual behaviour.

PROSOCIAL BEHAVIOUR, BASIC ATTACHMENT
AND THEIR NEURAL CORRELATES

The fact that psychopaths are unable to function in our society, shows us just how important prosocial moral sentiments are for a successful life in a social context. Indeed, helping others has been proposed to be evolutionary favourable: individuals that cooperate when the helping of others provides long term benefits over competing with others have better chances of survival and procreation. There has been a long debate on how helping others, often at one's own expense (altruism), would be evolutionary adaptive. A big step in modelling the evolution of helping behaviour is the extension of reciprocal altruism ("I'll help you if you help me") by "indirect reciprocity" (Nowak & Sigmund, 2005) in which prosocial behaviour pays off by improving one's reputation, which elicits cooperation from others at a later point in time. Reputation is a powerful force for the development and consolidation of social communities. When players know each others" reputations in repeated-play behavioural economics games, cooperation rates improve substantially (Fehr & Henrich, 2003). Evolutionary models show that indirect reciprocity can solve the problem of selfish behaviour known as free-rideing (which doomed simpler models of altruism) in moderately large groups (Panchanathan & Boyd, 2004), when people have access to information about reputations (Haidt, 2007). Being socially successful by maintaining a good reputation is highly predictive of both chances of survival of the individual and for successful passing on of the genes that lead to this behaviour. By this process, it is very much in the interest of the individual to help others and work for the common interest of the group in order to achieve and maintain a good reputation.

However, as often happens in evolution, the impulse to help close others to maintain good standing in the social group, became separated from the consequences that caused the evolution of this behaviour in the first place. By this process, this impulse also occurred when the chance of reciprocity was slim, so that also strangers could benefit. This is why we usually also treat people we do not really know in a just and ethical manner. It is important to realize that, certainly in evolutionary terms, it is not so long ago that meeting strangers was an extremely rare event. All social interactions were with a very limited number of people that were of the same family, clan or village. That we humans now live in what has been called a global village is in evolutionary terms a very recent novelty. Our brains evolved under circumstances were social groups were much smaller and the prosocial emotions generated in our brains still guide us toward behaviour that benefits others that we perceive to be close to us. For example, a huge number of people donated money to help victims of the tsunami in Thailand and Indonesia, whom they had never met and never will meet and who will never be able to return the favour. Moreover, we feel indignation when we hear of innocent people being imprisoned and tortured in some country far away from our own, when it is absolutely clear that those people are completely unrelated to us.

While moral behaviour towards other people in our global society can be viewed as a generalization of prosocial behaviour towards close group members, at a very basic level, the inclination to help next of kin and close others may in itself be a generalization from the basic attachment between mother and infant. In this relationship, it is of course of primary importance for the survival of the infant that the mother not only pursues her own immediate interests, but is also sensitive to the needs of her child. In non-human animals, the neuropeptide oxytocin has a central role in stimulating this maternal care (Pedersen, 1997). In addition, oxytocin receptors are distributed in various brain regions associated with behaviour such as pair bonding, sexual behaviour and the ability to form normal social attachments (Insel & Young, 2001). Given these findings, recent studies have begun to investigate the role of oxytocin in the promotion of prosocial behaviours in humans.

Kosfeld and colleagues (2005) analyzed the effect of exogenously administered oxytocin (using a nasal spray) on individuals" decisions in a trust game with real monetary stakes. In this trust game, two subjects interacting anonymously play either the role of an investor or a trustee. First, the investor has the option of choosing a costly trusting action by giving money to the trustee. If the investor transfers money, the total amount available for distribution between the two players is tripled by the experimentor but, initially, the trustee reaps the whole increase. The trustee is then informed about the investor's transfer and can honour the investor's trust by sharing the monetary increase generated by the investor's transfer. Thus, if the investor gives money to the trustee and the latter shares the proceeds of the transfer, both players end up with a higher monetary payoff. However, the trustee also has the option of violating the investor's trust. As sharing the proceeds is costly for the trustee, a selfish trustee will never honour the investor's trust, because the investor and the trustee interact only once during the experiment. Administration of Oxytocin by Kosfeld and colleagues, increased trust considerably: subjects that were administered Oxytocin on average transferred 17% more money to the trustee, with 45% of the treated subjects transferring all of their money, while only 21% of non-treated subjects transferred the entire amount.

In another study, subjects were administered either Oxytocin or placebo and played the ultimatum game (Zak, Stanton, & Ahmadi, 2007). The results showed that Oxytocin-administered proposers offered a significantly larger (21%) amount of money to the responders. The authors propose that Oxytocin selectively affected the understanding of how the other would experience, receiving a stingy offer and were motivated to reduce these expected negative emotions in others.

Although it does not become clear from these studies exactly how Oxytocin affects neural processing in terms of enhancing activity in certain brain areas, there is some evidence from animal studies that the mPFC may play a role. For example, microinjection of an OT receptor agonist into the mPFC enhances pair bond formation in female prairie voles (a small rodent living in North America; Young, Lim, Gingrich, & Insel, 2001). In addition the mPFC has been found to integrate information from brain structures involved in empathy and social behaviour and that are rich in OT receptors. The reader will recall that it also was the mPFC that was shown to be activated in studies on human morality (Greene et al., 2002; Moll et al., 2005; Koenigs et al., 2007).

All of this thus suggests that our sense of morality originates from a "hard wired" neural system that may be based on an evolutionary old system of basic attachment. For the survival of a newborn infant, it is of great importance that the mother feels connected to and responsible for the infant; its interest should be of equal or even greater importance to the mother than her own interests. If this were not the case, the infant would not survive and indeed its entire species would be doomed for extinction. For social animals (including humans), these feelings of attachment are not limited to mother and child, but extend also to next of kin, or even non related group members. As already mentioned, in a social setting it is of primary importance for the individual to maintain good relations with group members: all member are dependent on each other, and in the end chances of survival are greater when the individual not just acts out of immediate self interest, but instead cooperates with others. Indeed pure selfish behaviour may lead to social exclusion, and once excluded from the group, chances of survival are often limited. This is why moral behaviour is so fundamental to our being, and is associated with such strong emotions. Moral behaviour is prosocial behaviour and prevents exclusion from our social group. Violating moral norms (thus compromising our good reputation) or observing others violate moral norms (thus compromising the integrity of our social group) evokes strong aversive emotions such as shame, indignation or anger. It is these emotions that push our behaviour away from pure selfishness towards behaviour that promotes the wellbeing of others.

THE ROLE OF REASONING: THEORY OF MIND

Although morality or ethics has traditionally been posited to depend on a "higher," typically human capacity to reason in order to come to the "right" conclusion regarding how one should act in a given situation, it appears that reasoning may play only a relatively minor role in moral decision making. Indeed, Haidt (2001) argues in his social intuitionist model of morality, that "moral judgment is much like aesthetic judgment: we see an action or hear a story and we have an instant feeling of approval or disapproval. These feelings are best thought of as affect-laden intuitions, as they appear suddenly and effortlessly in consciousness, with an affective valence (good or bad), but without any feeling of having gone through steps of searching, weighing evidence, or inferring a conclusion. People certainly do engage in moral reasoning, but, as suggested by studies of informal reasoning, these processes are typically one-sided efforts in support of pre-ordained conclusions."

While our reasoning abilities appear to play only a minor role in morality, most people would agree that our moral behaviour is something more than prosocial behaviour in "lower" mammals or even primates. Although this difference may not be nearly as great as has been accepted until recent years, humans do excel at a form of reasoning that is highly social in nature. Our evolution in social groups has shaped our brain in such a way so that it is particularly good at thinking about what others may be thinking about. This capacity for social-cognitive processing has been proposed to enable us to go from empathy (which has also been observed in other primates and even mammals) to sympathy, which has so far has only been observed in humans.

To be able to take the interests of others into account (i.e., display prosocial behaviour), it is fundamental to be able to understand what those interests are, and to be able to realize that these interests may differ from one's own. This capacity has been termed mentalizing or theory of mind (ToM), and involves the process of inferring the feelings and thoughts of others from their observed behaviour (Blakemore & Decety, 2001; Frith & Frith, 1999). To be able to accurately predict what others are thinking is essential for the initiation of social interactions: it enables us to predict how others may react to our actions and what the subjective and emotional consequences of our actions will be for these others.

ToM emerges at around four years of age in young children, as is evidenced by their performance on the so-called "Sally Ann" task. In this task, infants are shown a scenario in which Sally has a pram, and Ann has a box of toys. In the scenario, Sally puts one of her toys in the pram and then leaves the scene. When Sally has left, Ann takes the toy out of the pram and puts it in her box. After a while, Sally returns for her toy. Where will she look for the toy? Normal children of about four years of age and older correctly answer that she will look in the pram, where she believes the toy to be, although the child knows it is actually in the box. Younger children or children with disorders like autism answer that she will look in the box (where they know the toy actually is, not realizing that Sally's mind, being different from their own, does not contain this information).

Studying ToM in adults is a bit more complex but is generally also done using scenarios or cartoons. Contrasting scenarios in which ToM is necessary to understand what is going on to scenarios for which this is not required results in increased activation in several brain areas, but particularly in the vmPFC (Frith & Frith, 1999; Berthoz et al., 2002). The tendency to attribute intentions and feelings to others is so strong and automatic that we even do it with objects that are clearly non-social. A classic example involves subjects watching a screen on which basic shapes (triangles, squares) moving about. Subjects readily ascribe intentions to these objects like: "The big red square is trying to persuade the little square to move," or "The blue triangle is trying to sneak up on the red triangle" (e.g. Heider & Simmel, 1944). Interestingly, watching these scenes activates the same areas that have been shown to be involved in mentalizing or ToM (Castelli, Happe, Frith, & Frith, 2000).

In recent years, the discovery of so-called "mirror neurons" has had a large impact on the theory of ToM (see Rizzolatti, Fogassi, & Gallese, 2001). The existence of these cells was discovered more or less by accident (or so the story goes). Researchers were studying the neural activity in macaque monkeys involved in grasping and picking up food items. After they were done, they forgot to turn off the recording equipment. At a certain moment, someone walks in with an ice-cream cone. To the surprise of all present, the monkeys "grasping neurons" began to fire spontaneously without any observed movement. Apparently, these cells simulated the movement of grasping for the ice-cream, without actually doing it.

Of course, instead of offering the monkey some of the ice-cream, this prompted the researchers to submit this monkey to various additional tests, showing that these cells not only fire when the monkey performs a certain motor act, but also when it views someone else performing the action. In particular, it was shown that these cells respond to the *intention* of the observed acts. This mechanism would allow for understanding the intentions of the behaviours of others, by simulating these actions internally. Although probably not representing the complete neural substrate of ToM, coding the intentions behind movements observed in others may be an essential part of what makes full blown ToM possible.

CONCLUSION

Together, our ability to understand the intentions of others and our strong prosocial sentiments that have evolved from basic attachment to important others in our social group, allow for morality to be a driving force in our social setting, guiding behaviour away from pure self interest and towards interests that we share with significant others. However, it is important to realize that selfishness and prosocial behaviour are not as diametrically opposed as they may seem. As already mentioned, displaying prosocial behaviour is often in the best interest of the individual, increasing chances of a successful life. Therefore, even prosocial behaviour can be seen as being ultimately selfish. Indeed, as becomes clear from reading the newspapers or watching the news on TV, people are often remarkably unconstrained in violating moral norms when individual profits can be made and they feel they can get away with it (i.e., when it will not diminish their social standing). While moral behaviour is aimed at preventing social exclusion, if chances of exclusion are slim (when moral violations will remain undetected), certain people may be less inclined to behave morally when there is a clear self interest motive. A similar process may occur in situations when the entire group with which individuals identify themselves displays unethical behaviour, as may happen within a bad ethical climate in companies. If certain ethical violations become the norm for a group (of CEOs, for example), individual group members may not feel a risk of exclusion and self interest motives may become dominant. An extreme example may be wartime situations in which people commit atrocities against other human beings. In these circumstances, in-group vs. out-group sentiments are very strong and amoral behaviour against out-group members (i.e., the enemy) may not be perceived as such because it will not lead to exclusion from the in-group (see also Optow et al., 2005). Indeed, it may even increase one"s standing in the in-group.

In summary, we propose that moral behaviour is an evolutionary adaptation to living in a highly social environment wherein taking into account the interests of significant others is of central importance to maintaining good standing in the group, in turn preventing social exclusion. We have suggested that the required prosocial sentiments have evolved from basic attachment mechanisms between mother and infant and have been transferred to close group members and finally also to individuals that are not able or likely to reciprocate prosocial acts. We have shown that the neuropeptide Oxytocin may play a central role in prosocial and moral behaviour and that certain brain areas, particularly the vmPFC are primarily involved in moral evaluations and decision making. Through our capacity for ToM, we have the uniquely human ability to display true sympathy for our fellow humans. Together, these evolutionary old neural systems drive ethical behaviour which is still such an important issue in our modern day society.

REFERENCES

Adolphs, R., Tranel, D., & Damasio, A. R. (1998). The human amygdala in social judgment. *Nature, 393*(6684), 470–474.

Anderson, S. W., Bechara, A., Damasio, H., Tranel, D., & Damasio, A. R. (1999). Impairment of social and moral behavior related to early damage in human prefrontal cortex. *Nature Neuroscience, 2*(11), 1032–1037.

Berrios, G. E. (1999). J. C. Prichard and the concept of "moral insanity." *History of Psychiatry, 10*(37), 111–116.

Berthoz, S., Armony, J. L., Blair, R. J. R., & Dolan, R. J. (2002). An fMRI study of intentional and unintentional (embarrassing) violations of social norms. *Brain, 125*, 1696–1708.

Berthoz, S., Grezes, J., Armony, J. L., Passingham, R. E., & Dolan, R. J. (2006). Affective response to one"s own moral violations. *Neuroimage, 31*(2), 945–950.

Birbaumer, N., Viet, R., Lotze, M., Erb, M., Hermann, C., Grodd, W., et al. (2005). Deficient fear conditioning in psychopathy–A functional magnetic resonance imaging study. *Archives of General Psychiatry, 62*(7), 799–805.

Blair, R. J. R. (2007). The amygdala and ventromedial prefrontal cortex in morality and psychopathy. *Trends in Cognitive Sciences, 11*(9), 387–392.

Blair, R. J. R., & Cipolotti, L. (2000). Impaired social response reversal–A case of "acquired sociopathy." *Brain, 123*, 1122–1141.

Blakemore, S. J., & Decety, J. (2001). From the perception of action to the understanding of intention. *Nature Reviews Neuroscience, 2*(8), 561–567.

Bolton, G. E., & Zwick, R. (1995). Anonymity versus punishment in ultimatum bargaining. *Games and Economic Behavior, 10*(1), 95–121.

Castelli, F., Happe, F., Frith, U., & Frith, C. (2000). Movement and mind: A functional imaging study of perception and interpretation of complex intentional movement patterns. *Neuroimage, 12*(3), 314–325.

Eisenberg, N. (2000). Emotion, regulation, and moral development. *Annual Review of Psychology, 51*, 665–697.

Fehr, E., & Henrich, J., (2003). In P. Hammerstein (Ed), *Genetic and Cultural Evolution of Cooperation*, Cambridge, MA: MIT Press.

Finger, E. C., Marsh, A. A., Kamel, N., Mitchell, D. G. V., & Blair, J. R. (2006). Caught in the act: The impact of audience on the neural response to morally and socially inappropriate behavior. *Neuroimage, 33*(1), 414–421.

Frith, C. D., & Frith, U. (1999). Cognitive psychology–Interacting minds–A biological basis. *Science, 286*(5445), 1692–1695.

Greene, J. D., Nystrom, L. E., Engell, A. D., Darley, J. M., & Cohen, J. D. (2004). The neural bases of cognitive conflict and control in moral judgment. *Neuron, 44*(2), 389–400.

Greene, J. D., Sommerville, R. B., Nystrom, L. E., Darley, J. M., & Cohen, J. D. (2001). An fMRI investigation of emotional engagement in moral judgment. *Science, 293*(5537), 2105–2108.

Haidt, J. (2001). The emotional dog and its rational tail: A social intuitionist approach to moral judgment. *Psychological Review, 108*(4), 814–834.

Haidt, J. (2007). The new synthesis in moral psychology. *Science, 316*(5827), 998–1002.

Heekeren, H. R., Wartenburger, I., Schmidt, H., Prehn, K., Schwintowski, H. P., & Villringer, A. (2005). Influence of bodily harm on neural correlates of semantic and moral decision-making. *Neuroimage, 24*(3), 887–897.

Heekeren, H. R., Wartenburger, I., Schmidt, H., Schwintowski, H. P., & Villringer, A. (2003). An fMRI study of simple ethical decision-making. *Neuroreport, 14*(9), 1215–1219.

Heider, F., & Simmel, M. (1944). An experimental study of apparent behavior. *American Journal of Psychology, 57*, 243–259.

Insel, T. R., & Young, L. J. (2001). The neurobiology of attachment. *Nature Reviews Neuroscience, 2*(2), 129–136.

Kiehl, K. A., Smith, A. M., Hare, R. D., Mendrek, A., Forster, B. B., Brink, J., et al. (2001). Limbic abnormalities in affective processing by criminal psychopaths as revealed by functional magnetic resonance imaging. *Biological Psychiatry, 50*(9), 677–684.

Koenigs, M., & Tranel, D. (2007). Irrational economic decision-making after ventromedial prefrontal damage: Evidence from the ultimatum game. *Journal of Neuroscience, 27*(4), 951–956.

Koenigs, M., Young, L., Adolphs, R., Tranel, D., Cushman, F., Hauser, M., et al. (2007). Damage to the prefrontal cortex increases utilitarian moral judgements. *Nature, 446*(7138), 908–911.

Kosfeld, M., Heinrichs, M., Zak, P. J., Fischbacher, U., & Fehr, E. (2005). Oxytocin increases trust in humans. *Nature, 435*(7042), 673–676.

Lynam, D. R., Caspi, A., Moffitt, T. E., Loeber, R., & Stouthamer-Loeber, M. (2007). Longitudinal evidence that psychopathy scores in early adolescence predict adult psychopathy. *Journal of Abnormal Psychology, 116*(1), 155–165.

Moll, J., & de Oliveira-Souza, R. (2007). Moral judgments, emotions and the utilitarian brain. *Trends in Cognitive Sciences, 11*(8), 319–321.

Moll, J., de Oliveira-Souza, R., Bramati, I. E., & Grafman, J. (2002). Functional networks in emotional moral and nonmoral social judgments. *Neuroimage, 16*(3), 696–703.

Moll, J., de Oliveira-Souza, R., Moll, F. T., Ignacio, F. A., Bramati, I. E., Caparelli-Daquer, E. M., et al. (2005). The moral affiliations of disgust–A functional MRI study. *Cognitive and Behavioral Neurology, 18*(1), 68–78.

Moll, J., Krueger, F., Zahn, R., Pardini, M., de Oliveira-Souzat, R., & Grafman, J. (2006). Human fronto-mesolimbic networks guide decisions about charitable donation. *Proceedings of the National Academy of Sciences of the United States of America, 103*(42), 15623–15628.

Nowak, M. A., & Sigmund, K. (2005). Evolution of indirect reciprocity. *Nature, 437*(7063), 1291–1298.

Opotow, S., Gerson, J., & Woodside, S. (2005). From moral exclusion to moral inclusion: Theory for teaching peace. *Theory into Practice, 44*(4), 303–318.

Panchanathan, K., & Boyd, R. (2004). Indirect reciprocity can stabilize cooperation without the second-order free rider problem. *Nature, 432*(7016), 499–502.

Pedersen, C. A. (1997). Oxytocin control of maternal behavior–Regulation by sex steroids and offspring stimuli. In *Integrative Neurobiology of Affiliation* (Vol. 807, pp. 126–145).

Phillips, M. L., Young, A. W., Senior, C., Brammer, M., Andrew, C., Calder, A. J., et al. (1997). A specific neural substrate for perceiving facial expressions of disgust. *Nature, 389*(6650), 495–498.

Pillutla, M. M., & Murnighan, J. K. (1996). Unfairness, anger, and spite: Emotional rejections of ultimatum offers. *Organizational Behavior and Human Decision Processes, 68*(3), 208–224.

Rizzolatti, G., Fogassi, L., & Gallese, V. (2001). Neurophysiological mechanisms underlying the understanding and imitation of action. *Nature Reviews Neuroscience, 2*(9), 661–670.

Sanfey, A. G., Rilling, J. K., Aronson, J. A., Nystrom, L. E., & Cohen, J. D. (2003). The neural basis of economic decision-making in the ultimatum game. *Science, 300*(5626), 1755–1758.

van't Wout, M., Kahn, R. S., Sanfey, A. G., & Aleman, A. (2006). Affective state and decision-making in the Ultimatum Game. *Experimental Brain Research, 169*(4), 564–568.

Young, L. J., Lim, M. M., Gingrich, B., & Insel, T. R. (2001). Cellular mechanisms of social attachment. *Hormones and Behavior, 40*(2), 133–138.

Zak, P.J., Stanton, A.A., Ahmadi, S. (2007). Oxytocin Increases Generosity in Humans. *PLoS ONE, 2*(11), e1128.

PART IV

THE SOCIAL CONTEXT AND ETHICAL BEHAVIOR

CHAPTER 10

THE TWO-FOLD INFLUENCE OF SANCTIONS ON MORAL CONCERNS

Laetitia B. Mulder
Tilburg University

When, in present society, policy makers wish to discourage undesirable behaviors such as illegal downloading of music, buying environmentally unfriendly products, or speeding on the motorway, the first measure that comes to mind is installing a punishment system. By forbidding undesirable behaviors or by making people pay a fine when performing these behaviors, it is reasoned that they become less attractive and are thus less often chosen. In social psychology there is indeed evidence that sanctioning antisocial behavior may successfully increase pro-social behavior (Caldwell, 1976; Eek, Loukopoulos, Fujii, & Gärling, 2002; Fehr & Gächter, 2002; McCusker & Carnevale, 1995; Van Vugt & De Cremer, 1999; Wit & Wilke, 1990; Yamagishi, 1986, 1992).[1]

But what kind of effect do sanctions have on people's judgments of the undesired behavior? Do sanctions create the feeling that downloading music, buying environmentally unfriendly products or speeding are *unethical and morally wrongful actions*? In other words, do sanctions boost moral

Psychological Perspectives on Ethical Behavior and Decision Making, pages 169–180
Copyright © 2009 by Information Age Publishing
169

judgments? This question is essential because sanctions that fail to increase moral judgments may also fail to improve behavior. When sanctions do not convince people that complying with a rule is the morally right thing to do, people may show non-compliance when, for example, chances of getting caught are low, when there is a possibility to escape the sanction (Mulder, Van Dijk, De Cremer, & Wilke, 2006b) or when the sanction is removed (Mulder, Van Dijk, De Cremer, & Wilke, 2006a). Considering that people are strongly influenced by moral norms (Biel, Von Borgstede, & Dahlstrand, 1999; Cialdini, Kallgren, & Reno, 1991; Goldstein & Cialdini, 2007; Kerr, Garst, Lewandowski, & Harris, 1997), one can easily imagine that a sanction that succeeds in convincing people that the sanctioned behavior is immoral will be a much stronger motivator than a sanction that does not.

So, do sanctions influence moral concerns? And if so, do they influence them for the better? A first intuitive answer may be "yes." After all, sanctions and norms of morality are strongly related. In science of law, sanctions are seen to have not only the function of deterring people from performing undesired behavior, but also of signaling the underlying attitudes in society regarding this behavior. In this sense, sanctions (and laws) have an expressive function of showing what is morally right and wrong (McAdams, 2000). They convey the message that the sanctioned behavior is the morally wrong thing to do and may thus bring about social disapproval towards perpetrators of the rule and moral condemnation towards rule perpetration (Cooter, 1998). As such they have the function of providing normative validation for (social) rules and regulations and may actually contribute to the moral conviction that the sanctioned behavior is "bad" (Williams & Hawkins, 1986). Seen in this way, sanctions should be able to change individual values and increase awareness of moral norms (cf., Nyborg, 1999). Findings in field research is in line with this reasoning. Van Vugt (1999) and Van Vugt and Samuelson (1999) argue that policy interventions (in their case metering personal energy use) signal severity of the problem (e.g. energy scarcity) and therefore encourage individuals to take up responsibility toward solving the problem. Research by Thøgersen (2003) showed that the positive influence of economic incentives on recycling garbage was largely due to a change in personal norms in favor of recycling.

However, recent literature from psychology and economics suggests also that sanctions do *not* increase moral concerns and that, in fact, they may even *decrease* them (Fehr & Falk, 2001; Gneezy & Rustichini, 2000; Tenbrunsel & Messick, 1999). An example is Gneezy and Rustichini's study (2000) which took place in Israelian day-care centers, where teachers were faced with the problem of parents picking up their children late. To counter this behavior, a fine was installed on picking up one's children more than 10 minutes late. However, rather than decreasing late coming behavior, the installment of the fine made even more parents pick up their children late. The explana-

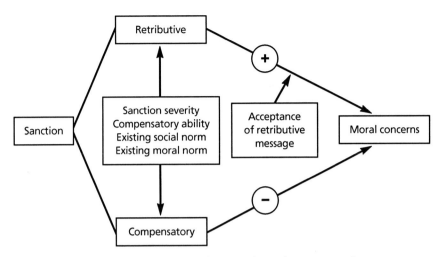

Figure 10.1 Model of the two-fold influence of sanctions on moral concerns.

tion of the researchers was that the sanction made picking up one's children late seem "all right" as the sanction itself was seen as a way to pay for it. It thus converted a moral decision into a business transaction.

So, both the theoretical and empirical literature and previous research both suggest that sanctions may increase and may decrease moral concerns. Therefore, the next logical step does not seem to be what the effect of sanctions on moral concerns is, but rather raise the question *what circumstances* make sanctioning systems exert *positive* influences and *what circumstances* make sanctioning systems exert *negative* influences on moral concerns. In this chapter I will present a model that offers a possible answer to this question. The key message of this model is that sanctions increase moral concerns when they are interpreted as a retributive measure and decrease moral concerns when they are interpreted as a compensatory measure. If the former is the case, the retributive message of a sanction also needs to be accepted in order to increase moral concerns. I will explicate this model, which is pictured in Figure 10.1, in the following.

RETRIBUTION AND COMPENSATION

Sanctions generally have two functions: compensating for the harm being done to the victim or fulfilling the desire to punish the perpetrator (Darley & Pittman, 2003). Whenever some kind of injustice has been done, the need to "resolve justice" arises. This need can manifest itself in the impulse to compensate (i.e., restoring victims to the state they were in before the justice violation) or the impulse to punish (i.e., inflicting punishment upon the perpetrator for causing the justice violation) (see also Carlsmith, Darley, & Robinson, 2002; McFatter, 1982). The latter impulse (also called "giving just deserts") more strongly arises the more a justice violation is morally condemned, for example when it clearly violates moral principles or when the violation was intentional.

These two reasons for sanctioning may mirror how people *interpret* a sanctioning system that is installed by a super ordinate authority. Sanctioning systems installed by an authority may either be interpreted as mechanisms to compensate for the damage being done to the victim or as mechanisms to give the offender his or her just deserts. So, by making either a compensatory or retributive action salient, a sanction may either elicit the idea of compensatory justice or the idea of retributive justice. For example, having to pay a fine if you return your library books late can be interpreted either as a compensation payment for the library or as a message that returning your library books late is discouraged and disapproved of. Whether a sanction is interpreted in the former or the latter way will largely affect how it influences moral concerns. Only if a sanction is interpreted in a retributive way it actually expresses a moral norm as it shows that the sanctioned behavior is disapproved. It may only be then that it affects moral concerns in a positive way. If a sanction is interpreted as a way to compensate for the consequences of one's behavior, however, the situation is perceived in terms of a financial pay-off and will make people feel that they merely complete a transaction than that they are being punished for an immoral act. The feeling of paying in a transaction may bring about that people regard the sanctioned behavior as "immoral" to a lesser extent, and even *remove* the moral aspects of the behavioral decision.

So, all in all, I propose that sanctions are more likely to increase moral concerns if they are interpreted in a retributive way and are more likely to decrease moral concerns if they are interpreted in a compensatory way. So what causes a sanction to be interpreted in a retributive or a compensatory way? This may depend on various aspects of the situation, such as sanction severity, the compensatory ability of a sanction, the existing social norm and the existing moral norm. These factors will be discussed in the following.

SANCTION SEVERITY

First, when a sanction is severe rather than mild, it will more easily trigger retributive concerns. After all, sanctions imply something about the seriousness of the undesired behavior. Serious crimes are usually more severely punished than less serious crimes. Indeed, mild crimes usually evoke the need for compensation, whereas serious crimes evoke the motivation to give an offender his or her just deserts (Darley & Pittman, 2003). Research by Mulder, Verboon and De Cremer (2009) has shown that severity of sanctions influences moral disapproval regarding the sanctioned behavior. They reasoned that sanction severity shows *how* undesired the sanctioned behavior is and thus allows people to make inferences to what extent an authority disapproves of the sanctioned behavior and thus how morally wrong it is to show it. Indeed, their data show that when certain behavior is severely sanctioned, stronger moral norms are evoked regarding this behavior and stronger disapproval towards people showing the behavior than when this behavior is mildly sanctioned. This suggests that severe sanctions communicate more than mild sanctions that the sanctioned behavior is regarded as morally wrong and thus evoke a retributive rather than a compensatory interpretation.

COMPENSATORY ABILITY

In Gneezy and Rustichini's study (Gneezy & Rustichini, 2000) the fine for picking up one's children late was, according to the authors, unintentionally regarded as a payment to compensate for the teachers who worked late to take care of the children. This suggests that a compensatory rather than a retributive interpretation of a sanction is more likely when the situation is constructed in such a way that the sanction can be regarded as a way to make up for the negative consequences of the behavior. Different circumstances may induce this interpretation of a sanction. For example, when a sanction is *financial* in nature it gives more liberty to think that the sanction compensates for something and therefore leaves less room to interpret it in a retributive way. Indeed, support has been found that, in social dilemmas, financial sanctions, compared to disapproval, fail to induce internalization of the norm of cooperation (Nelissen & Mulder, 2008). Also, when the negative consequences can actually be repaired by a sanction, a sanction will be more likely seen as a way to repair them. So a fine for disposing unseparated garbage may evoke a compensatory interpretation as the fine may be regarded as money to pay the local cleansing department so they can separate it themselves. This interpretation may be less likely when it is clear that garbage will be processed in the condition in which it is collected or when the sanction is not a fine but, for example, deprivation of certain privileges. Further, whether the situation concerns a business context or a social context may either make a compensatory or a retributive interpretation of a sanction more likely. Such situational framing has proven to influence social decisions (Pillutla & Chen, 1999). For example, when a commercial organization asks a payment for certain behavior, it is more likely to be interpreted in a compensatory sense than when a non-profit or governmental organization does the same.

EXISTING SOCIAL NORMS

The influence of social norms (What do other people do? What is "normal" to do?) on behavior has proven to be substantial. People are strongly influenced by such "descriptive norms" and adapt their behavior to those of others (Cialdini, 2005; Nolan, Schultz, Cialdini, Goldstein, & Griskevicius, 2008; Schultz, Nolan, Cialdini, Goldstein, & Griskevicius, 2007). Behavior of others may also influence how a sanctioning system is received. More specifically, the number of people showing behavior on which a sanction is installed may determine the extent to which a sanction is interpreted in a compensatory or a retributive way. When only few people show the sanctioned behavior, the installation of the sanction corresponds to and expresses the existing social norm. This makes it likely that the sanction will be perceived as a retributive measure to deter and punish norm deviants. However, if many people show the sanctioned behavior it is less likely to be interpreted as a retributive measure (and insofar as it *is*, it is unlikely to be accepted as one; we will address this issue later on in this chapter). Then, there is more liberty for a compensatory interpretation. With many people showing the behavior, a sanction may be seen merely as a practical measure to overcome the consequences of this very common behavior.

All in all, a sanction is more likely to be interpreted in a retributive way the more it is in line with the social norm present (i.e., the less people show the sanctioned behavior) and is more likely to be interpreted in a compensatory way the less it is in line with the social norm present (i.e., the more people show the sanctioned behavior).

EXISTING MORAL NORMS

People are not only influenced by what other people *do* (descriptive norms) but also, and even more so, by what behaviors other people *(dis)approve* of (injunctive norms) (Cialdini et al., 2006; Reno, Cialdini, & Kallgren, 1993). Research on tax compliance has shown that when tax fraud is strongly disapproved of by others, a sanction has a positive effect on tax-compliance (Wenzel, 2004). More specific, the extent of disapproval of the behavior that is sanctioned may greatly impact how the sanction is *interpreted* and the extent to which the sanctioned behavior clearly violates *moral* standards may determine this. Does it concern behavior that seems to break moral rules aimed at human welfare and justice? A specific function of giving just deserts is that people feel the need to reassert moral rules and values within their community (Tyler & Boeckmann, 1997). The stronger a behavior is seen as a violation of such moral values (for example, because the behavior harms others or leads to injustice), the more likely it is that sanctioning will be regarded as a retributive rather than as a compensatory measure. In other words, a sanctioning system may evoke moral concerns when the possible immoral aspects of the sanctioned behavior are salient.

ACCEPTANCE OF RETRIBUTIVE MESSAGE

So far I have argued that the impact of sanctions on moral concerns depends on whether the sanction is perceived in a retributive way or compensatory way. In order to increase moral norms it needs to be perceived in a retributive way. The chances of this are higher when the sanction is severe, when its compensatory ability is low, and the sanction is in line with existing social and moral norms. But does a retributive perception of a sanction guarantee an increase in moral concerns? Does it mean that when a sanction is seen as an authority's retributive message, people automatically *agree* that the behavior is morally wrong and should be punished? Not always. In order to affect moral concerns positively, a sanction should communicate a moral norm, but people also have to accept this message. One could imagine that this is not always the case. In fact, whether the retributive message is accepted may depend on several factors such as trust in the authority and the justice of the sanctioning system.

Previous research has shown that trust in authorities influences the extent to which people accept authorities' decisions and comply by their rules (Tyler, 2001; Tyler & Degoey, 1996; Tyler & Huo, 2002). Similarly, people may be more receptive to the opinion of an authority and hence adopt an authority's position the more trust they have in the authority. This is supported by research by Mulder et al. (2009) on sanction severity. In their research the influence of sanction severity depended on the extent to which people were inclined to trust authorities. Sanction severity only increased their moral judgments when trust in authorities was high rather than low. So, only when trust in authorities was high, people based their own opinion of what was morally right and wrong on the authority's moral judgment that was expressed by the sanction.

Another factor that may determine whether people accept the retributive message of a sanction is whether the sanction itself is perceived as unjust. This may depend on several features of the sanction or situation. First, how the sanction is executed will affect its perceived (in)justice. A sanction that is procedurally unfair has been shown to decrease compliance (Van Prooijen, Gallucci, & Toeset, 2008). Such a sanction is unlikely to advance accepting the moral norm expressed by the sanction. Second, as pointed out earlier, when a majority of people shows the behavior that is sanctioned, a sanction may fail to increase a moral concern. This may for a great part be because a sanction for behavior that is regarded as "normal" is evaluated as contradicting an existing social norm and thus as unjust. So, a sanction may express that an authority disapproves of the behavior, but when it is in contrast with the descriptive norm, an individual will perceive the sanction as illegitimate and will be less motivated to adapt the norm expressed by an authority. Third, whereas I previously argued that severe sanctions increase moral concerns more than mild ones, the severity of a sanction may also *prevent* that it convinces people that something is morally wrong. This may be the case when a sanction is *too* severe. So, a $50 fine on littering may increase people's moral judgment with regard to littering compared to a $1 fine, but a $10,000 fine is likely to be regarded as an extremely unreasonable fine in light of the act of littering. This may lead people to distrust the authority and to feel that their freedom of choice is too strongly restricted, which usually leads to reactance (see also Brehm, 1966; Wilson & Lassiter, 1982). Hence, the sanction's (and authority's) retributive message will not be accepted and it therefore will fail to affect personal moral judgments about littering. Support for this idea is found in research by Depoorter and Vanneste (2005) on legal sanctions in copyright law. They showed that excessive legal sanctions did not increase (and even *decreased*) the norm that copying music is wrong.

CONCLUSIONS

In this chapter I have argued that sanctions in modern society can trigger either compensatory or retributive concerns and that each of these two concerns affect awareness of moral norms in opposite ways. A compensatory interpretation of a sanction does not evoke, or may even reduce, moral concerns, whereas a retributive interpretation is necessary to evoke moral concerns. Whether a compensatory or a retributive interpretation is more likely depends on sanction severity, the sanction's compensatory ability, and the existing social and moral norm. Once a sanction is perceived as a retributive message by an authority, it also needs to be accepted for the expressed norm to be used by individuals. This is influenced by trust in authorities, justice of the sanction, and sanction severity.

The model presented in this chapter thus goes beyond arguing that sanctions either boost or undermine moral concerns in social decision making. It recognizes that sanctions can work both ways and tries to distinguish conditions that determine whether sanctions positively or negatively affect moral concerns. By doing this it also provides leads for practical implications. For example, it suggests that for a sanction to boost moral concerns there should already be some public support for the norm that is communicated by the sanction. This means that merely installing a sanctioning system may often not be enough: It may be necessary to make clear to individuals *why* the sanctioned behavior is immoral (for example, because it harms others or the collective) and, preferably, the feeling should be created that most other people do not show the behavior and disapprove of it. Also, it should be made clear that the sanction is not a payment that softens the consequences of one's behavior. Instead, people should realize that performing the behavior is anyhow "bad" and that the sanction is a way to deter people from this behavior and to give individuals that *do* show the behavior their just deserts. Another practical implication is that the sanction should be severe enough so that it shows disapproval, but not so severe that it is perceived as unreasonable and illegitimate. So, when installing extremely large sanctions an authority may encounter strong resistance, like the Belgium government did after they introduced "super fines" for traffic offenses in March, 2004 (Britishembassy.gov.uk, 2004), which is why they reversed these super fines two years later.

Although it may be possible that there are more circumstances than identified in this chapter that determine whether a sanction is interpreted as retributive or compensatory, I argue that the distinction between the two interpretations is vital to understand and predict how, when installing a sanction, one can prevent negative side effects and make it strengthen moral reasoning. With this insight, it may even be possible with the external incentive of a sanction to induce the motivation to behave in the requested way because people have become convinced it is the morally right thing to do. Of course, this is a more intrinsic motivation than merely trying to avoid a sanction. This motivation is most likely to make people refrain from the sanctioned behavior even when the chances of getting caught are low, or when there are possibilities to dodge the sanction. In other words, by creating this motivation such imperfect sanctioning systems will work perfectly despite their imperfections.

NOTE

1. In this chapter, sanctions are defined as punishments and can range from financial fines to prison sentences.

REFERENCES

Biel, A., Von Borgstede, C., & Dahlstrand, U. (1999). Norm perception and cooperation in large scale social dilemmas. In M. Foddy, M. Smithson, S. Schneider & M. Hogg (Eds.), *Resolving social dilemmas: Dynamic, structural, and intergroup aspects.* (pp. 245–252). Philadelpia: Psychology Press.

Brehm, J. W. (1966). *A Theory of Psychological Reactance.* Oxford, England: Academic Press.

Britishembassy.gov.uk. (2004). New traffic fines ("super fines") as from 1 March 2004. Retrieved December, 11, 2007, from http://www.britishembassy.gov.uk/servlet/Front?pagename=OpenMarket/Xcelerate/ShowPage&c=Page&c id=1079977509390

Caldwell, M. D. (1976). Communication and sex effects in a five-person Prisoner's Dilemma Game. *Journal of Personality and Social Psychology, 33,* 273–280.

Carlsmith, K. M., Darley, J. M., & Robinson, P. H. (2002). Why do we punish? Deterrence and just deserts as motives for punishment. *Journal of Personality and Social Psychology, 83,* 284–299.

Cialdini, R. B. (2005). Basic social influence is underestimated. *Psychological Inquiry, 15,* 158–161.

Cialdini, R. B., Demaine, L., Sagarin, B. J., Barret, D. W., Rhoads, K., & Winter, P. L. (2006). Managing social norms for persuasive impact. *Social Influence, 1,* 3–15.

Cialdini, R. B., Kallgren, C. A., & Reno, R. R. (1991). A focus theory of normative conduct: A theoretical refinement and reevaluation of the role of norms in human behavior. *Advances in Experimental Social Psychology, 24,* 201–234.

Cooter, R. (1998). Expressive law and economics. *Journal of Legal Studies, 27,* 585–608.

Darley, J. M., & Pittman, T. S. (2003). The psychology of compensatory and retributive justice. *Personality and Social Psychology Review, 7,* 324–336.

Depoorter, B., & Vanneste, S. (2005). Norms and enforcement: the case against copyright law. *Oregon Law Review, 84,* 1127–1179.

Eek, D., Loukopoulos, P., Fujii, S., & Gärling, T. (2002). Spill-over effects of intermittent costs for defection in social dilemmas. *European Journal of Social Psychology, 32,* 801–813.

Fehr, E., & Falk, A. (2001). Psychological foundations of incentives. *European Economic Review, 46,* 687–724.

Fehr, E., & Gächter, S. (2002). Altruistic punishment in humans. *Nature, 415,* 137–140.

Gneezy, U., & Rustichini, A. (2000). A fine is a price. *Journal of Legal Studies, 29,* 1–17.

Goldstein, N. J., & Cialdini, R. B. (2007). Using social norms as a lever of social influence. In A. R. Pratkanis (Ed.), *The science of social influence: Advances and future progress* (pp. 167–191). NY: Psychology Press.

Kerr, N. L., Garst, J., Lewandowski, D. A., & Harris, S. E. (1997). That still, small voice: Commitment to cooperate as an internalized versus a social norm. *Personality and Social Psychology Bulletin, 23,* 1300–1311.

McAdams, R. H. (2000). An attitudinal theory of expressive law. *Oregon Law Review, 79,* 339.

McCusker, C., & Carnevale, P. J. (1995). Framing in resource dilemmas: Loss aversion and the moderating effects of sanctions. *Organizational Behavior and Human Decision Processes, 61,* 190–201.

McFatter, R. (1982). Purpose of punishment: Effects of utilities of criminal sanctions on perceived appropriateness. *Journal of Applied Psychology, 67,* 255–267.

Mulder, L. B., Van Dijk, E., De Cremer, D., & Wilke, H. A. M. (2006a). Undermining trust and cooperation: The paradox of sanctioning systems in social dilemmas. *Journal of Experimental Social Psychology, 42,* 147–162.

Mulder, L. B., Van Dijk, E., De Cremer, D., & Wilke, H. A. M. (2006b). When sanctions fail to increase cooperation in social dilemmas: Considering the presence of an alternative defection option. *Personality and Social Psychology Bulletin, 32,* 1312–1324.

Mulder, L. B., Verboon, P., & De Cremer, D. (2009). Sanctions and moral judgments: The moderating effect of sanction severity and trust in authorities. *European Journal of Social Psychology, 39,* 255–269.

Nelissen, R. M. A., & Mulder, L. B. (2008). What makes a sanction 'stick'? The effects of financial and social sanctions on norm compliance. *Unpublished Manuscript.*

Nolan, J. M., Schultz, P. W., Cialdini, R. B., Goldstein, N. J., & Griskevicius, V. (2008). Normative social influence is underdetected. *Personality and Social Psychology Bulletin, 34,* 913–923.

Nyborg, K. (1999). Informational aspect of environment policy deserves more attention: Comment on the paper by Frey. *Journal of Consumer Policy, 22,* 419–427.

Pillutla, M. M., & Chen, X. P. (1999). Social norms and cooperation in social dilemmas: The effects of context and feedback. *Organizational Behavior and Human Decision Processes, 78,* 81–103.

Reno, R. R., Cialdini, R. B., & Kallgren, C. A. (1993). The transsituational influence of social norms. *Journal of Personality and Social Psychology, 64,* 104–112.

Schultz, P. W., Nolan, J. M., Cialdini, R. B., Goldstein, N. J., & Griskevicius, V. (2007). The constructive, destructive, and reconstructive power of social norms. *Psychological Science, 18,* 429–434.

Tenbrunsel, A. E., & Messick, D. M. (1999). Sanctioning systems, decision frames, and cooperation. *Administrative Science Quarterly, 44,* 684–707.

Thøgersen, J. (2003). Monetary incentives and recycling: Behavioural and psychological reactions to a performance-dependent garbage fee. *Journal of Consumer Policy, 26,* 197–228.

Tyler, T. R. (2001). The psychology of public dissatisfaction with government. In J. R. Hibbing & E. Theiss Morse (Eds.), *What is it about government that Americans dislike? Cambridge studies in political psychology and public opinion.* (pp. 227–242). Cambridge, UK: Cambridge University Press.

Tyler, T. R., & Boeckmann, R. J. (1997). Three strikes and you are out, but why? The psychology of public support for punishing rule breakers. *Law and Society Review, 31,* 237–265.

Tyler, T. R., & Degoey, P. (1996). Trust in organizational authorities: The influence of motive attributions on willingness to accept decisions. In R. M. Kramer & T. R. Tyler (Eds.), *Trust in organizations: Frontiers of theory and research.* (pp. 331–356). Thousand Oaks, CA, US: Sage.

Tyler, T. R., & Huo, Y. J. (2002). *Trust in the law: Encouraging public cooperation with the police and courts.* New York, NY: Russell Sage Foundation.

Van Prooijen, J. W., Gallucci, M., & Toeset, G. (2008). Procedural justice in punishment systems: Inconsistent punishment procedures have detrimental effects on cooperation. *British Journal of Social Psychology, 47,* 311–324.

Van Vugt, M. (1999). Solving natural resource dilemmas through structural change: The social psychology of metering water use. In M. Foddy, M. Smithson, S.

Schneider & M. Hogg (Eds.), *Resolving social dilemmas: Dynamic, structural, and intergroup aspects.* (pp. 121–133). Philadelphia: Psychology Press.

Van Vugt, M., & De Cremer, D. (1999). Leadership in social dilemmas: The effects of group identification on collective actions to provide public goods. *Journal of Personality and Social Psychology, 76,* 587–599.

Van Vugt, M., & Samuelson, C. D. (1999). The impact of personal metering in the management of a natural resource crisis: A social dilemma analysis. *Personality and Social Psychology Bulletin, 25,* 731–745.

Wenzel, M. (2004). The social side of sanctions: Personal and social norms as moderators of deterrence. *Law and Human Behavior, 28,* 547–567.

Williams, K. R., & Hawkins, R. (1986). Perceptual research on general deterrence: A critical review. *Law and Society Review, 20,* 545–572.

Wilson, T. D., & Lassiter, G. D. (1982). Increasing intrinsic interest with superfluous extrinsic constraints. *Journal of Personality and Social Psychology, 42,* 811–819.

Wit, A., & Wilke, H. A. M. (1990). The presentation of rewards and punishments in a simulated social dilemma. *Social Behaviour, 5,* 231–245.

Yamagishi, T. (1986). The provision of a sanctioning system as a public good. *Journal of Personality and Social Psychology, 51,* 110–116.

Yamagishi, T. (1992). Group size and the provision of a sanctioning system in a social dilemma. In W. B. G. Liebrand, D. M. Messick & H. Wilke (Eds.), *Social dilemmas: Theoretical issues and research findings. International series in experimental social psychology.* (pp. 267–287). Elmsford, NY: Pergamon Press.

CHAPTER 11

MAKING ETHICAL CLIMATE A MAINSTREAM MANAGEMENT TOPIC

A Review, Critique, and Prescription for the Empirical Research on Ethical Climate

David M. Mayer
University of Central Florida

Maribeth Kuenzi
Southern Methodist University

Rebecca L. Greenbaum
University of Central Florida

The plethora of corporate scandals in recent years at companies such as Enron, Tyco, and Worldcom has thrust the issue of business ethics to center stage in the media and in the minds of many consumers. In the scientific literature,

Psychological Perspectives on Ethical Behavior and Decision Making, pages 181–213

181

there is growing acceptance of the notion that corporate indiscretions are the result of more than just a few "bad apples" and that the organizational environment has a strong influence on employees' unethical behavior (Treviño, Weaver, & Reynolds, 2006). With the importance of the organizational context in mind, approximately 20 years ago Victor and Cullen (1987, 1988) introduced the concept of *ethical climate* to describe how the organizational environment impacts unethical behavior. Victor and Cullen (1987) define ethical climate as "the shared perception of what is correct behavior, and how ethical situations should be handled in an organization" (p. 51). A premise of this construct is that the social context in organizations plays a pivotal role in determining whether employees will behave unethically.

Victor and Cullen's (1987, 1988) seminal work on ethical climate has been well received in the business ethics literature prompting over 70 empirical studies in the past 20 years. Interestingly, however, the vast majority of published articles on ethical climate are in business ethics journals as opposed to mainstream management journals. This is problematic because whereas research on other climate constructs such as service climate (Schneider, Bowen, Ehrhart, & Holcombe, 2000), safety climate (Zohar, 1980, 2000), and justice climate (Naumann & Bennett, 2000) is commonly found in top-tier mainstream management journals, ethical climate research has been relegated to niche journals thus limiting the visibility, impact, perceived scientific rigor, and attributed importance of the topic. In this chapter we argue that there are a number of conceptual, operational, methodological, and analytical issues that are largely responsible for the current state of empirical research on ethical climate. In general, we believe that although Victor and Cullen's (1987, 1988) initial conceptualization and operationalization of ethical climate was extremely useful in sparking interest in the topic, a number of changes are now necessary for ethical climate research to continue to prosper and to become a mainstream management topic like other well-known climate constructs.

The primary goal of this chapter is to provide a critique of the ethical climate literature and to highlight a number of ways future research can be improved. It should be noted that the primary purpose is not to simply review the extant literature on ethical climate. Although we do provide a brief review of the conceptualization, operationalization, and empirical work on ethical climate, our focus is more on where we believe the literature should go in the future as opposed to summarizing where it has been in the past. For more detailed information on the extant literature on ethical climate we suggest reading excellent qualitative (Arnaud & Schminke, 2007) and quantitative (Martin & Cullen, 2006) reviews that have been recently published.

This chapter is divided into the following four sections: (a) a brief description of the conceptualization and operationalization of ethical climate; (b) a short review of the antecedents and consequences of ethical climate;

(c) a critique of the extant literature; and (d) a prescription for where we believe the field should go in the future.

CONCEPTUALIZATION AND OPERATIONALIZATION OF ETHICAL CLIMATE

Conceptual Basis and Measurement of Ethical Climate

Victor and Cullen (1987, 1988) are known as the "fathers" of ethical climate. They utilized philosophical and sociological perspectives in developing a theoretical basis for creating a measure of ethical climate. More specifically, they used a two-dimensional theoretical perspective to describe the different types of ethical climates that exist in organizations. The first dimension, *ethical criterion*, maps on to the three major classes of ethical theory: egoism (i.e., maximizing self-interest), benevolence (i.e., maximizing joint interests), and deontology or principle (i.e., adhering to a principle) (Fritzche & Becker, 1984; Williams, 1985). The second dimension is referred to as the *locus of analysis* and draws heavily on the work by Merton (1957) on roles and reference groups. Locus of analysis relates to who the referent is for one's actions. The three loci of analysis include: self (i.e., oneself), local (i.e., one's organization or subunit), and cosmopolitan (i.e., the environment external to the organization).

This three (ethical criteria) by three (loci of analysis) matrix forms nine theoretical dimensions of ethical climate. These nine theoretical dimensions include: (a) self-interest; (b) company profit; (c) efficiency; (d) friendship; (e) team interest; (f) social responsibility; (g) personal morality; (h) company rules and procedure; (i) and laws and professional codes (see Victor & Cullen, 1987, 1988 for a detailed description of each dimension). However, the dimensionality across studies tends to yield different factor structures (a topic we return to in our critique). The five dimensions that have been most commonly examined include instrumental (includes self-interest and company profit), caring (includes friendship and team interest), personal morality, company rules and procedure, and laws and professional codes (Martin & Cullen, 2006).

Victor and Cullen (1987, 1988) wrote four items to tap each of these dimensions for a total of 36 items which make up the Ethical Climate Questionnaire (ECQ). Although other measures have been used as well (see Arnaud & Schminke, 2007 for a qualitative review), the ECQ has been by far the most commonly used measure of ethical climate (Martin & Cullen, 2006). In what follows, we briefly summarize the empirical literature examining antecedents and consequences of ethical climate—most of which draws on Victor and Cullen's (1987, 1988) conceptualization and measure of ethical climate.

EMPIRICAL RESEARCH REVIEW

Because other reviews of ethical climate have been recently conducted, our focus is primarily on providing a critique and prescription for the empirical research on ethical climate. However, we deemed it important to provide a brief summary of the extant empirical literature examining antecedents and consequences of ethical climate. To provide a succinct summary of the extant work, in addition to the following sections, we also provide a summary table (see Table 11.1). Table 11.1 provides the following information for each published empirical article on ethical climate: (a) author and year; (b) journal published in; (c) measure used; (d) level of analysis of the study; (e) antecedents examined; and (f) consequences examined. We chose to highlight these specific article characteristics in Table 11.1 because they provide a good summary of the key characteristics of the findings and highlight some of the limitations and inconsistencies in the research.

Antecedents of Ethical Climate

A considerable amount of research has examined antecedents of ethical climate. We categorize these antecedents into individual, organizational, and environmental antecedents.

Individual antecedents. Individual antecedents concern characteristics of both employees and leaders. First, few studies have examined *employee* characteristics. The studies that have examined characteristics such as demographics (e.g., gender and age) and personality variables (e.g., individual moral values and moral ethical development). Dawson (1992) and Luthar, Dibattista, and Gautschi (1997) found that females had a higher expectation about what the ethical climate of an organization should be. Luthar et al. (1997) found that older students were more cynical and that the more education an individual had about business ethics, the more they expected an ethical climate in any organization they would later work in. Only two studies have examined personality-related variables of employees and employees' ethical climate perceptions. Research has demonstrated a positive link between ethical climates and moral values (Herndon, Ferrell, LeClair, & Ferrell, 1999) and cognitive moral development (Weeks, Loe, Chonko, Martinez, & Wakefield, 2006).

There has been more research focusing on the relationship between the development of ethical climates and *leaders.* This includes some theoretical work linking leaders to the development of ethical climates (e.g., Dickson, Smith, Grojean, & Ehrhart, 2004; Logsdon & Yuthas, 1997; Sims & Brinkman, 2002), as well as empirical work. More specifically, researchers have examined variables such as demographic characteristics (e.g., age, tenure,

TABLE 11.1 Characteristics of Empirical Studies on Ethical Climate

Authors	Journal	Measure	Level of Analysis	Antecedents	Consequences
Agarwal & Malloy (1999)	*Journal of Business Ethics*	Ethical Climate Questionnaire (ECQ) (Individual caring, machiavellianism, independence, social caring, and law and code)	Psychological climate		
Ambrose, Arnaud, & Schminke (2007)	*Journal of Business Ethics*	ECQ (Instrumental, caring, and independence)	Organizational climate		*Job satisfaction, organizational commitment, turnover intention*
Aquino (1998)	*Journal of Conflict Management*		Psychological climate		*Deception, ethical behavior, personally favorable outcomes*
Aquino & Becker (2005)	*Journal of Organizational Behavior*		Psychological climate		*Neutralization strategies in negotiation*
Babin, Boles, & Robin (2000)	*Journal of the Academy of Marketing Science*	Own Measure (Responsibility/trust, peer behavior, ethical norms, selling practices)	Psychological climate		*Job satisfaction, organizational commitment, role conflict, role ambiguity*
Barnett & Schubert (2002)	*Journal of Business Ethics*	ECQ (Benevolence 1 – social responsibility, benevolence 2 – team, principle-laws and code, egoism-self interest)	Psychological climate		*Covenantal relationship*

(continued)

TABLE 11.1 Characteristics of Empirical Studies on Ethical Climate (continued)

Authors	Journal	Measure	Level of Analysis	Antecedents	Consequences
Barnett & Vaicys (2000)	*Journal of Business Ethics*	ECQ (Egoistic, utilitarian, deontological)	Psychological climate		*Ethical judgments, ethical intentions*
Bartels, Harrick, Martell, & Strickland (1998)	*Journal of Business Ethics*	Own measure	Psychological climate		*Seriousness of ethical problem within organizations, success in dealing with ethical issues*
Bourne & Snead (1999)	*Journal of Business Ethics*	Own Measure (Cultural environment, external stakeholder interaction, employee ethics, ethical conflict situations, determinant of ethical behavior)	Psychological climate		
Brower & Shrader (2000)	*Journal of Business Ethics*	ECQ (Principle, benevolence, egoism)	Psychological climate	*Organization type (for-profit versus not-for-profit)*	
Buchan (2005)	*Journal of Business Ethics*	ECQ (instrumental climate)	Psychological climate		Ethical intentions
Caldwell & Moberg (2007)	*Journal of Business Ethics*		Psychological climate		*Moral imagination*
Cullen, Parboteeah, & Victor (2003)	*Journal of Business Ethics*	ECQ (General egoistic, general benevolent, general principled, self interest, company profit, efficiency, friendship, personal morality, rules, standard operating procedures, laws, professional codes)	Organizational climate		*Organizational commitment*

Cullen, Victor, & Bronson (1993)	*Psychological Reports*	ECQ (Self-interest, company profit efficiency, friendship and team interest, social responsibility, rules, standard operating procedures, laws, professional codes)	Organizational climate	
Dawson (1992)	*Journal of Personnel Selling & Sales Management*	No Measure	Gender	
DeConinck (2003)	*The Marketing Management Journal*	Ethical Work Climate (Babin, Boles, & Robin, 2000) (Responsibility/trust, peer behavior, ethical norms)	Psychological climate	*Perceptions of an ethical situation, willingness to engage in ethical behavior, moral intensity towards an unethical situation*
DeConinck & Lewis (1997)	*Journal of Business Ethics*	ECQ (Caring, law and code, rules, instrumental, independence)	Psychological climate	Managers' decisions to reward or punish unethical sales force behavior
Deshpande (1996a)	*Journal of Business Ethics*	ECQ (Professionalism, caring, rules, instrumental, efficiency, independence)	Psychological climate	*Job Satisfaction*
Deshpande (1996b)	*Journal of Business Ethics*	ECQ (Professionalism, caring, rules, instrumental, efficiency, independence)	Psychological climate	*Perceived ethical practices of successful managers*

(continued)

TABLE 11.1 Characteristics of Empirical Studies on Ethical Climate (continued)

Authors	Journal	Measure	Level of Analysis	Antecedents	Consequences
Deshpande, George, & Joseph (2000)	*Journal of Business Ethics*	ECQ (Professionalism, caring, rules, instrumental, efficiency, independence)	Psychological climate		Perceived ethical behavior by successful managers
Elm & Nichols (1993)	*Journal of Business Ethics*	ECQ (Egoism, utilitarianism, principled)	Psychological climate	Moral reasoning level	
Engelbrecht, van Aswegen, & Theron (2005)	*South African Journal of Business Management*	ECQ (Law and code, rules, independence, caring)	Psychological climate	*Transformational leadership, integrity*	
Erondu, Sharland, & Okpara (2004)	*Journal of Business Ethics*	Measure not specified (Self-interest, company profit, friendship, team interest, personal morality, rules & procedures)	Psychological climate		*Efficiency, social responsibility, law and professional codes*
Flannery & May (2000)	*Academy of Management Journal*	ECQ (dimensions not specified)	Psychological climate		*Managers' environmental ethical decision intentions*
Forte (2004a)	*Journal of Business Ethics*	ECQ (Rule, caring, law and code, instrumental, independence)	Psychological climate	*Manager's age, management level*	Manager moral reasoning
Forte (2004b)	*Journal of Business Ethics*	ECQ (Caring, law and code, rules, instrumental, independence)	Psychological climate	Locus of control, *age, work tenure, gender, management levels*, SIC code	Manager moral reasoning

				Individual moral values	Ethical decision making
Fritzche (2000)	Journal of Business Ethics	ECQ (caring, law and codes, efficiency, rules, independence, company)	Psychological climate		Ethical decision making
Gonzalez-Padron, Hult, & Calantone (2008)	Industrial Marketing Management	Ethical dimension of corporate citizenship (Maignan & Ferrell, 2000)	Psychological climate		Learning, entrepreneurial innovation, relationship quality, cycle time
Hart (2005)	Journal of Nursing Scholarship	Hospital Ethical Climate Survey (Olson, 1995)	Psychological climate		Positional turnover intentions, professional turnover intentions
Herndon, Ferrell, LeClair, & Ferrell (1999)	Research in Marketing	ECQ (1 dimension)	Psychological climate	Individual moral values	Job satisfaction, organizational commitment, turnover intentions
Jaffe & Tsimerman (2005)	Journal of Business Ethics	ECQ (Law and codes, caring, rules, instrumental, efficiency, independence,)	Psychological climate		
Jaramillo, Mulki, & Solomon (2006)	Journal of Personal Selling & Sales Management	Schwepker's (2001) 7-item ethical climate scale	Psychological climate		Role conflict, role ambiguity, organizational commitment, job satisfaction
Joseph & Deshpande (1997)	Health Care Management Review	ECQ (Professionalism, caring, rules, instrumental, efficiency, independence)	Psychological climate		Job Satisfaction

(continued)

TABLE 11.1   Characteristics of Empirical Studies on Ethical Climate (continued)

Authors	Journal	Measure	Level of Analysis	Antecedents	Consequences
Kelley & Dorsch (1991)	*Journal of Personal Selling & Sales Management*	ECQ (Caring, rules, instrumental)	Psychological climate		*Organizational Commitment,* indebtedness (characterized by discomfort and *repayment*)
Koh & Boo (2001)	*Journal of Business Ethics*	Own measure adapted from ECQ (Egoistic, benevolent, principled)	Psychological climate		*Job Satisfaction*
Logsdon & Young (2004)	Book chapter in *Positive Psychology in Business Ethics and Corporate Social Responsibility*				
Luthar, DiBattista, & Gautschi (1997)	*Journal of Business Ethics*	No Measure		*Gender, age, Education Level, Ethics Education*	
Martin & Cullen (2006)	*Journal of Business Ethics*	ECQ	Meta-analysis		*Organizational commitment, job satisfaction, psychological well-being, lying, stealing, falsifying reports, accepting gifts and favors*
McKendall & Wagner (1997)	*Organization Science*	Bentley College Center for Business Ethics Questionnaire (no dimensions)	Psychological climate		*Corporate illegality, industry concentration of illegality*

Author (Year)	Journal	Measure	Climate type	Moderators/Antecedents	Outcomes
Mulki, Jaramillo, & Locander (2006)	Journal of Personal Selling & Sales Management	Schwepker (2001)	Psychological climate		Job satisfaction, organizational commitment, trust
Neubaum, Mitchell, & Schminke (2005)	Journal of Business Ethics	ECQ (instrumental, caring, independence, rules, law & code)	Organizational climate	Entrepreneurial orientation, firm newness, firm size	
Parboteeah, Cullen, Victor, & Sakano (2005)	Management International Review	ECQ (egoism-individual climate, benevolent-local climate, benevolent-cosmopolitan climate, principle-cosmopolitan climate)	Psychological climate	National culture (US vs Japanese)	
Peterson (2002a)	Journal of Business and Psychology	ECQ (rules, law, employee focus, community focus, personal ethics, self-interest, efficiency)	Psychological climate		Production deviance, political deviance, property deviance, personal aggression
Peterson (2002b)	Journal of Business Ethics	ECQ (self-interest, company profit, efficiency, friendship, team interest, social responsibility, personal morality, rules, laws)	Psychological climate	Code of ethics	Unethical behavior
Ross & Robertson (2000)	Business Ethics Quarterly	Own Measure (no dimensions)	Psychological climate		Lying, lying to competitors
Rothwell & Baldwin (2006)	Review of Public Personnel Administration	ECQ (independence, instrumental, caring, rules, law & code)	Psychological climate		Whistle blowing intentions, whistle blowing actions
Rothwell & Baldwin (2007)	Journal of Business Ethics	ECQ (law & rules, friendship or team interest, social responsibility, company profit or efficiency, independence)	Psychological climate		Willingness to whistle blow (minor, major, misdemeanors, felonies), frequency of whistle-blowing

(continued)

TABLE 11.1 Characteristics of Empirical Studies on Ethical Climate (continued)

Authors	Journal	Measure	Level of Analysis	Antecedents	Consequences
Ruppel & Harrington (2000)	*Journal of Business Ethics*	ECQ (individual interests, organizational interests, principled individual, principled organizational, principled cosmopolitan	Psychological climate		*Employee trust, atmosphere of trust, employee communication*
Schminke, Ambrose, & Neubaum (2005)	*Organizational Behavior and Human Decision Processes*	ECQ (instrumental, independence, rules, caring, law & code)	Organizational climate	*Leader moral development, moral development utilization, organizational age*	
Schwepker (2001)	*Journal of Business Research*	Own Measure (1 dimension)	Psychological climate		*Job satisfaction, organizational commitment, turnover intention*
Schwepker & Good (2007)	*Journal of Personal Selling & Sales Management*	Own Measure (1 dimension)	Psychological climate		*Unethical sales force, sales manager's ethical attitudes*
Schwepker, Ferrell, & Ingram (1997)	*Journal of the Academy of Marketing Science*	Own Measure (1 dimension)	Psychological climate		*Ethical conflict with sales managers, ethical conflict with TM*
Schwepker & Hartline (2005)	*Journal of Service Research*	Qualls & Puto (1989) and Herndon (1991)	Psychological climate	Enforcement of code of ethics, *internalization of code of ethics, punishment of ethical violations,* discussion of ethical issues	*Role conflict, job satisfaction, commitment to service quality*
Sims & Keon (1997)	*Journal of Business Ethics*	ECQ (instrumental, caring, law & code, rules, independence)	Psychological climate		

Sims & Kroeck (1994)	*Journal of Business Ethics*	ECQ (instrumental, caring, law & code, rules, independence)	Psychological climate	
Stone & Henry (2003)	*Journal of Business Ethics*	ECQ plus own items (cosmopolitan egoistic, cosmopolitan principle, organizational egoistic, organizational utilitarian/ individual utilitarian, organizational egoistic/ workgroup egoistic, workgroup principle, individual egoistic, individual principle)	Psychological climate	
Treviño, Butterfield, McCabe (1998)	*Business Ethics Quarterly*	ECQ (ethical environment, employee-focused, community-focused, self-interest, efficiency, rules & procedures, personal ethics, law & professional codes)	Psychological climate	*Organizational commitment*
Ulrich, O'Donnell, Taylor, Farrar, Danis, & Grady (2007)	*Social Science & Medicine*	Oldham's Hospital ethical climate scale	Psychological climate	*Job satisfaction, intentions to leave*

(continued)

TABLE 11.1 Characteristics of Empirical Studies on Ethical Climate (continued)

Authors	Journal	Measure	Level of Analysis	Antecedents	Consequences
Upchurch & Ruhland (1996)	Journal of Business Ethics	ECQ (egoism, benevolence, principle)	Psychological climate	Gender, years of management experience, educational level, *property classification, individual level, local level,* cosmopolitan level	
Vaicys, Barnett, & Brown (1996)	Psychological Reports	ECQ (team spirit, rules & codes, social responsibility, self interest, efficiency, personal morality)	Psychological climate		
VanSandt, Shepard, & Zappe (2006)	Journal of Business Ethics	ECQ (self-interest, company interest, efficiency, friendship, team play, social responsibility, personal morality, rules & procedures, law & code)	Psychological climate		*Moral awareness*
Vardi (2001)	Journal of Business Ethics	ECQ (caring, law & code, rules, instrumental, interdependence)	Psychological climate		*Organizational Misbehavior*
Verbeke, Ouwerkerk, & Peelen (1996)	Journal of Business Ethics	Ruch & Newstom (1975)	Psychological climate	*Control system, career orientation,* communication	*Ethical decision-making, attraction of lower Machiavellists*
Victor & Cullen (1988)	Administrative Science Quarterly	ECQ (instrumental, caring, independence, rules, law & code)	Type of company	Satisfaction	

Study	Journal	Measure	Level of analysis	Moderator/Variable	Outcomes
Webber (2007)	*The Journal of Academic Librarianship*	RECQ (reflexive, peer directed, self-directed, rule-directed, patriotic, self-preserving, socially responsible)	Psychological climate		
Weber (1995)	*Organizational Science*	ECQ (instrumental, caring, independence, rules, law & code)	Psychological climate	*Department Type (technical core, buffer, boundary spanning)*	
Weber, Kurke, & Pentico (2003)	*Business & Society*	ECQ (instrumental, caring, independence, rules & procedures, law & code)	Psychological climate	*Theft vs no theft groups*	*Morally preferred EWC*
Weber & Seger (2002)	*Journal of Business Ethics*	ECQ (instrumental, caring, independence, rules, law & code)	Psychological climate	*Department Type*	
Weeks, Loe, Chonko, & Wakefield (2004)	*Journal of Personal Selling & Sales Management*	Schwepker et al. (1997)	Psychological climate		*Commitment to quality, organizational commitment, individual performance*
Weeks, Loe, Chonko, Martinez, & Wakefield (2006)	*Journal of Personal Selling & Sales Management*		Psychological climate	*Moral ethical development*	*Commitment to quality, organizational commitment, sales performance*
Wimbush, Shepard, & Markham (1997a)	*Journal of Business Ethics*	ECQ (caring, law & rules, service, independence, instrumental)	Psychological climate	*Operating units*	
Wimbush, Shepard, & Markham (1997b)	*Journal of Business Ethics*	ECQ (independence, caring, instrumental, law & rules, service)	WABA (district level)		*Stealing, lying, disobeying company rules, being an accomplice*
Wittmer & Coursey (1996)	*Journal of Public Administration Research & Theory*	ECQ and Menzel (1991)	Psychological climate	*Public vs private companies*	
Wotruba, Chonko, & Loe (2001)	*Journal of Business Ethics*	Schwepker et al. (1997)	Psychological climate		*Usefulness of code of ethics*

Note: Significant relationships in italics.

gender, management level), personality characteristics (e.g., leader moral development, leader integrity, moral development utilization, locus of control), and types of leadership (e.g., transformational leadership).

Related to the demographics of leaders, Forte (2004a) found that younger managers perceived stronger ethical climates and top management perceived their organization to have a rules climate. They found no differences for work tenure, education, or gender.

In addition to demographic characteristics, researchers have found a positive relationship between personality characteristics of leaders such as moral development (Schminke, Ambrose, & Neubaum, 2005) and integrity (Englebrecht, van Aswegen, & Theron, 2005) and ethical climates. However, no support was found for the link between leader moral reasoning (Elm & Nichols, 1993) or locus of control (Forte, 2004b) on ethical climates.

Lastly, researchers have only just begun to examine how different types of leadership affect the development of ethical work climates. Englebrecht et al. (2005) found that transformational leadership is positively related to ethical climates.

Organizational antecedents. Most of the research examining antecedents of ethical climate has focused on organizational antecedents. This work includes type of department/unit, type of company, characteristics of the organization (e.g., firm newness, organizational age, entrepreneurial orientation, high theft organizations, and punishment of ethical violations), and structure (e.g., firm size, code of ethics, control orientation, and career goals).

Researchers have examined various types of organizations and departments and their relationship to ethical work climates. Wimbush, Shepard, and Markham (1997a) found that distinct ethical climates predominated in the various departments, suggesting that the structure of a department impacts the formation of ethical climates. However, Weber conducted two studies on the type of departments in organizations (Weber, 1995; Weber & Seger, 2002) and found that ethical subclimates may be determined by the strength of an organization's overall ethical climate, rather than the department's function.

Related to the types of organizations, Brower and Shrader (2000) found that boards of directors in not-for-profit organizations were more likely to describe their organizations' climate as "benevolent," whereas boards of directors from for-profit firms tended to view their organization as having an "egoistic" climate. Further, Wittmer and Coursey (1996) found that employees working at public institutions had less favorable perceptions of ethical climate than those working in private institutions. Finally, Upchurch and Ruhland (1996) found that different types of hotel properties affected ethical climate perceptions.

Some research has also been conducted on specific characteristics of the organization such as enforcement of ethical codes, internalization of ethical codes, high-theft companies, and firm newness. Schwepker and Hartline (2005) found that organizations that enforced and punished ethical codes had more positive ethical climates. Weber, Kurke, and Pentico (2003) found that organizations that reported no theft had higher rules and procedures, caring, and law and professional codes climates or what the authors label morally preferred climates. Finally, Neubaum, Mitchell, and Schminke (2004) examined the newness of organizations and found that new firms were more strongly related to independence climate, but exhibited weaker relationships to instrumental climate. Further, they found that the relationship between leader moral development and ethical climate was stronger in younger organizations for instrumental, caring, law and codes, and rules climates, and independence climate was stronger in older organizations.

More directly related to structure, Verbeke, Ouwerkerk, and Peelen (1996) examined different aspects of organizational structure and found that behavior-controlled oriented organizations had more positive ethical climates than outcome-focused organizations. Further, organizations that have a career orientation also had more favorable ethical climates. Also related to structure, Neubaum et al. (2005) found that smaller firms exhibited more positive ethical climates for caring, rules, and law and code.

Environmental antecedents. Finally, the impact of the outside environment on an organization's ethical climates has been studied. These environmental influences come from institutionalized societal norms such as regional differences, national culture, and type of industry.

Bourne and Snead (1999) found regional differences in ethical climates lending support for the important role of community norms in impacting the ethical components of an organization. Deshpande, George, and Joseph (2000) found that rules climate was most common and independence climate was least likely to be found within a Russian organization. Although there was no comparison made to other countries, they suggest that national culture may impact ethical climate. Parboteeah, Cullen, Victor and Sakano (2005) examined the effects of Japanese and U.S. national cultures on ethical climates in accounting organizations. They found that there were no differences in egoistic-individual climates, but that the U.S. employees had higher individual- and local-benevolent, and principled-cosmopolitan climates. Finally, Forte (2004b) did not find any differences between different industry types.

Summary of Antecedents

In sum, a number of individual, organizational, and environmental variables have been examined as antecedents of ethical climate. Unfortunately, there is not strong theoretical support for expecting many of these relationships and the results do not paint a clear picture of the factors that influence the perception of an ethical climate. The majority of studies are cross-sectional, correlational studies and they often use different measures of ethical climate. Thus, although there is considerable research on antecedents of ethical climate, the conceptual and methodological limitations of the extant research make it difficult to make definitive conclusions regarding the antecedents of ethical climate.

Consequences of Ethical Climate

In the previous section, we highlighted a number of empirical studies that examined antecedents of ethical climate. Beginning in the late 1990s, a body of research emerged focusing on the consequences of ethical climate. To date, research has primarily examined three major outcomes of ethical climate: (a) job attitudes and affect, (b) ethical behavior, and (c) miscellaneous ethical outcomes.

Job attitudes and affect. The first set of outcome variables that we examined includes job attitudes and affective reactions of organizational incumbents. Job satisfaction has received the most attention. In particular, a number of studies have demonstrated that certain dimensions of ethical climate lead to more satisfied employees (Ambrose, Arnaud, & Schminke, 2008; Babin, Boles, & Robin, 2000; Deshpande, 1996a; Herndon et al., 1999; Jaramillo, Mulki, & Solomon, 2006; Joseph & Deshpande, 1997; Koh & Boo, 2001; Martin & Cullen, 2006; Mulki, Jaramillo, & Locander, 2006; Schwepker, 2001; Schwepker & Hartline, 2005; Sims & Keon, 1997; Ulrich, O'Donnell, Taylor, Farrar, Danis, & Grady, 2007). However, although the relationship between types of ethical climate and job satisfaction appears to be robust, the mechanism(s) by which these two variables should be related have not been adequately enumerated or tested in the literature.

In addition to job satisfaction, organizational commitment is another variable that has been frequently examined in the literature. Extant research suggests that there is a relationship between various dimensions of ethical climate and organizational commitment (Ambrose et al., 2007; Babin et al., 2000; Cullen, Parboteeah, Victor, 2003; Herndon et al., 1999; Kelly & Dorsch, 1991; Martin & Cullen, 2006; Mulki et al., 2006; Schwepker, 2001; Treviño, Butterfield, & McCabe, 1998; Weeks, Loe, Chonko, & Wakefield, 2004; Weeks, Loe, Chonko, Martinez, & Wakefield, 2006). While construct validity concerns are abundant in that different climate measures were used across most of these studies, statistically significant relationships between ethical climate and commitment were consistently found.

Some studies have also found statistically significant relationships between ethical climate and turnover intentions (Ambrose et al., 2007; Hart,

2005; Schwepker, 2001; Ulrich et al., 2007). In addition, scholars have linked ethical climate and psychological well-being (Martin & Cullen, 2006). Finally, extant research suggests that ethical climate is related to affective reactions, including employee trust (Mulki et al., 2006; Ruppell & Harrington, 2000). Overall, these results lend support for the relationship between ethical climate and attitudinal and affective variables (e.g., job satisfaction, commitment, turnover intentions, trust).

Ethical behavior. A second set of consequences that have been systematically examined within the ethics literature includes (un)ethical behaviors. In particular, extant research has found relationships between ethical climate and a number of unethical behaviors including deception (Aquino, 1998), lying (Martin & Cullen, 2006; Ross & Robertson, 2000; Wimbush, Shepard, & Markham, 1997b), stealing (Martin & Cullen, 2006; Wimbush et al., 1997b), falsifying reports (Martin & Cullen, 2006), disobeying company rules, being an unethical accomplice (Wimbush et al., 1997b), production deviance, political deviance, property deviance, personal aggression (Peterson, 2002a), unethical sales (Schwepker & Good, 2007), organizational misbehavior (Vardi, 2001), and general unethical behaviors (Peterson, 2002b). Relationships have also been found between ethical climate and ethical or prosocial behaviors. Statistically significant relationships exist between various dimensions of ethical climate and ethical behavior (Aquino, 1998), perceptions of ethical management (Deshpande, 1996b; Deshpande, George, & Joseph, 2000) success in handling ethical issues (Bartels, Harrick, Martell, & Strickland, 1998), and whistle-blowing (Rothwell & Baldwin, 2007; Rothwell & Baldwin, 2006). Overall, the results of these empirical studies suggest that ethical climate is a predictor of a number of ethical and unethical outcomes.

Miscellaneous ethical and job/organizational outcomes. Within the ethics literature, ethical climate also emerged as a frequent predictor of miscellaneous ethical outcomes. For example, empirical findings suggest that ethical climate is related to ethical judgments (Barnett & Vaicys, 2000; Bartels et al., 1998; DeConinck, 2003), ethical intentions (Buchan, 2005), ethical decision-making (Fritzche, 2000; Verbeke, Ouwerkerk, & Peelen, 1996), moral imagination (Caldwell & Moberg, 2007), and moral intensity (DeConinck, 2003). Additionally, relationships have been found between ethical climate and a number of ethics-related job and organizational outcomes. Dimensions of ethical climate have been found to affect role conflict (Schwepker & Hartline, 2005), role ambiguity (Babin et al., 2000; Jaramillo et al., 2006), and levels of communication (Ruppel & Harrington, 2000). Results suggest that ethical climate is also related to organizational outcomes including efficiency, social responsibility, law and professional codes (Erondu, Sharland, & Okpara, 2004), managers' environmental ethical intentions (Flannery & May, 2000), learning, entrepreneurial innovation, inter-organizational relationship quality, product cycle time (Gonzalez-Padron, Hult, & Calantone, 2008), corporate illegality, industry concentration of illegality (McKendall & Wagner, 1997), commitment to product quality, and performance (Weeks et al., 2004; Weeks et al., 2006).

Summary of Consequences

Considerably more empirical research has examined consequences of ethical climates compared to antecedents. Results provide fairly strong support for the relationships between ethical climates and job attitudes and (un)ethical behavior. However, this research suffers from many of the conceptual and methodological limitations noted for the antecedents. For example, it is unclear *why* ethical climate is associated with the various outcomes. Thus, although there is support for the relationship between ethical climate and the outcomes, there are some conceptual and methodological issues that limit the conclusions that can be confidently drawn from this research.

CRITIQUE OF EXTANT LITERATURE ON ETHICAL CLIMATE

Thus far we have outlined how ethical climate was initially conceptualized, the way it has been operationalized, and detailed empirically derived antecedents and consequences of ethical climate. Although there is clearly interest in ethical climate, we believe there are a number of limitations of the extant literature that has limited its broad appeal in the field of management. Below we highlight a number of important issues that should be addressed regarding the empirical research on ethical climate.

Issues in Ethical Climate Research

Definition. A major dilemma in ethical climate research is how this construct has been defined. Victor and Cullen (1988, p. 51) define ethical climate as the "shared perception of what is correct behavior and how ethical issues should be handled." This definition is problematic on at least two fronts. First, it is unclear from this definition whether the determination of what is "correct behavior" is specific to a particular organization or must also coincide with general societal norms. Dickson et al. (2001) highlight this point and instead choose the term "climate regarding ethics." They use this new terminology because it is difficult to describe an organization that has a shared perception about morality that does not fit general societal values of what is right. One can imagine how a terrorist group such as Al Qaeda may meet Victor and Cullen's criteria for ethical climate because people in that group tend to agree on what is just behavior. However, this perception is not acceptable to the majority of society. Thus, the question is raised, does Al Qaeda have an ethical climate?

Second, this definition is not consistent with the generally accepted definition for organizational climate that focuses on employees' perceptions of the policies, practices, and procedures, that get rewarded, encouraged, and supported with regard to *something* (Schneider & Reichers, 1983). The definition used by Victor and Cullen (1987, 1988) does not say anything about policies, practices, and procedures and all are key components of climate.

Conceptualization. As discussed previously, Victor and Cullen (1987, 1988) draw on philosophical and sociological theories to develop the nine theoretical dimensions of ethical climate. Although some have argued for the marriage of philosophical and social science approaches to ethics (Treviño & Weaver, 2003), the fact that there has been so much difficulty establishing a consistent factor structure of the ECQ highlights the difficulty in trying to translate a philosophical theory to an empirical domain.

Measurement. Measurement in ethics research has been a long standing issue and the work on ethical climate is no exception (Babin et al., 2000). As evidenced by Table 11.1, it is clear that although the ECQ is the primary measure utilized in the literature, there is little consistency in terms of the items scholars have used. Scholars have used the measure in many different ways such as using the 36-item ECQ measure, a 26-item version of the ECQ, a 16-item version of the ECQ, or choosing specific items from the ECQ. In addition to the inconsistency in terms of the item used, there is inconsistency in terms of the factor structure of the ECQ. Although most ethical climate researchers agree that ethical climate is multidimensional, there is no consensus as to what these dimensions should be. In the literature there are anywhere from three (Wimbush, Shepard, & Markham, 1997a) to nine (Peterson, 2002b) dimensions of ethical climate with over 20 different ethical climate types discussed. Without a psychometrically sound measure, it is difficult to imagine the ethical climate field progressing.

Experimental designs and methodology. The predominate methodology in ethical climate research involves providing a cross-sectional survey to an organizational member who provides data on ethical climate and either an antecedent or consequence of ethical climate and then a correlation is calculated. A major problem with this correlational design is same source bias that may artificially inflate the magnitude of the relationships. Further, the use of strictly correlational designs does not allow for causal tests between variable—tests that have been called for by ethical climate researchers (Bourne & Snead, 1999). In addition, there is a dearth of research using structural equation modeling (SEM) to test theoretically-derived causal relationships involving ethical climate. In addition, the response rates for many of the studies are between 10–20% which may call into question whether there is a systematic bias in the way the data are collected (Bartels et al., 1998; DeConinck & Lewis, 1997).

Organizational versus psychological climate. A point to keep in mind when reviewing the ethical climate literature is that most of the ethical climate research has been conducted at the psychological climate level, or in other words the measures were not aggregated (see Cullen, Parboteeah, & Victor, 2003; Neubaum, Mitchell, & Schminke, 2004; Schminke, Ambrose, & Neubaum, 2005 for exceptions). However, almost all of these studies use the term organizational climate. Given the focus on psychological climate, it is perhaps not surprising that the use of aggregation statistics has been largely ignored. Victor and Cullen (1987) define ethical climate as a "shared" perception of members of an organization or work group. However, the appropriate measure of within-group agreement, the r_{wg}, is generally not mentioned in the literature. Thus, the empirical research has not attempted to empirically examine within-group agreement in an effort to be consistent with the initial conceptualization of ethical climate. Further, a fundamental proposition put forth by Victor and Cullen (1987, 1988) is that there is more within-group agreement than between-group agreement. The statistical measure this statement describes is the ICC(1). The ICC(1) is a comparison between the within-group agreement and between-group variability and demonstrates whether there is a group or organizational level effect. Thus, if we want to statistically confirm the propositions set forth by Victor and Cullen (1987, 1988), then it is important to ensure that there is more agreement within an organization than between organizations. Unfortunately, research has generally not tested this proposition (see Cullen et al., 2003 for an exception).

Visibility of the Topic. Although ethical climate is a relevant construct for a mainstream management audience, the majority of articles have been published in business ethics journals. If research on ethical climate is published in more mainstream journals, it would add some more visibility to this area of research. Other forms of climate (e.g., service, safety, justice) have broken into mainstream management journals and it may provide more visibility to ethics in organizations if empirical research on ethical climate could do the same.

PRESCRIPTIONS FOR EMPIRICAL RESEARCH ON ETHICAL CLIMATE

The empirical research presented thus far has illustrated a number of antecedents and consequences of ethical climate. Despite these gains, in the previous section we described a number of critical issues facing this body of research. To address some of these concerns, we now present a number of research ideas to help this burgeoning field to continue to grow.

Future Directions for Ethical Climate Research

Measurement of ethical climate. A number of measures of ethical climate have been used such as a measure of the ethical context (Treviño et al., 1998), ethical culture (Kaptein, 2008) moral climate (Vidaver-Cohen, 1995), and organizational ethical climate (Schwepker, Ferrell, & Ingram, 1997). Although a lot of measures of ethical climate have been used, the ECQ has clearly been used the most. Unfortunately, the ECQ has not undergone a formal validation process by which it is compared to related constructs in its nomological network and subjected to confirmatory factor analyses that have held up over time. Indeed, the factor structure of the ECQ (when formally examined) has been inconsistent. Without a psychometrically sound measure of ethical climate, it calls into question the validity of extant empirical findings.

Although the ECQ has provided a much needed measure of ethical climate, we believe given the limitations of the measure it is time to call a moratorium on the use of the ECQ. Indeed, we believe it is important to develop a new measure of ethical climate using a behavioral ethics framework that focuses on how employees actually do behave as opposed to how they should behave (i.e., descriptive instead of prescriptive). This framework is consistent with other climate constructs that have made it into mainstream management journals such as service, safety, and justice. A key aspect of the development of any new measure is that it is based in existing theory. For example, Kaptein's (2008) ethical culture measure draws on the *corporate ethics virtue model* as a theoretical basis for developing a measure. Although this measure is inconsistent with how we defined organizational climate, this ethical culture measure was validated in a rigorous manner and has a strong conceptual framework, which is a step in the right direction.

One particularly fruitful approach for developing a new measure is to draw on Treviño and Nelson's (1998) framework of ethical context. Treviño and Nelson highlight many different dimensions that comprise ethical context such as decision making processes, recruitment and selection systems, orientation and training programs, reward and punishment systems, formal policies and codes, and structures in place to increase accountability. A nice aspect of Treviño and Nelson's model is that it focuses on practices, policies, and procedures—all hallmarks of organizational climate.

Multilevel designs. The use of multilevel designs will also aid this literature. Given that ethical climate is a group or organizational-level construct, it would be interesting to examine the effects of ethical climate on individual, group, and organizational outcomes. Further, it is important to report aggregation statistics (e.g., r_{wg}, ICCs) to demonstrate that some assumptions of ethical climate are met before relating the construct to other variables. In addition, the use of multilevel designs will allow researchers to examine if ethical sub-climates exist within a single organization. Although this type of research has been examined in a few studies (cf., Weber, 1995, Wimbush et al., 1997b), ICC(1) values showing a comparison between within-group and between-group agreement were not reported.

Conceptual basis for construct and predictions. As mentioned previously, there are some inherent difficulties in taking a theory based on philosophy and sociology and translating it into a measure to be used for empirical research. Thus, as suggested previously, we suggest drawing on a theoretical framework that is based in the social sciences and is consistent with other types of climate.

In addition to the conceptualization of ethical climate, there is little theory provided for why ethical climate should be associated with various outcomes. Is the mechanism for the relationship between job attitudes the same for unethical behavior? Some theories that may be particularly useful to draw on include theories of social influence, such as social learning theory (Bandura, 1977, 1986), social exchange theory (Blau, 1964), and social information processing theory (Salancik & Pfeffer, 1978). All of these theories highlight how individuals look to their social environment for cues about the appropriate way to behave.

Alternate research paradigms. The traditional research design in ethical climate studies involves mailing a survey to an organization (or multiple organizations) where ethical climate and some other variables are measured and then correlated. This design has allowed us to infer that ethical climate is related to a number of different outcomes. However, it is a theoretical leap to draw causal conclusions from correlational research. The use of both experimental designs and causal modeling will be very helpful in this regard. Structural equation modeling, particularly with longitudinal designs, is a useful approach to understanding causal relationships between variables. Thus, an expansion of present research designs and analytical techniques could enrich the literature.

Expanding the dependent variables. As discussed previously, ethical climate has been empirically linked to both attitudinal and ethics-related outcomes. However, there is no research linking ethical climate to bottom line organizational performance despite suggestions from some scholars that the link exists (Treviño & Nelson, 1998). Although Victor and Cullen (1988) state that ethical climate should lead to organizational performance, this relationship has not been empirically examined in the literature. Dickson et al. (2001) provide a potentially useful explanation for how ethical climate can translate into bottom line performance. They suggest that when an ethical climate exists, this can lead to more cohesion and/or morale within a work group or organization and this cohesion/morale translates into positive bottom-line returns. If researchers find that ethical climate is related to firm performance, whether it is directly or through some mediating mechanism, undoubtedly there will be more interest given to this body of research. Future research should seek to examine both direct and mediated relationships that link ethical climate to financial performance. Indeed, such research would meet calls for linking ethical climate to important organizational outcomes (Kaptein, 2008).

In addition, although unethical behaviors have been examined, there is a dearth of research on the relationship between ethical climate and prosocial behaviors. For instance, it would be interesting to examine whether ethical climates promote citizenship behaviors aimed at improving group and organizational functioning.

Exploring antecedents of ethical climate. Many business ethics researchers have described the importance of leadership in developing and sustaining ethical climates (Dickson et al., 2001; Mendonca & Kanungo, 1996; Treviño & Nelson, 1998, Wimbush & Shepard, 1994). Indeed, some have said that leadership is the single biggest factor in predicting whether an ethical climate will exist (Treviño & Nelson, 1998). However, to date there is a dearth of empirical research examining the role of leadership on ethical climates. It is important for future research to determine what type of leader is able to create and sustain an ethical climate. One potentially useful construct in this regard is Brown, Treviño, and Harrison's (2005) measure of ethical leadership. Ethical leadership draws on principles of social learning theory (Bandura, 1977, 1986) to explain how managers influence employees. It would be particularly interesting to examine which level of leadership (i.e., top management or supervisory) has the strongest influence on the development of ethical climates.

In addition to leadership, it is important to examine the role of followers' characteristics in the development of ethical climates. In the leadership literature there is growing interest in the role of followers in understanding leadership effects (Van Knippenberg, van Knippenberg, De Cremer, & Hogg, 2004). Indeed, the effects of leadership on ethical climate are likely dependent on follower personality, values, and identity. Future research should examine the joint influence of leaders and followers as antecedents of ethical climates.

Finally, Kaptein (2008) suggests that future research also examine how ethical climates vary as a function of hierarchical level, sector, and nation. Indeed, aspects of the industry or organizational context could influence the emergence of ethical climates.

The effects of other stakeholders' perceptions of ethical climate. Almost all research on ethical climate has focused on employees' perceptions. However, it would be interesting to examine the effects of other stakeholders' perceptions of ethical climate. For example, are the effects of ethical climate rated by employees similar to that of supervisors or top management? Do customers' perceptions of ethical climate influence the likelihood of remaining a consumer? Do investors consider the ethical climate of an organization before purchasing stock? These are all potentially interesting questions to examine in future research.

Exploring ethical climate strength. One issue that is often confounded when people talk about ethical climate is that reporting a high score on ethical climate means that there is a strong climate. However, climate strength has been operationalized as the amount of agreement within a particular organization or work group (Schneider, Salvaggio, & Subirats, 2002). Thus, it is possible to have a mean score on ethical climate that is high but with a lot of variability in responses. This issue is discussed by Dickson et al. (2001) and provided a rationale for why they use the term "climate regarding ethics." These authors argue that people often inadvertently confuse the term ethical climate (i.e., the mean level of ethical climate) with a strong ethical climate (i.e., the variance in perceptions of ethical climate). However, it is possible for the ethical climate to be high or low as well as strong or weak.

It is possible that ethical climate strength (i.e., the variability in ratings) may be an important moderator of the relationship between ethical climate level (i.e., the mean score) and organizational outcomes. Indeed, empirical research on service climate (Schneider et al., 2002) and justice climate (Colquitt, Noe, & Jackson, 2002) has found climate strength to be important. For example, perhaps the relationship between ethical climate and organizational commitment is even stronger when organizational members agree that the climate is ethical. This issue should be explored in future research.

Relative impacts of personal values and ethical climate on behavior. A recurring theme in the literature on ethical climate is whether unethical behavior is more a function of personal or organizational characteristics (Treviño & Nelson, 1998). There is general consensus among scholars that both factors impact unethical acts. However, an implicit assumption of research on ethical climate is that the way an organization is structured can influence the display of ethical behavior among organizational members. In other words, it is not just a "few bad apples" that cause ethical problems in organizations (Treviño & Nelson, 1998). However, there have not been empirical investigations into the relative impact of personal characteristics and ethical climate on individual and organizational outcomes. This could prove to be a fruitful area of research and could help empirically demonstrate that the organization's environment is important in influencing ethicality over and above the effects of characteristics of individuals in an organization.

CONCLUSIONS

The media attention given to corporate indiscretions in recent years has put ethical issues into the forefront of the minds of many people. In these times, the importance of research on ethical climate cannot be overstated. Some important conclusions are starting to be drawn based on the empirical work on ethical climate. However, the scientific study of business ethics, and ethical climate specifically, must meet the high standards of conceptual and methodological rigor to help make sure it emerges as a mainstream management topic. Given the development of research on climate, the time is ripe to take research on ethical climate to the next level. This paper highlighted the gains that have been made and a number of avenues to aid in the progression of research in this domain.

REFERENCES

Agarwal, J., & Malloy, D. C. (1999). Ethical work climate dimensions in a not-for-profit organization: An empirical study. *Journal of Business Ethics, 20,* 1–14.

Ambrose, M., Arnaud, A., & Schminke, M. (2008). Individual moral development and ethical climate: The influence of person-organization fit on job attitudes. *Journal of Business Ethics, 77,* 323–333.

Aquino, K. (1998). The effects of ethical climate and the availability of alternatives on the use of deception during negotiation. *International Journal of Conflict Management, 9,* 195–217.

Aquino, K., & Becker, T. E. (2005). Lying in negotiations: How individual and situational factors influence the use of neutralization strategies. *Journal of Organizational Behavior, 26,* 661–679.

Arnaud, A., & Schminke, M. (2007). Ethical work climate: A weather report and forecast. In S. W. Gilliland, D. D. Steiner, & D. P. Skarlicki (Eds.), *Research in social issues in management: Managing social and ethical issues in organizations* (Vol. 5, pp. 181–227). Greenwich, CT: IAP.

Babin, B. J., Boles, J. S., & Robin, D. P. (2000). Representing the perceived ethical work climate among marketing employees. *Journal of the Academy of Marketing Science, 28,* 345–358.

Bandura, A. (1997). *Self-efficacy: The exercise of control.* New York: W. H. Freeman.

Bandura, A. (1986). *Social foundations of thought & action.* Englewood Cliffs, NJ: Prentice-Hall.

Barnett, T., & Vaicys, C. (2000). The moderating effect of individuals' perceptions of ethical work climate on ethical judgments and behavioral intentions. *Journal of Business Ethics, 27,* 351–362.

Bartels, L. K., Harrick E., Martell, K., & Strickland, D. (1998). The relationship between ethical climate and ethical problems with human resource management. *Journal of Business Ethics, 17*, 799–804.

Beu, D. S., & Buckley, M. R. (2004). Using accountability to create a more ethical climate. *Human Resource Management Review, 14*, 67–83.

Blau, P. (1964). *Exchange and power in social life.* New York: John Wiley.

Bourne, S., & Snead, J. D. (1999). Environmental determinants of organizational ethical climate: A community perspective. *Journal of Business Ethics, 21*, 283–290.

Brower, H. H., & Shrader, C. B. (2000). Moral reasoning and ethical climate: Not-for-profit vs. for-profit boards of directors. *Journal of Business Ethics, 26*, 147–167.

Brown, M. E., Treviño, L. K., & Harrison, D. A. (2005). Ethical leadership: A social learning perspective for construct development and testing. *Organizational Behavior and Human Decision Processes, 97*, 117–134.

Buchan, H. F. (2005). Ethical decision making in the public accounting profession: An extension of Ajzen's theory of planned behavior. *Journal of Business Ethics, 61*, 165–181.

Caldwell, D. F., & Moberg, D. (2007). An exploratory investigation of the effect of ethical culture in activating moral imagination. *Journal of Business Ethics, 73*, 193–204.

Cullen, J. B., Parboteeah, K., & Victor, B. (2003). The effects of ethical climates on organizational commitment: A two-study analysis. *Journal of Business Ethics, 46*, 127–141.

Cullen, J. B., Victor, B., & Bronson, J. W. (1993). The ethical climate questionnaire: An assessment of its development and validity. *Psychological Reports, 73*, 667–674.

Dawson, L. M. (1992). Will feminization change the ethics of the sales profession? *Journal of Personal Selling & Sales Management, 12*, 21–32.

DeConinck, J. B. (2003). The impact of a corporate code of ethics and organizational justice on sales managers' ethical judgments and reaction to unethical behavior. *Marketing Management Journal, 13*, 23–31.

DeConinck, J. B., & Lewis, W. F. (1997). The influence of deontological and teleological considerations and ethical climate on sales. *Journal of Business Ethics, 16*, 497–506.

Deshpande, S. P. (1996a). The impact of ethical climate types on facets of job satisfaction: An empirical investigation. *Journal of Business Ethics, 15*, 655–660.

Deshpande, S. P. (1996b). Ethical climate and the link between success and ethical behavior: An empirical investigation of a non-profit organization. *Journal of Business Ethics, 15*, 315–320.

Deshpande, S. P., George, E., & Joseph, J. (2000). Ethical climates and managerial success in Russian organizations. *Journal of Business Ethics, 23*, 211–217.

Dickson, M. W., Smith. D. B., Grojean, M. W., & Ehrhart, M. (2001). An organizational climate regarding ethics: The outcome of leader values and the practices that reflect them. *Leadership Quarterly, 12*, 197–217.

Elm, D. R., & Nichols, M. P. (1993). An investigation of the moral reasoning of managers. *Journal of Business Ethics, 12*, 817–833.

Engelbrecht, A. S., van Aswegan, A. S., & Theron, C. C. (2005). The effect of ethical values on transformational leadership and ethical climate in organizations. *South African Journal of Business Management, 36*, 19–26.

Erondu, E. A., & Sharland, A., & Okpara, J. O. (2004). Corporate ethics in Nigeria: A test of the concept of an ethical climate. *Journal of Business Ethics, 51*, 349–357.

Flannery, B. L., & May, D. R. (2000). Environmental ethical decision making in the U.S. metal-finishing industry. *Academy of Management Journal*, 43, 642–662.

Forte, A. (2004a). Business Ethics: A study of the moral reasoning of selected business managers and the influence of organizational ethical climate. *Journal of Business Ethics, 51*, 167–173.

Forte, A. (2004b). Antecedents of manager's moral reasoning. *Journal of Business Ethics, 51*, 315–347.

Fritzche, D. J. (2000). Ethical climates and the ethical dimension of decision making. *Journal of Business Ethics, 24*, 125–140.

Fritzche, D. J., & Becker, H. (1984). Linking management behavior to ethical philosophy. *Academy of Management Journal, 27*, 166–175.

Gonzalez-Padron, T., & Hult, T. M. (2008). Exploiting innovative opportunities in global purchasing: An assessment of ethical climate and relationship performance. *Industrial Marketing Management, 37*, 69–82.

Herndon, N. C., Jr., Ferrell, O. C., LeClair, D. Y., & Ferrell, L. K. (1999). Relationship of individual moral values and perceived ethical climate to satisfaction, commitment, and turnover in a sales organization. *Research in Marketing, 15*, 25–48.

Jaffe, E. D., & Tsimerman, A. (2005). Business ethics in a transition economy: Will the next Russian generation be any better? *Journal of Business Ethics, 62*, 87–97.

Joseph, J., & Deshpande, S. P. (1997). The impact of ethical climate on job satisfaction of nurses. *Health Care Management Review, 22*, 76–83.

Kaptein, M. (2008). Developing and testing a measure for the ethical culture of organizations: The corporate ethical virtues model. *Journal of Organizational Behavior, 29*, 923–947.

Kelley, S. W., & Dorsch, M. J. (1991). Ethical climate, organization commitment, and indebtedness among purchasing executives. *Journal of Personal Selling & Sales Management, 11*, 55–66.

Koh, H. C., & Boo, E. H. Y. (2001). The link between organizational ethics and job satisfaction: A study of managers in Singapore. *Journal of Business Ethics, 29*, 309–324.

Logsdon, J. M., & Young, J. E. (2004). Executive influence on ethical culture. In R. Giacalone, C. Jurkeiwicz, & C. Dunn (Eds.), *Positive psychology in business and ethics and corporate social responsibility* (pp. 103–122). Greenwich, CT: Information Age.

Logsdon, J. M., & Yuthas, K. (1997). Corporate social performance, stakeholder orientation, and organizational moral development. *Journal of Business Ethics, 16*, 1213–1226.

Luthar, H. K., & Karri, R. (2005). Exposure to ethics education and the perception of linkage between organizational ethical behavior and business outcomes. *Journal of Business Ethics, 61*, 353–368.

Malloy, D. C., & Agarwal, J. (2001). Ethical climate in nonprofit organizations: Propositions and implications. *Nonprofit Management & Leadership, 12*, 39–54.

Martin, K., & Cullen, J. (2006). Continuities and extensions of ethical climate theory: A meta-analytic review. *Journal of Business Ethics, 69,* 175–194.

McKendall, M. A., & Wagner III, J. A. (1997). Motive, opportunity, choice, and corporate illegality. *Organization Science, 8,* 624–647.

Mendonca, M., & Kanungo, R. N. (1996). *The ethical dimensions of leadership.* Thousand Oaks, CA: Sage.

Merton, R. K. (1957). *Social theory and social structure.* New York: Free Press.

Meyer, J. W., & Rowan, B. (1977). Formal structure of organizations as myth and ceremony. *American Journal of Sociology, 83,* 340–263.

Mulki, J., Jaramillo, J., & Locander, W. (2006). Effect of ethical climate on turnover intention: Linking attitudinal- and stress theory. *Journal of Business Ethics, 78,* 559–574.

Naumann, S., & Bennett, N. (2000). A case for procedural justice climate: Development and test of a multilevel model. *Academy of Management Journal, 43,* 881–889.

Neubaum, D. O., Mitchell, M. S., & Schminke, M. (2004). Firm newness, entrepreneurial orientation, and ethical climate. *Journal of Business Ethics, 52,* 335–347.

Parboteeah, K. P., Cullen, J. B., Victor, B., Sakano, T. (2005). National culture and ethical climates: A comparison of U.S. and Japanese accounting firms. *Management International Review (MIR), 45,* 459–481.

Peterson, D. K. (2002a). Deviant workplace behavior and the organization's ethical climate. *Journal of Business and Psychology, 17,* 47–61.

Peterson, D. K. (2002b). The relationship between unethical behavior and the dimensions of the ethical climate questionnaire. *Journal of Business Ethics, 41,* 313–326.

Ross, W. T., & Robertson, D. C. (2000). Lying: The impact of decision context. *Business Ethics Quarterly, 10,* 409–440.

Rothwell, G. R., & Baldwin, J. N. (2006). Ethical climates and contextual predictors of whistle-blowing. (2006). *Review of Public Personnel Administration, 26,* 216–244.

Rothwell, G. R., & Baldwin, J. N. (2007). Ethical climate theory, whistle blowing, and the code of silence in police agencies in the State of Georgia. *Journal of Business Ethics, 70,* 341–361.

Ruppel, C. P., & Harrington, S. J. (2000). The relationship of communication, ethical work climate, and trust to commitment and innovation. *Journal of Business Ethics, 25,* 313–328.

Salancik, G. R., & Pfeffer, J. (1978). A social information processing approach to job attitudes and task design. *Administrative Science Quarterly, 23,* 224–253.

Schminke, M., Ambrose, M. L., & Neubaum, D. O. (2005). The effects of leader moral development on ethical climate and employee attitudes. *Organizational Behavior and Human Decision Processes, 97,* 135–151.

Schneider, B., Bowen, D. E., Ehrhart, M. G., & Holcombe, K. M. (2000). The climate for service: Evolution of a construct. In N. M. Ashkanasy, C. Wilderom, & M. F. Peterson (Eds.), *Handbook of organizational culture and climate* (pp. 21–36). Newbury Park, CA: Sage.

Schneider, B., & Reichers, A. (1983). On the etiology of climates. *Personnel Psychology, 36*, 19–41.

Schneider, D., Salvaggio, A. N., & Subirats, M. (2002). Climate strength: A new direction for climate research. *Journal of Applied Psychology, 87*, 220–229.

Schwepker, C. H. Jr. (2001). Ethical climate's relationship to job satisfaction, organizational commitment, and turnover intention in the salesforce. *Journal of Business Research, 54*, 39–52.

Schwepker, C. H. Jr., Ferrell, O. C., & Ingram, T. N. (1997). The influence of ethical climate and ethical conflict on role stress in the sales force. *Journal of the Academy of Marketing Science, 25*, 99–108.

Schwepker, C. H., & Good, D. J. (2007). Exploring sales manager quota failure from an ethical perspective. *Marketing Management Journal, 17*, 156–168.

Schwepker, C. H. Jr., & Hartline, M. D. (2005). Managing the ethical climate of customer-contact service employees. *Journal of Service Research, 7*, 377–397.

Sims, R. L., & Keon, T. L. (1997). Ethical work climate as a factor in the development of person-organization fit. *Journal of Business Ethics, 16*, 1095–1105.

Sims, R. L., & Kroeck, K. G. (1994). The influence of ethical fit on employee satisfaction, commitment and turnover. *Journal of Business Ethics, 13*, 939–947.

Sims. R. R., & Brinkmann, J. (2003). Enron ethics (Or: Culture matters more than codes). *Journal of Business Ethics, 45*, 243–256.

Treviño, L. K., & Butterfield, K. D., & McCabe, D. L. (1998). The ethical context in organizations: Influences on employee attitudes and behaviors. *Business Ethics Quarterly, 8*, 447–476.

Treviño, L. K., & Nelson, K. A. (1998). *Managing business ethics: Straight talk about how to do it right.* Wiley, John & Sons.

Treviño, L. K., & Weaver, G. R. (2003). *Managing ethics in business organizations: Social scientific perspectives.* CA: Stanford University Press.

Treviño, L. K., Weaver, G. R., & Reynolds, S. J. (2006). Behavioral ethics in organizations: A review. *Journal of Management, 32*, 951–990.

Ulrich, C., O'Donnell, P., Taylor, C., Farrar, A., Danis, M., & Grady, C. (2007). Ethical climate, ethics stress, and the job satisfaction of nurses and social workers in the United States. *Social Sciences & Medicine, 65*, 1708–1719.

Upchurch, R. S., & Ruhland, S. K. (1996). The organizational bases of ethical work climates in lodging operations as perceived by general managers. *Journal of Business Ethics, 15*, 1083–1093.

Vaicys, C., Barnett, T., & Brown, G. (1996). An analysis of the factor structure of the ethical climate questionnaire. *Psychological Reports, 79*, 115–120.

VanSandt, C. V., Shapard, J. M., & Zappe, S. M. (2006). An examination of the relationship between ethical work climate and moral awareness. *Journal of Business Ethics, 68*, 409–432.

Van Knippenberg, D., van Knippenberg, B., De Cremer, D., & Hogg, M. A. (2004). Leadership, self, and identity: A review and research agenda. *The Leadership Quarterly, 15*, 825–856.

Vardi, Y. (2001). The effects of organizational and ethical climates in misconduct at work. *Journal of Business Ethics, 29*, 325–337.

Verbeke, W., Ouwerkerk, C., & Peelen, E. (1996). Exploring the contextual and individual factors on ethical decision making of salespeople. *Journal of Business Ethics, 15,* 1175–1187.

Victor, B., & Cullen, J. B. (1987). A theory and measure of ethical climate in organizations. *Research in Corporate Social Performance and Policy, 9,* 51–71.

Victor, B., & Cullen, J. B. (1988). The organizational bases of ethical work climates. *Administrative Science Quarterly, 33,* 101–125.

Vidaver-Cohen, D. (1995). Moral climate in business firms: A framework for empirical research. *Academy of Management Proceedings,* 386–390.

Weber, J. (1995). Influences upon organizational ethical subclimates: A multi-departmental analysis of a single firm. *Organizational Science, 6,* 509–523.

Weber, J., Kurke, L. B., Pentico, D. W. (2003). Why do employees steal? *Business and Society, 42,* 359–381.

Weber, J., & Seger, J. E. (2002). Influences upon organizational ethical subclimates: A replication study of a single firm at two points in time. *Journal of Business Ethics, 41,* 69–84.

Weeks, W. A., Loe, T. W., Chonko, L. B., & Wakefield, K. (2004). The effect of perceived ethical climate on the search for sales force excellence. *Journal of Personal Selling & Sales Management, 24,* 199–214.

Weeks, W. A., Loe, T. W., Chonko, L. B., Martinez, C. R. Wakefield, K. (2004). Organizational readiness for change, individual fear of change, and sales manager performance: An empirical investigation. *Journal of Personal Selling & Sales Management, 24,* 7–17.

Weeks, W. A., Loe, T. W., Chonko, L. B., Martinez, C. R. Wakefield, K. (2006). Cognitive moral development and the impact of perceived organizational ethical climate on the search for sales force excellence: A cross-cultural study. *Journal of Personal Selling & Sales Management, 26,* 205–217.

Williams, B. (1985). *Ethics and the limits of philosophy.* Cambridge, MA: Harvard University Press.

Wimbush, J. C., & Shepard, J. M. (1994). Toward an understanding of ethical climate: Its relationship to ethical behavior and supervisory influence. *Journal of Business Ethics, 13,* 637–647.

Wimbush, J. C., Shepard, J. M., & Markham, S. E. (1997a). An empirical examination of the multi-dimensionality of ethical climate in organizations. *Journal of Business Ethics, 16,* 67–77.

Wimbush, J. C., Shepard, J. M., & Markham, S. E. (1997b). An empirical examination of the relationship between ethical climate and ethical behavior from multiple level of analysis. *Journal of Business Ethics, 16,* 1705–1716.

Wittmer, D, & Coursey, D. (1996). Ethical work climates: Comparing top managers in public and private organizations. *Journal of Public Administration Research & Theory, 6,* 559–570.

Wotruba, T. R., Chonko, L. B., & Loe, T. W. (2001). The impact of ethics code familiarity on manager behavior. *Journal of Business Ethics, 33,* 59–69.

Zohar, D. (1980). Safety climate in industrial organizations: Theoretical and applied implications. *Journal of Applied Psychology, 65*, 96–102.

Zohar, D. (2000). A group-level model of safety climate: Testing the effect of group climate on microaccidents in manufacturing jobs. *Journal of Applied Psychology, 85*, 587–596.

CHAPTER 12

ETHICS AND RULE ADHERENCE IN GROUPS

Tom Tyler
New York University

David De Cremer
Erasmus University

A wide variety of topics can be placed under the broad umbrella of ethics. In this discussion we are concerned with one issue—what motivates ethical behavior. By ethical behavior we mean adherence to social rules defining appropriate conduct within a particular group, organization or society (Tyler, 2006a,b). If we look within current American social institutions we find a pervasive focus on motivating rule adherence via deterrence, i.e by threatening to punish those who break rules (Tyler, 2007). This is true irrespective of whether we look at law, politics or management. Within each authorities and institutions are viewed as shaping behavior through their possession of the ability to reward or punish group members (Tyler, 2006a,b). We argue that an alternative approach is to encourage rule adherence by appealing to people's values. The key empirical question is whether such approaches work. In this chapter we present evidence supporting the argument that they do.

Psychological Perspectives on Ethical Behavior and Decision Making, pages 215–232
Copyright © 2009 by Information Age Publishing
215

In our experience authorities acknowledge the problems associated with deterrence approaches, but say that there is no better system available. Hence, they accept the high cost—low impact—deterrence system by default. They then live with its troubling side effects. The difficulty over time has been that many of these side effects are cumulative. So, for example, in the criminal justice system the costs of incarceration are increasing as the prison population grows (Tyler, 2007). Within management the undermining effects of deterrence on trust and confidence in authorities, as well as in intrinsic motivations for rule following, pose problems because employees become increasingly adept at circumventing organizational monitoring and thereby more able to engage in practices ranging from stealing office supplies to avoiding regulations (Greenberg, 2002; Mulder, Van Dijk, De Cremer, & Wilke, 2006; Tenbrunsel & Messick, 1999). An excellent example is cheating on tests in educational settings. Students are continually devising new and clever ways to exchange information—for example, texting to each other during exams (McCabe & Treviño, 1996). As these social dynamics unfold, the pressure to find other solutions increases. The purpose of this chapter is to propose such an alternative solution.

We want to make two arguments about the motivations that lead to compliance in these types of situations. These arguments form the basis for a *self-regulatory model of authority*, the model we wish to advocate in this chapter.

The first argument is that values matter. People are more likely to obey rules if those rules accord with two important values: legitimacy and morality. Perhaps most centrally, people obey rules when they view those rules as being more legitimate. Further, they obey them when the rules accord with their personal views about what is right and wrong.[1] These effects are distinct from the influence of people's fears of sanctioning for noncompliance, and we will argue that they are stronger. We argue that ethics involves appeals to these values (Tyler, Dienhart, & Thomas, 2008).

Second, we will argue that values are rooted in procedural justice. In particular, people think that rules are legitimate if they believe that the authorities are exercising their authority in fair ways (Tyler, 2007). Further, we will argue, that procedural justice facilitates the belief that laws and rules are morally appropriate. In other words, when people see authorities exercising their authority in just ways, they are more likely to indicate that the rules themselves are consistent with their moral values. This assumption fits well with the idea that respectful treatment (the interpersonal form of procedural fairness; De Cremer et al., 2004; Tyler & Blader, 2000,2003) communicates that one belongs to a moral community with strong humanitarian values, as such facilitating the maintenance of one's moral values and identity (see De Cremer & Mulder, 2007).

AN ALTERNATIVE MODEL BASED ON LEGITIMACY AND MORALITY

Most recent scholarship on rule following addresses issues of motivation and rule-following in the context of deterrence and social control, that is, by imposing external constraints on people largely through the threat of punishment. Social psychologists can contribute to a broader understanding of compliance. Specifically, a good deal of research indicates that self-regulatory motivations are activated when people believe that the rules reflect their views about right and wrong and that it is therefore both a moral responsibility and even an obligation to conform to the rules. Consequently, people who identify with legal authorities and imbue the legal system with legitimacy and morality behind it will voluntarily abide by rules and defer to authorities (Darley, Tyler, Bilz, 2003; Jost & Major, 2001; Tyler, 2006a; Tyler & Blader, 2000). We argue that we can motivate rule following in a different way, i.e., by focusing on these values.

Ever since Kurt Lewin's field theory, social psychologists have assumed that behavior is determined by two main forces. The first is the pressure of the situation or the environment, and the second includes the motives and perceptions that the person brings to the situation. In Lewin's famous equation, behavior is understood to be a function of the person and the environment: $B = f(P, E)$. An expanded conception of the person term includes the set of social and moral values that shape the individual's thoughts and feelings about what is ethical or normatively appropriate to do. We will focus on two such values: (a) commitment to the notion that if the rules are fair and legitimate, then they ought to be obeyed (moral value congruence), and (b) the conviction that following the rules of the community is (in most cases) the morally appropriate thing to do (legitimacy).

1. VALUES: LEGITIMACY AND MORAL VALUES

From a social psychological perspective, the first step is to recognize that the authorities in groups, organizations and societies depend at least in part on the willingness of members to consent to the operation of authorities and to actively cooperate with them. Second, willing acceptance comes most quickly and completely to the extent that people view the rules, regulations and rules as (a) legitimate and (b) consistent with cherished moral values.

Legitimacy

Modern discussions of legitimacy are usually traced to the writings of Weber (1968) on authority and the social dynamics of authority (e.g., Zelditch, 2001). Weber, like Machiavelli and others before him, argued that successful leaders and institutions use more than brute force to execute their will. More specifically, they strive to win the consent of the governed so that their commands will be voluntarily obeyed (Tyler, 2006a). As Kelman (1969) puts it:

> It is essential to the effective functioning of the nation-state that the basic tenets of its ideology be widely accepted within the population.... This means that the average citizen is prepared to meet the expectations of the citizen role and to comply with the demands that the state makes upon him, even when this requires considerable personal sacrifice. (p. 278)

Widespread voluntary cooperation with authorities and institutions allows authorities to concentrate their resources most effectively on pursuing the long term goals of society. The authorities do not need to provide incentives or sanctions to all citizens to get them to support every rule or policy they enact.

When people ascribe legitimacy to the system that governs them, they become willing subjects whose behavior is strongly influenced by official (and unofficial) doctrine. They also internalize a set of moral values that is consonant with the aims of the system, and—for better or for worse—they take on the ideological task of justifying the system and its particulars (see also Jost & Major, 2001).

Kelman & Hamilton (1989) refer to legitimacy as "authorization" to reflect the idea that a person authorizes an authority to determine appropriate behavior within some situation, and then feels obligated to follow the directives or rules that authority establishes. As they indicate, the authorization of actions by authorities

> seem[s] to carry automatic justification for them. Behaviorally, authorization obviates the necessity of making judgments or choices. Not only do normal moral principles become inoperative, but—particularly when the actions are explicitly ordered—a different type of morality, linked to the duty to obey superior orders, tends to take over. (Kelman & Hamilton, 1989, p. 16)

One way to think about legitimacy is as a property of an institution. For example, studies of confidence in government ask people to rate the overall government, and its institutions and authorities. Studies of the legitimacy of legal authorities similarly ask people to evaluate their general feelings of responsibility and obligation to obey the law and legal authorities (see

Tyler, 2006a). This focus on the importance of legitimacy reflects concern with the circumstances under which people follow the directives of social rules and social authorities. Legitimacy is important to the success of such authorities because they are enabled to gain public deference to a range of decisions by virtue of their social role. This deference is not unlimited, since legitimacy may exist within a certain sphere, but within that sphere, acceptance of the right of authorities to make decisions that ought to be accepted and obeyed is broad (Tyler, 2006b).

Legitimacy can also be the property of a person. For example, recent research has shown that charismatic leaders are also attributed legitimacy as charisma reinforced the trustworthiness of their vision, strategy and goals they wish to pursue, consequently promoting cooperation and compliance (De Cremer, 2002). Also, in early policing, for example, the beat officer patrolled a particular area, and area in which he/she often lived. They developed personal relationships with the public—i.e., people knew them. So, they had legitimacy as individuals, and they build or undermined that legitimacy by the manner in which they exercised their authority. In modern police forces, which are rooted in police cars, the officer who steps out of a car to respond to a particular situation is generally someone that the people involved do not know. That officer has institutional legitimacy, marked by a uniform, a cap, and a badge. Their authority comes from the authority of their office, not from anything about them as particular people.

The value of cultivating system legitimacy consists in its enabling the effective exercise of social authority. While authorities can exercise power directly through the promise of rewards or the threat of punishment, such approaches to deterrence are expensive, inefficient, and psychologically naive. They may be especially problematic during times of instability or crisis, when authorities need the support of the people at a time in which they lack control over resources. An organization or society whose governance is motivated only by incentives and sanctions is at risk of disintegrating during times of trouble or change. In contrast, if a system enjoys widespread legitimacy, authorities can appeal to members based upon their shared purposes and values, providing the system with much-needed stability. From this perspective, legitimacy is a highly desirable feature of social systems (see also Tyler, 2006a, 2006b; Tyler & Huo, 2002).

Underlying this generally positive view of the role of legitimacy and social values in motivating cooperation with the social system is the belief that there is a mutual benefit that comes from voluntarily accepting societal norms. According to this view, the rulers and the ruled alike gain from having "a stable social and political order" that is helped by widespread shared beliefs that the system is legitimate and consistent with people's moral values (Sears, 2003, p. 322). Clearly, legitimacy and stability facilitate regulation—the process whereby authorities seek to bring the behavior of individuals into line with system rules.

Legitimacy in particular has many appealing features as a possible basis for the management of groups. On its face it appears to be an all-purpose mechanism of social coordination, insofar as people feel obligated to obey whatever rules or decisions authorities make, within some realm of legitimacy. Much as studies of confidence and trust in government focus on people's overall evaluations of the government, its institutions, and its authorities, studies of "legal consciousness" focus on whether people have "trust and confidence" in the legal system, whether they think that the rules work to help everyone, and how and when people have duties and obligations to legal institutions and authorities (Ewick & Silbey, 1988).

Moral Values

Legitimacy is not the only social value upon which a system might potentially be based. A second social value is personal morality—the motivation to behave in accord with one's sense of what is appropriate and right to do in a given situation. This personal morality is internal and shapes actions distinct from consideration of being caught and punished for wrongdoing. Indeed, personal morality in fact constitutes people's core values as reflected in their moral identity and thus represents an important self-relevant resource that people across situations wish to maintain and uphold (Aquino & Reed, 2002; cf., Griffin & Ross, 1991; Sedikides & Strube, 1997). What unites the study of legitimacy and morality? In both cases, the key is that people accept as their own feelings of responsibility and obligation for their actions in society. In other words, both are ethical values which lead people to behave in rule consistent ways.

The influence of moral values is based on the internalization of feelings of responsibility to follow principles of personal morality (see Robinson & Darley, 1995; Tyler & Darley, 2000). A core element of moral values is that people feel a personal responsibility to follow those values, and feel guilty when they fail to do so. That is, because of people's tendency to maintain a positive identity and self-concept (Sedikides & Strube, 1997), they are motivated to stay close to their true values, or, in other words, to comply with their moral standards in order to avoid anticipated feelings of guilt. In fact, being a moral person can be seen as equally deeply rooted as our visceral reactions such as, for example, hunger, implying that people will go through considerable regulatory efforts to satisfy their moral needs. Hence, moral values, once they exist, are self-regulatory in character, and those who have such values are personally motivated to bring their conduct into line with their moral standards.

The internalized sense of morality is central to the work of, among others, Freud, Weber, and Durkheim. Hoffman (1977) writes:

> The legacy of both Sigmund Freud and Emile Durkheim is the agreement among social scientists that most people do not go through life viewing society's moral norms as external, coercively imposed pressures to which they must submit. Though the norms are initially external to the individual and often in conflict with [a person's] desires, the norms eventually become part of [a person's] internal motive system and guide [a person's] behavior even in the absence of external authority. Control by others is thus replaced by self control [through a process labeled internalization]. (p. 85)

The idea is that internalized values become self-regulating, so that people accept and act on the basis of values that produce respect for societal institutions, authorities, and rules. Public standards are taken on as private values that are associated with a moral responsibility to act in accordance with ethical judgments about what is right and wrong. Presumably, this occurs during childhood as part of the socialization process. Robinson and Darley (1995) argue that people's moral values form during childhood socialization, and are not easy to change later in their lives.

The significance of morality is illustrated by research on punishment. Studies demonstrate that people's views about appropriate sentencing decisions in criminal cases are driven by moral judgments about deservingness rather than by instrumental judgments concerning how to deter future criminal conduct (Carlsmith, Darley, & Robinson, 2002; Darley, Carlsmith, & Robinson, 2000). People accept that a punishment is appropriate when it accords with their moral sense of what is appropriate given the level and type of wrong committed (Robinson & Darley, 1995; Tyler, 2006a). As a consequence, an important question for authorities is the degree to which rules are congruent with public moral values. If people correctly understand the rules, and if the rules truly reflect moral standards of the community, then the internalized sense of morality acts as a force for rule-abidingness.

Values and Institutional Design

A value-based perspective on human motivation suggests the importance of developing and sustaining a civic culture in which people abide by the rules because they feel that it is morally appropriate/just and that legal authorities are legitimate and ought to be obeyed. For this model to work, society must create and maintain public values that are conducive to following justice norms. Political scientists refer to this set of values as a "reservoir of support" for government and society (Dahl, 1956). Although it may not always be easy for authorities to maintain high reservoir levels, a value-based model is consistent with a social psychological understanding of how authorities can effectively regulate citizen behavior, maintain social order, and promote an effective, well-functioning society by developing and maintaining a culture of supportive social values that will be internalized by the citizenry.

The value-based model outlined in this section avoids many of the pitfalls of the deterrence model. Specifically, it does not require extensive surveillance efforts, is more sophisticated concerning the genuine causes of human behavior, engages intrinsic (and not just extrinsic) motivation, and fosters a positive social climate based on a shared commitment to moral values rather than a negative social climate based on suspicion and distrust. But there is yet another important advantage of our value-based model to which we have only alluded thus far. To the extent that people are in fact internalizing appropriate moral values, deferring to legal authorities who implement fair procedures, and obeying rules that are truly just, then the model of human behavior sketched will lead not only to an efficient and well-ordered society but also to one that has a profoundly legitimate basis for regulating the behavior of its citizenry. The crucial empirical question is whether or not values actually shape rule related behavior.

Values and Everyday Rule Related Behavior

The focus upon the relationship between legal authorities and members of the communities over which they exercise authority is the traditional concern of discussions of law and criminal justice. The issues outlined are addressed in that context in Tyler (2006a). That study involved interviews with random sample of the residents of the city of Chicago about their law related values and behaviors. The results indicated that compliance with everyday laws was shaped by three factors: risk of detection; legitimacy of legal authority; and the morality of the law. Of these factors risk was the least important. Legitimacy was five times as important as was risk, while morality was fifteen times as important.

This finding is typical of empirical findings in this area. Studies find that values shape rule following (Sunshine & Tyler, 2003; Tyler, 2006a, 2006b; Tyler & Fagan, in press). Second, they find that their influence is stronger than the effect of risk estimates. Subsequent research extends this finding beyond compliance and shows that cooperation with legal authorities is also shaped by legitimacy and moral value congruence (Sunshine & Tyler, 2003).

Beyond general rule following, legitimacy also shapes deference to the particular decisions made by legal authorities, either directly (Tyler & Huo, 2002) or by influencing judgments about the experience (Tyler & Fagan, in press). When people view the police as more legitimate, before they deal with them, they are more likely to accept the decisions that police officers make during a subsequent personal interaction.

VALUES IN ORGANIZATIONAL SETTINGS

We consider the role of values among employees in profit organizations.

Corporate Wrongdoing and Organizational Legitimacy

Can businesses effectively engage in internal regulation of employee behavior, and if so, what strategies should they use to best achieve that objective? Recent corporate scandals have evoked a heightened concern among members of the public, government officials, and business leaders about both whether businesses can regulate the conduct of their employees, as well as about how to effectively secure employee adherence with corporate rules and policies. Such adherence is important in a wide variety of work settings, and involves organizational policies that cover, among other things, accurate accounting, conflicts of interest, product or service quality, environmental safety, sexual harassment, and race, gender and/or sexual orientation discrimination. In these and many other ways gaining adherence to organizational policies that control everyday employee behavior is critical for successful organizational functioning.

To avoid these types of problems, organizations rely on their employees to follow the formal rules and procedures they establish. Such rule following is critical for organizations to function effectively, a reality that is apparent in the significant time and resources devoted to controlling employee behavior. While there is little question that gaining adherence to organizational policies is critical for successful organizational functioning, the strategies organizations should use to best achieve that objective is more debatable.

The importance of identifying optimal strategies to engender rule following is linked to the significant challenge that is presented by trying to achieve employee adherence to organizational rules and policies. Indeed, there has long been extensive evidence that noncompliance within organizations is widespread (Tyler, 2007). Recent corporate scandals similarly reinforce this point, and have heightened the concern among business and government officials over successfully regulating the conduct of employees. These events, as well as the more mundane and common rule-breaking in organizations that occurs daily, make clear why organizational researchers should be concerned with identifying optimal strategies for achieving employee rule and policy adherence.

In this essay we compare the utility of two approaches to achieving rule adherence: the command-and-control approach and the self-regulatory approach. Here our concern is to apply this distinction to the rule following behavior of employees in for profit work organizations.

The command-and-control model represents a traditional approach to encouraging rule following, insofar as it operates via extrinsic forces and draws upon employees' instrumental concerns and utility maximization goals. It is based on the view that people follow rules as a function of the costs and benefits they associate with doing so. It is rooted in traditional economic theory, insofar as it assumes that employees are rational actors who are primarily concerned about maximizing their own outcomes in work settings, and it embodies the principles of approaches such as agency theory that emphasize the influence of self-interested outcome maximization on employee behavior. The command and control approach argues that employees are instrumentally motivated and are thus primarily interested in the resources and outcomes they receive from their organizations. Therefore, organizations need to take an active role in enforcing rules by providing incentives (to encourage desired behavior) and sanctions (to discourage undesirable behavior). Interestingly, while there is much discourse in the organizational literature over incentives (Kohn, 1999), there has not been a parallel discussion regarding the potential strengths and pitfalls of punishments as motivational tools.

Do such techniques work? Some studies supporting this argument in work settings (Jenkins, Mitra, Gupta, & Shaw, 1998), but, the efficacy of command-and-control strategies has likewise been questioned (Tenbrunsel & Messick, 1999). Skepticism of this approach is less common among organizational scholars, than in the field of law, and thus the managerial relevance of critiques of social control remains an open issue. One reason for the greater support of the instrumental model in work settings is the possibility of using incentives as well as sanctions to motivate behavior. Incentives are more effective than sanctions (Podsakoff, Bommer, Podsakoff, & MacKenzie, 2006).

We empirically examined the influence of the command-and-control approach on employee rule-following in the two employee studies (see Tyler & Blader, 2005). We did so by examining employee perceptions of the likelihood that their behavior would be detected, combined with their perceptions regarding the sanctions and incentives presented to them for engaging in undesirable and desirable behavior (respectively). By considering both sanctions and incentives, we covered the breadth of instrumental or extrinsic motivations that shape employee behavior. That is, we covered the range of cost/benefit analyses that may underlie employees' decisions whether to follow organizational rules or not.

The *self-regulatory model* represents an alternative approach to encouraging rule following because it focuses on employees' intrinsic motivations. It identifies rule-following as originating with an individual's intrinsic desire to follow organizational rules, and not with external contingencies in the environment that are linked to rule-following.

As we discussed earlier, the value based approach examines the influence of two judgments regarding an employee's work organization: (a) the perceived legitimacy of the organization's rules and authorities and (b) the congruence of those rules with an employee's moral values. Legitimacy refers to the view that "the actions of an entity are desirable, proper, or appropriate within some socially constructed system of norms, values, beliefs and definitions" (Suchman, 1995, p. 574), and thus feelings of legitimacy are expected to be related to adherence to rules and policies. Congruence between rules and an individual's moral values should also motivate adherence, as people strive to follow their inclinations to do what they feel is morally right. The self-regulatory approach argues that the concerns embodied in these two judgments can intrinsically motivate employees to feel a personal responsibility and desire to bring their behavior into line with corporate rules and policies.

The first study was based on questionnaires distributed to the employees of one division of a multinational banking firm. The second study was based on an internet-based survey conducted on a national panel of employees, with supervisor ratings of respondent's rule following behavior for a subset of these employees. The studies complemented one another, since one was conducted within the division of a single organization and the other represented a broader cross-section of occupations, industries, and organizations.

Together, the findings largely confirmed the hypothesized influence of a self-regulatory approach to employee rule following. They indicated that employees follow organizational rules, and are perceived by their supervisors as following those rules, when they hold favorable social values that promote rule following. Command and control concerns, such as detection of behavior and incentives and sanctions associated with behavior, were important predictors of whether employees reported following organizational rules, but were not predictive of supervisor ratings of employee rule following nor were they even the primary predictors of employee reports of deference and rule following. These results provide additional support for the premise that self-regulatory strategies, and the variables associated with them, are particularly useful for gaining employee adherence to organizational rules.

Social Values and Workplace Rule Adherence

Our above studies support the argument that employees' social value judgments shape their behavior, and in particular their rule-following behavior. Those judgments are a major motivation leading to employee adherence with company policies and rules, and they also lead to lower levels of rule breaking behavior on the part of employees. These results suggest that one promising way to bring the behavior of corporate employees into line with corporate codes of conduct is to tap into their social values. To gain acceptance for corporate rules and policies, companies should activate employee values. These values are central to the self-regulatory strategy for achieving employee compliance.

Of course, the activation of employee values is not the only way to influence rule-related behavior. As is the practice in many organizations, organizational efforts to monitor employees and sanction/reward their behavior may likewise motivate employees to follow organizational policies, consistent with the command-and-control approach. However, in the two studies reported the utility of that approach overall appears to be relatively weaker than that of a self-regulatory approach.

These findings suggest that companies have a great deal to gain by going beyond instrumental strategies of social control and focusing attention on the activation of employee values that are consistent with a self-regulatory strategy. Overall, the two studies discussed indicate the viability of such a strategy and, furthermore, the potential superiority of that strategy over the more traditional command-and-control approach. This alternative strategy leads to employee cooperation much more efficiently and effectively, since employees become self-regulatory and take the responsibility of following rules onto themselves. Further, they do so without reference to the likelihood of being punished for wrongdoing or rewarded for acting appropriately.

The current findings also extend previous work by considering not only the social value of legitimacy but also that of moral value congruence (i.e., the match between the person's moral values and those of the organization). When employees feel that the values of their work organization are congruent with their own, their own motivation to behave morally leads them to follow organizational rules out of their intrinsic motivation to behave appropriately.

The argument advanced here is for a broader view of the employee and of the antecedents of rule-following behavior among employees. This approach looks at the influence of both instrumental and value-based motivations in shaping rule-following behavior. The results presented suggest that the consideration of both models together better explains such behavior than is possible via either model taken alone.

The view presented here includes not only the motivations traditionally studied, motivations that are linked to sanctions and incentives, but also includes value based motivations for following group rules. These motivations are linked to concerns about acting in fair ways in work settings. The case for this broader model rests on the finding that, in two different studies, corporate actors are found to be motivated in their rule-following by their social values concerning legitimacy and morality. These findings suggest that we would be better able to understand rule following behavior in work organizations, as well as other settings, if we adopted a broader model of human motivation that added an account of value based motivations to our models of employee behavior.

Procedures and Rule Following in Organizational Contexts

It is important to understand the factors that shape whether or not employees come to hold ethical values that encourage such adherence. Drawing upon the literature on procedural justice, we argue that employees' ethical values will be activated and will be more salient in decision making when employees evaluate their organization as being governed in procedurally just ways. Usually, both employees and researchers distinguish two forms of fairness: distributive and procedural. Distributive fairness is concerned with the fairness of a person's outcomes, while procedural justice is concerned about the fairness of the way that decisions are made. In particular, however, the studies we outlined indicate that it is primarily a *procedurally* just workplace that encourages ethical values and rule-following behavior.

As a matter of fact, the findings of these studies suggest that work organizations can motivate their employees is by exercising authority in ways that will be judged by those employees as fair. Those employees who feel that they work in a fair work environment are especially willing to take the responsibility to follow company policies upon themselves, with the obvious advantage the company does not then have to compel such behavior. Both studies show that procedural justice judgments have the potential to shape rule related behavior, and that that influence is primarily explained by the impact that procedural justice has on ethical values. These findings support the arguments of the group engagement model (Tyler & Blader, 2000) and the self-based model of cooperation (De Cremer & Tyler, 2005), which suggests that cooperation is linked to procedural justice judgments (via self-regulatory processes).

These findings directly support the argument that fair behavior on the part of management motivates desirable behavior by employees. Hence, it is important for companies to be concerned about acting in ways that employees will judge to be fair. By acting fairly, companies motivate employees to both follow company policies and refrain from engaging in actions that undermine the company, actions ranging from theft to sabotage. These actions are costly to the company, undermining efficiency and effectiveness, and make clear why companies should be motivated to understand and respond to employee's feelings about what is fair.

Of course, companies are hierarchical, with rules and policies flowing down from top levels of management. If upper management does not itself support the value of rule following and conformity to ethical codes of conduct, as appears to have been the case in the recent Enron scandal, then the motivation to create a supportive corporate culture may not exist among managers. In that case knowing how to create an ethical culture will be unimportant since upper management will not be motivated to act toward the objective. Further, employees are likely to become aware that company policies do not follow their own moral values, and they will become less committed to following company rules and policies. In a situation of this type the effectiveness of regulation falls on the ethical values of semiautonomous groups, such as external lawyers or accountants, whose ethical values may have been activated by their own organizations, and/or to government regulators, who again may be motivated by their own ethical concerns.

These findings have optimistic implications for the ability of organizational authorities to encourage rule following behavior among their employees. Authorities are seldom in the position to expend excessive organizational resources on monitoring and punishing employee misbehavior. The procedural justice perspective suggests that people will comply with, and more strikingly, voluntarily defer to rules when they feel that the rules and authorities within their organization are following fair procedures when they exercise their authority and make managerial decisions. This strategy similarly promotes the view amongst employees that organizational authorities are legitimate and that the moral values of the organization correspond with their own personal moral values (respectful treatment indeed reinforces a view of a moral community; De Cremer & Mulder, 2007). What makes such a finding optimistic from an organizational point of view is that the creation and implementation of procedures that all individuals perceive as fair is not restricted in the same way that allocations of resources are. Procedural fairness is not finite, particularly since it is based on ethical criterion.

Interestingly, the procedural justice perspective is consistent with emerging trends in law and the legal regulation of business. As command and control based strategies of regulation have increasingly been questioned, government regulatory agencies have developed a variety of strategies for enlisting businesses and other "stakeholders" in the formulation and implementation of regulatory policy.

These studies suggest that one promising approach to stopping employee misbehavior, and thus the recent wave of corporate scandals that have dominated the business press, is to emphasize the ability of appropriate work cultures to motivate employees to act based upon their feelings of responsibility and obligation to both company codes of conduct and to their own personal feelings of morality. Encouraging such motivations leads to an enhanced likelihood that companies can bring their own behavior into line with their internal principles, as well as formal laws and government regulations, even in the absence of government and corporate regulation

SUMMARY

This chapter suggests that there is a similar benefit to developing the second aspect of the utility model—our understanding of what people value, i.e., of creating an expanded version of what it is that motivates people in social settings. While they are motivated by material incentives, such as opportunities for pay and promotion, and seek to avoid losses, such as sanctions for rule breaking, people are motivated by a broader set of issues, issues loosely collected here and labeled value based motivations.

Value based motivations are distinct from instrumental motivations, conceptually, and as a consequence they have distinct strengths and weaknesses. A distinct strength is, as has been noted, that they do not require organizational authorities to possess the ability to provide incentives for desired behavior, or to be able to create and maintain a credible system of sanctions. At all times groups benefit from having more resources available that can be directed toward long-term group goals. If everyday group actions are shaped by self-regulating motivations, groups have more discretionary resources.

And, as the findings of this study make clear, value based motivations are important because they are more powerful and more likely to produce changes in cooperative behavior than are instrumental motivations. Hence, value based motivations are both more powerful and less costly than are incentives and sanctions. Of course, this does not mean that value based motivations can be immediately and automatically deployed in all situations.

NOTE

1. In the present chapter we note that our conceptualization of personal views about what is right or wrong (i.e., personal moral values) is not the same as the notion of "moral mandates"(Skitka, 2002). A moral mandate refers to people's strong attitudes that are rooted in moral conviction and that is related to a specific position (e.g. being against abortion). Our notion of per-

sonal moral values can best be seen as a moral building stone for a moral and humanitarian community. From this point of view, our idea of personal moral values thus reflects more a community or collective-based value (see also De Cremer & Mulder, 2007).

REFERENCES

Aquino, K., & Reed, A., II. (2002). The self-importance of moral identity. *Journal of Personality and Social Psychology, 83,* 1423.

Carlsmith, K. M., Darley, J. M. & Robinson, P. H. (2002). Why do we punish. J*ournal of Personality and Social Psychology, 83,* 284–299.

Dahl, R. (1956). *A preface to democratic theory.* University of Chicago Press.

Darley, J. M., Carlsmith, K. M., & Robinson, P. H. (2000). Incapacitation and just deserts as motives for punishment. *Law and Human Behavior, 24,* 659–683.

Darley, J. M., Tyler, T. R., & Bilz, K (2003). Enacting justice: The interplay of individual and institutional practices. In M.A. Hogg & J. Cooper (Eds.), *The Sage Handbook of Social Psychology* (pp. 458–476). London: Sage.

De Cremer, D. (2002). Charismatic leadership and cooperation in social dilemmas: A matter of transforming motives? *Journal of Applied Social Psychology, 32,* 997–1016.

De Cremer, D., & Mulder. L. B. (2007). A passion for respect: On understanding the role of human needs and morality. *Gruppendynamik und Organisationsberatung (Group Dynamics and Organization Consulting), 38,* 439–449.

De Cremer, D., & Tyler, T. R. (2005). Managing group behavior: The interplay between procedural fairness, self, and cooperation. In M. Zanna (Ed.), *Advances in Experimental Social Psychology* (Vol. 37, pp. 151–218). New York: Academic Press.

De Cremer, D., van Knippenberg, D., van Dijke, M., & Bos, A. E. R. (2004). How self-relevant is fair treatment? Social self-esteem moderates interactional justice effects. *Social Justice Research, 17*(4), 407–419.

Ewick, P., & Silbey, S. S. (1988). *The common place of law.* University of Chicago Press.

Greenberg, J. (2002). Who stole the money, and when? Individual and situational determinants of employee theft. *Organizational Behavior and Human Decision Processes, 89,* 985–1003.

Griffin, D. A., & Ross, L. (1991). Subjective construal, social inference, and human misunderstanding. In M. Zanna (Ed.), *Advances in Experimental Social Psychology* (Vol. 24, pp. 319–359). New York: Academic Press.

Hoffman, M. (1977). Moral internalization: Current theory and research. *Advances in Experimental Social Psychology, 10,* 85–133.

Jenkins, G. D., Mitra, A., Gupta, N. & Shaw, J. D. (1998). Are financial incentives related to performance? A meta-analytic review of empirical research. *Journal of Applied Psychology, 83,* 777–787.

Jost, J. T., & Major, B. (2001). Emerging perspectives on the psychology of legitimacy. In J. T. Jost & B. Major (Eds.), *The psychology of legitimacy* (pp. 3–32). Cambridge, UK: Cambridge University Press.

Kelman, H. C. (1969). Patterns of personal involvement in the national system: A social-psychological analysis of political legitimacy. In J. Rosenau (Ed.), *International politics and foreign policy* (pp. 276–288). New York: Free Press.

Kelman, H. C., & Hamilton, V. L. (1989). *Crimes of obedience.* New Haven, CT: Yale.

Kohn, A. (1999). *Punished by rewards.* New York: Houghton Mifflin Company.

McCabe, D. L., & Treviño, L. K. (1996). What we know about cheating in college: Longitudinal trends and recent developments. *Change, 28,* 28–34.

Mulder, L., van Dijk, E., De Cremer, D., & Wilke, H. A. M. (2006). Undermining trust and cooperation: The paradox of sanctioning systems in social dilemmas. *Journal of Experimental Social Psychology, 42,* 147–162.

Podsakoff, P. M., Bommer, W. H., Podsakoff, N. P., & MacKenzie, S. B. (2006). Relationships between leader reward and punishment behavior and subordinate attitudes, perceptions, and behaviors. *Organizational Behavior and Human Decision Processes, 99,* 113–142.

Robinson, P. H., & Darley, J. (1995). *Justice, liability, and blame.* Boulder, CO: Westview.

Sears, D. O. (2003). The psychology of legitimacy. *Political psychology, 25,* 318–323.

Sedikides, C., & Strube, M. J. (1997). Self-evaluation: To thine own self be good, to thine own self be sure, to thine own self be true, and to thine own self be better. In M. P. Zanna (Ed.), *Advances in Experimental Social Psychology, 29,* (pp. 209–269). New York, NY: Academic Press.

Skitka, L. J. (2002). Do the means justify the ends, or do the ends justify the means? A test of the value protection model of justice. *Personality and Social Psychology Bulletin, 28,* 588–597.

Suchman, M. C. (1995). Managing legitimacy: Strategic and institutional approaches. *Academy of Management Review, 20,* 571–610.

Sunshine, J., & Tyler, T. R. (2003). The role of procedural justice and legitimacy in shaping public support for policing. *Law and Society Review, 37,* 513–548.

Tenbrunsel, A. E., & Messick, D. M. (1999). Sanctioning systems, decision frames, and cooperation. *Administrative Science Quarterly, 44,* 684–707.

Tyler, T. R. (2005). Promoting employee policy adherence and rule following in work settings: The value of self-regulatory approaches. *Brooklyn Law Review, 70,* 1287–1312.

Tyler, T. R. (2006a). *Why people obey the law: Procedural justice, legitimacy, and compliance.* NJ: Princeton University Press..

Tyler, T. R. (2006b). Legitimacy and legitimation. *Annual Review of Psychology, 57,* 375–400.

Tyler. T. R. (2007). *Psychology and the design of legal institutions.* Nijmegen, the Netherlands: Wolf Legal.

Tyler, T. R., & Blader, S. (2000). *Cooperation in groups: Procedural justice, social identity, and behavioral engagement.* Philadelphia, Pa.: Psychology Press.

Tyler, T. R., & Blader, S. (2003). Procedural justice, social identity, and cooperative behavior. *Personality and Social Psychology Review, 7,* 349–361.

Tyler, T. R., & Blader, S. L. (2005). Can businesses effectively regulate employee conduct?: The antecedents of rule following in work settings. *Academy of Management Journal, 48,* 1143–1158.

Tyler, T. R., Dienhart, J., & Thomas, T. (2008). The ethical commitment to compliance: Building value-based cultures that encourage ethical conduct and a commitment to compliance. *California Management Review, 50*, 31–51.

Tyler, T. R., & Fagan, J. (in press). Legitimacy and cooperation: Why do people help the police fight crime in their communities? *Ohio Journal of Criminal Justice.*

Tyler, T. R., & Huo, Y. J. (2002). *Trust in the law.* New York: Russell Sage Foundation.

Tyler, T. R., Sherman, L.W., Strang, H., Barnes, G. C., & Woods, D. J. (2007). Reintegrative shaming, procedural justice, and recidivism: The engagement of offenders' psychological mechanisms in the Canberra RISE drinking-and-driving experiment. *Law and Society Review, 41*(3), 553–586.

Weber, M. (1968). *Economy and society.* (G. Roth and C. Wittich, Eds.). Berkeley, CA: University of California Press.

Zelditch, M., Jr. (2001). Theories of legitimacy. In J. T. Jost & B. Major (Eds.), *The psychology of legitimacy* (pp. 33–53). Cambridge, UK: Cambridge University Press.

BIOGRAPHICAL SKETCHES

Maarten Boksem is a post doctoral researcher at the Centre of Justice and Social Decision Making (JuST) at Tilburg University, The Netherlands. Trained in neuroscience and biological psychology, he received his PhD from the University of Groningen in 2006. His research currently focuses on the neural correlates of fairness, morality and power, but also on more basic neural mechanisms and individual differences in the evaluation of punishments and rewards.

Daylian M. Cain is an assistant professor at the Yale School of Management. Prior to joining Yale, he was the Russell Sage Fellow of Behavioral Economics at Harvard. A former Canada Science Scholar, Cain has three master's degrees and earned his PhD from Carnegie Mellon. Cain's research—which focuses on decision-making—combines behavioral economics and moral philosophy; e.g., Cain is becoming a recognized expert on how people think through conflicts of interest. He is co-editor of Cambridge Press's *Conflicts of Interest* (2005), and he won the Herb Simon Dissertation Award for his work "The Dirt on Coming Clean: Perverse Effects of Disclosing Conflicts of Interest." Cain's research on disclosure has been discussed in the *New Yorker, Forbes, Harvard Business Review,* the *Washington Post, BusinessWeek,* and the *Wall Street Journal.* An award-winning educator in both business and philosophy, Cain is building a new Yale MBA course called "Leadership & Values."

Jessica S. Cameron is completing her PhD in Social Psychology at Stanford University. Her research focuses on unethical behavior, and on the situational factors that motivate it. She is interested in how people respond

Psychological Perspectives on Ethical Behavior and Decision Making, pages 233–237

when a key component of their identity is under threat—particularly when they choose to lie, cheat, or steal in order to neutralize that threat.

Tara L. Ceranic is an Assistant Professor of Business Ethics in the School of Business Administration at the University of San Diego. Her research focuses on ethical decision-making and behavior as it relates to emotion, gender and moral identity.

David De Cremer is professor of behavioral business ethics at Rotterdam School of Management, the Netherlands, head of the research group "Erasmus Center of Behavioural Ethics" and guest professor at the Departement of Developmental, Personality and Social Psychology, Ghent University, Belgium. He is the recipient of the British Psychology Society (BPS) award for "Outstanding Ph.D. in Social Psychology" (year 2000), of the Jos Jaspars Early Career Award for "Outstanding contributions to social psychology" (awarded by the European Association of Experimental Social Psychology; year 2005), of the "Comenius European Young Psychologist Award" (awarded by the European Federation of Psychology; year 2007), and of the International Society for Justice Research Early Career Contribution Award (year 2008). He is also a member of the Young Academy of Sciences in the Netherlands (Royal Netherlands Academy of Arts and Sciences, "De Jonge Akademie," KNAW).

Mario Gollwitzer is associate professor in the psychology department at the University of Koblenz-Landau, Germany, where he teaches statistics, methodology, and evaluation. His research focuses on the interplay between morality, justice, aggression, and antisocial behavior. Current research projects are the psychological foundations of individual differences in justice sensitivity, the negative (and positive) effects of playing violent computer games, and the evaluation of interventions that aim at reducing or preventing aggression among schoolchildren.

Rebecca Greenbaum is a doctoral candidate in the Department of Management in the College of Business Administration at the University of Central Florida. Her research interests focus on behavioral ethics and organizational justice. Her work has been published or accepted in the *Journal of Applied Psychology* and *Organizational Behavior and Human Decision Processes*.

Maribeth Kuenzi received her Ph.D. in management from the College of Business Administration at the University of Central Florida and is currently an assistant professor in the Management and Organizations Department at the Cox School of Business at Southern Methodist University. Her research interests focus on organizational climate, multilevel phenomena, and behavioral ethics. Her work has been published or accepted in the

Journal of Applied Psychology, Journal of Business Ethics, Journal of Management, and *Organizational Behavior and Human Decision Processes*

Katie Liljenquist is an assistant professor of organizational leadership and strategy at the Marriott School of Management at Brigham Young University. As a National Science Foundation fellow, she studied at the Kellogg School of Business at Northwestern University. Katie researches the psychology of decision-making in the domains of ethics, power, impression management, influence, and counterfactual thinking. Her research on the "Macbeth Effect" and moral cleansing was published in *Science* and recognized by the *New York Times'* annual "Year in Ideas" magazine as one of the most innovative ideas of 2006.

David M. Mayer received his Ph.D. in industrial and organizational psychology from the University of Maryland and is currently an assistant professor in the Department of Management in the College of Business Administration at the University of Central Florida. His research interests concern social and ethical issues in organizations and he has focused primarily on behavioral ethics, prosocial behavior, organizational justice, and diversity. His work has been published or accepted in the *Academy of Management Journal, Business Ethics Quarterly, European Journal of Work and Organizational Psychology, Human Performance, Journal of Applied Psychology, Organizational Behavior and Human Decision Processes,* and *Personnel Psychology.* He is on the editorial boards of a number of journals including the *Journal of Applied Psychology* and the *Journal of Management.*

Dale T. Miller is Professor of Psychology and Morgridge Professor of Organizational Behavior at Stanford University. His research focuses on the impact of social norms on social life. One of his main interests is how widespread misperceptions of norms develop and how these misperceptions influence group and individual behavior. A second line of research focuses on the origins and consequences of the norm that specifies that self-interest does and should exert a powerful influence over individual and group behavior

Celia Moore is Assistant Professor of Organisational Behaviour at London Business School. Her two main areas of research focus on ethics and organizational advancement, with a particular interest in topics that intersect these two interests. She received her Ph.D. from the Rotman School of Management at the University of Toronto after spending 8 years in human resources consulting and research.

Laetitia Mulder worked with Eric van Dijk at Leiden University and completed her PhD in 2004. In 2005 she became an assistant professor at the Center of Justice and Social Decision Making (JuST), Tilburg University

(Department of Social Psychology). Her research interests are moral decision making, norms, sanctioning systems, and social dilemmas.

Madan Pillutla is Professor and Chair of Organisational Behaviour at the London Business School. His research interests include the investigation of fairness, trust, and competition in interpersonal and work relationships. Among his current research projects are an investigation into the origin of fair behaviour in exchange situations, i.e., are we born with the capacity to be fair or is it something we learn? Other research projects are an investigation into how people can rebuild trust following transgressions in interpersonal relationships, and whether people like to associate with more competent or less competent people in their work-groups.

Chris Reinders Folmer is working as a postdoctoral researcher at Tilburg University, Center of Justice and Social Decision Making (JuST). His research focuses on social decision making, and currently in particular on ethical and moral decision making.

Scott J. Reynolds is an Assistant Professor Business Ethics and the Helen Moore Gerhardt Faculty Fellow in the Michael G. Foster School of Business at the University of Washington. His research focuses on the moral decision-making process, particularly on moral awareness and the intuitive and reflexive aspects of moral behavior. His research has appeared in several management and business ethics journals.

Tobias Rothmund is a pre-doctoral research assistant in the psychology department at the University of Koblenz-Landau, Germany. His research focuses on learning through video games and psychological reactions on injustice perceptions. He is involved in a research program on "Reception and Effects of Violent Video Games." Current research projects focus on suspiciousness as a psychological reaction on meanness in video games, indirect measures of automatic guilt reactions, and the evaluation of social learning in serious games.

Eric van Dijk is a professor of social psychology at Leiden University. His current interests include risky decision making, social decision making, social dilemmas, and bargaining.

Stefan Thau is an Assistant Professor of Organizational Behavior at the London Business School. Stefan earned his PhD in Behavioral and Social Sciences from the University of Groningen. His broad research interest is to explain why people harm and help themselves and others in groups and organizations. Stefan's research is published in *Human Relations, Journal of Applied Psychology, Journal of Experimental Social Psychology, Journal of Organi-*

zational Behavior, Organizational Behavior and Human Decision Processes, and *Social Justice Research.*

Tom Tyler is professor of psychology at the department of psychology, New York University. His research interests are concerned with a variety of issues related to the dynamics of authority within groups, organizations, and society.

Chen-Bo Zhong is an assistant professor at the Rotman School of Management, the University of Toronto. He received his Ph.D. from the Kellogg School of Management, Northwestern University and his B.A. from Renmin University. His research focuses on ethics, decision making, unconscious processes, social identity, and power. His publications include *Science, Psychological Science, Organization Science, Personality and Social Psychology Bulletin*, and *Journal of Conflict Resolution*. His research received national and international recognition and media mentions such as *The New York Times, Washington Post, National Public Radio, Toronto Star, The Times, BBC Radio*, and *The Telegraph,*. His work on the "Macbeth Effect" and moral cleansing was selected as one of the Ideas of the Year in 2006 by the *New York Times Magazine* and the 25 Great Ideas from Great Minds by the *Toronto Star.*

Printed in the United States
153856LV00001B/6/P